PERGAMON INSTITUTE OF ENGLISH (OXFORD)

Language Teaching Methodology Series

CONTRASTIVE LINGUISTICS
AND THE
LANGUAGE TEACHER

Other titles in this series include:

ALTMAN, Howard B and C Vaughan James
Foreign Language Teaching: meeting individual needs

BRUMFIT, Christopher J
Problems and Principles in English Teaching

CARROLL, Brendan J
Testing Communicative Performance: an interim study

DUFF, Alan
The Third Language: recurrent problems in translation into English

FREUDENSTEIN, Reinhold
Teaching Foreign Languages to the Very Young

FREUDENSTEIN, BENEKE, PONISCH (eds)
Language Incorporated: teaching foreign languages in industry

JOHNSON, Keith
Communicative Language Teaching: problems of syllabus design and methodology

KELLERMAN, Marcelle
The Forgotten Third Skill: reading a foreign language

KRASHEN, Stephen
Second Language Acquisition and Second Language Learning

LEONTIEV, Aleksei A
Psychology and the Language Learning Process

LEWIS, Glyn
Bilingualism and Bilingual Education

NEWMARK, Peter P
Approaches to Translation

ROBINSON, Pauline C
ESP (English for Specific Purposes)

SHARP, Derrick W H
English at School: the wood and the trees

STREVENS, Peter
Teaching English as an International Language

TOSI, Arturo
Immigration and Bilingual Education

See also *SYSTEM: the International Journal of Educational Technology and Language Learning Systems* (Sample copy available on request)

CONTRASTIVE LINGUISTICS
AND THE
LANGUAGE TEACHER

Edited by

JACEK FISIAK
Adam Mickiewicz University, Poznań, Poland

PERGAMON PRESS
Oxford · New York · Toronto · Sydney · Paris · Frankfurt

U.K.	Pergamon Press Ltd., Headington Hill Hall, Oxford OX3 0BW, England
U.S.A.	Pergamon Press Inc., Maxwell House, Fairview Park, Elmsford, New York 10523, U.S.A.
CANADA	Pergamon Press Canada Ltd., Suite 104, 150 Consumers Road, Willowdale, Ontario M2J 1P9, Canada
AUSTRALIA	Pergamon Press (Aust.) Pty. Ltd., P.O. Box 544, Potts Point, N.S.W. 2011, Australia
FRANCE	Pergamon Press SARL, 24 rue des Ecoles, 75240 Paris, Cedex 05, France
FEDERAL REPUBLIC OF GERMANY	Pergamon Press GmbH, 6242 Kronberg-Taunus, Hammerweg 6, Federal Republic of Germany

First edition 1981

British Library Cataloguing in Publication Data

Contrastive linguistics and the language teacher.
—(Language teaching methodology series)
1. Contrastive linguistics—Addresses, essays, lectures
I. Fisiak, Jacek   II. Series
410   P201

ISBN 0-08-027230-4

Printed in Great Britain by A. Wheaton & Co. Ltd., Exeter

Preface

The pedagogical application of contrastive linguistics has been the subject of numerous controversies since the mid-sixties. Despite strong critical voices, coming particularly, although not exclusively, from America, a large number of applied linguists and language teachers in Europe and elsewhere have found applied contrastive linguistics useful in language teaching, materials development and the analysis of errors.

The present collection of fourteen papers and a select bibliography is intended to indicate the direction in which applied contrastive linguistics has been developing in recent years and to suggest further areas of research, leading to a better understanding of the language-learning process and to the improvement of design and classroom techniques. It will be seen that these may profitably be supplemented under certain circumstances by the inclusion of the contrastive component.

Most of the papers here have appeared in various places since 1975. One (Sajavaara, 1980) was presented only in December 1980; one paper (Jackson) and the bibliography have been written specifically for this volume. Since even the earlier papers were printed in periodicals and serial publications of limited distribution, thereby reducing their accessibility to a wider audience, it was suggested by many colleagues that they should be made available to both teachers of English and students of TEFL/TESOL and contrastive linguistics (courses of which have now become permanent components of syllabuses of many American and European universities) by being collected in one volume. Presenting this volume to the interested reader, it is hoped that it will serve as a useful supplement to existing collections of essays on contrastive linguistics (Nickel, 1971, 1972; Fisiak, 1980)—none of which, incidentally, was devoted solely to pedagogical applications of contrastive linguistics.

The papers published in this volume have been reprinted from the following sources:

Sharwood Smith, M (1974) 'Contrastive studies in two perspectives.' *PSiCL* 2, 5–10.

Sanders, C (1976) 'Contrastive linguistics, past and present, and a communicative approach.' *Jyväskylä Contrastive Studies* 4, 9–30.

Krzeszowski, T P (1977) Contrastive analysis in a new dimension.' *PSiCL* 6, 5–15.

Sajavaara, K (1980) 'Psycholinguistic models, second language acquisition, and contrastive analysis.' Paper read at the 4th International Conference of Contrastive Projects at Charzykowy, Poland, December 4th, 1980.

Riley, P (1979) 'Towards a contrastive pragmalinguistics.' *PSiCL* 10, 57–78.

Marton, W (1973) 'Contrastive analysis in the classroom.' *PSiCL* 1, 15–22.

Marton, W (1972) 'Pedagogical implications of contrastive studies.' *SAP* 4, 115–125.

Marton, W (1979) 'Some more remarks on the pedagogical use of contrastive studies.' *PSiCL* 9, 35–45.

James C (1979) 'The transfer of communicative competence.' *PSiCL* 10, 99–108.

Janicki K (1977) 'On the feasibility of pedagogical contrastive sociolinguistics.' *PSiCL* 17–24.

Jackson, H (1979) 'Contrastive analysis as a predictor of errors, with reference to Punjabi learners of English' (previously unpublished).

Sridhar, S N (1980) 'Contrastive analysis, error analysis and interlanguage.' Croft, K, ed, 1980. *Readings on English as a second language.* Cambridge, Mass: Winthrop, 91–119.

Sajavaara, K and Lehtonen, J (1980) 'A bibliography of applied contrastive linguistics' (prepared for this volume).

The Editor would like to express his gratitude to the Adam Mickiewicz University, Poznań, Poland; the University of Jyväskylä, Finland; Winthrop Publishers and IRAL for their kind permission to reprint the contributions included in the present anthology.

Last but not least, thanks are also due to C Vaughan James for his interest and encouragement in the preparation of the volume.

Poznań, December 1980   Jacek Fisiak

Notes

Nickel, G, ed (1971) *Papers in contrastive linguistics.* Cambridge: University Press.

Nickel, G, ed (1972) *Reader zur kontrastiven Linguistik.* Frankfurt/M.: Athenäum.

Fisiak, J, ed (1980) *Theoretical issues in contrastive linguistics.* Amsterdam: Benjamins.

Abbreviations

The abbreviations listed below are those which are most frequently used in papers included in the present volume. The abbreviations used in the Bibliography are listed separately on pp 243–4.

BPTJ   *Builetyn Polskiego Towarzystwa Językoznawczego* (Bulletin of Polish Linguistics Association), Cracow, Poland.

BSE   *Brno Studies in English*, Brno, Czechoslovakia.

GURT   *Georgetown University Round Table* (also referred to as Monograph Series on Languages and Linguistics, Georgetown University).

IRAL   *International Review of Applied Linguistics, ed* by B Malmberg and G Nickel, Heidelberg, Germany.

ISB   *Interlanguage Studies Bulletin, ed* by M Sharwood-Smith and J Pankhurst, Utrecht, Holland.

ITL   *Review of Applied Linguistics ITL, ed* by L K Engels, Leuven, Belgium.

PSiCL   *Papers and Studies in Contrastive Linguistics, ed* by J Fisiak, Poznań, Poland and Washington, DC, USA.

SAP   *Studia Anglica Posnaniensia: An International Review of English Studies, ed* by J Fisiak, Poznań, Poland.

TCLP   *Traveaux de Cercle Linguistique de Prague*, Prague, Czechoslovakia.

Contents

ix

x   Contents

1. Some Introductory Notes Concerning Contrastive Linguistics

Jacek Fisiak

Adam Mickiewicz University, Poznań

Comparative studies in linguistics have a long history. Linguists have compared, for example, various stages in the development of a single language, or different but related languages at a certain stage of development, in order to reconstruct a proto-language. These activities have been known as *Comparative Historical Linguistics.*

For a different reason, ie to classify languages into certain groups on the basis of the occurrence of one or more features, linguists have also been comparing languages as they are used today. This type of activity has been termed *Comparative Typological Linguistics.*

Apart from these two types of comparative studies, there is still a third. Two languages—possibly more—can be compared to determine the differences and similarities between them. Since the forties this type of activity has been termed *Contrastive Analysis* or *Contrastive Study.*

These last two types of study (ie typological and contrastive) have different aims but share the comparative element and the interest in comparing (ie contrasting and confronting) languages synchronically.

It may therefore be said that contrastive and typological studies belong to one branch of linguistics—*Synchronic Comparative Linguistics.*

Contrastive Linguistics may roughly be defined as a subdiscipline of linguistics concerned with the comparison of two or more languages or subsystems of languages in order to determine both the differences and similarities between them (Fisiak *et al*, 1978; cf Jackson, 1976). The term contrastive linguistics is an unfortunate one. A number of linguists writing in German refer to contrastive linguistics as **konfrontative Linguistik** (cf L Zabrocki, 1970 and others); Ellis (1966) calls it **comparative descriptive linguistics**; Akhmanova and Melenčuk (1977) speak about **linguistic confrontation**. Nevertheless, for traditional reasons mainly, the term contrastive linguistics is most frequent and occurs in most languages which are the subject of this type of investigation.

There are two types of contrastive studies: theoretical and applied.

Theoretical contrastive studies give an exhaustive account of the differences and similarities between two or more languages, provide an adequate model for their comparison, and determine how and which elements are comparable, thus defining such notions as congruence, equivalence, correspondence, etc. Theoretical semantico-syntactic studies operate with universals, ie they specify how a given universal category is realized in the contrasted languages. In phonology, theoretical contrastive studies operate with phonological primes, ie features, and specify how these features function in the two or more languages being compared.

In other words, theoretical contrastive studies are language independent. They do not investigate how a given category present in language A is presented in language B. Instead, they look for the realization of a universal category X in both A and B. Thus, theoretical contrastive linguistics do not have a direction from A to B or vice versa, but rather as in Fig. 1.

Figure 1

Applied contrastive studies are part of applied linguistics. Drawing on the findings of theoretical contrastive studies they provide a framework for the comparison of languages, selecting whatever information is necessary for a specific purpose, eg teaching, bilingual analysis, translation, etc.

Applied contrastive studies are preoccupied with the problem of how a universal category X, realized in language A as Y, is rendered in language B, and what may be the possible consequences of this for a given field of application. Another task of applied contrastive studies is the identification of probable areas of difficulty in another language where, for example, a given category is not represented in the surface and interference is likely to occur.

Applied contrastive studies should not only deal with differences but also attach importance to similarities. The teacher should be able to point out the forms which are similar, so that the learner will not have to guess them, and will not attempt to construct forms which are more 'foreign' and therefore more likely to occur. Very often we express our surprise when an element of a foreign language is similar to what we have in our own language.

All in all, applied contrastive studies deal more, although not exclusively, with the surface representation of languages than do theoretical contrastive studies, which is understandable if one remembers that learners of foreign languages have immediate access to this representation before they begin to reconstruct the underlying representation and develop competence in the foreign language.

In contrastive studies one finds such sets of terms as source and target language, L1 and L2 or native and foreign language. Theoretical contrastive studies can do away with those distinctions, which imply a unidirectional linear relation, ie starting with the first member of each of the pairs and going towards the other. The avoidance of these terms is indeed necessary in theoretical contrastive studies because the languages being compared have an equal status, cf Figure 1.

The terms L1 and L2 have their place in applied contrastive studies and in bilingual studies; the terms source and target language, in translation; and both native and foreign language as well as the previous two pairs, in language didactics.

Contrastive studies are not a very recent linguistic phenomenon. Contrastive linguistics has roots that extend further back than the fifties or even the forties. Although it did not receive its present name until 1941 (Whorf), it goes back at least to the last decade of the nineteenth century and the beginning of the twentieth century. The first published studies were predominantly theoretical (Grandgent, 1892; Viëtor, 1894; Passy, 1912; J Baudouin de Courtenay, 1912; Bogorodickij, 1915). The applied aspect was not totally neglected (eg

Viëtor, 1903) but was definitely more peripheral and of secondary importance.

Theoretically oriented contrastive studies were continued from the late twenties throughout the interwar period and later well into the sixties by linguists of the Prague school, notably V. Mathesius (1928, 1936; cf Vachek, 1980) and his followers (Trnka, 1953–1955; Vachek, 1961; Isačenko, 1954–1960; and Firbas, 1964).

The Second World War aroused great interest in foreign language teaching in the United States, where almost unlimited funds and enormous efforts were devoted to working out the most effective and economical methods and techniques of teaching. Contrastive studies were recognized as an important part of foreign language teaching methodology and consequently more applied relevance was assigned to them. Fries (1945:9) pointed out that 'the most efficient materials are those that are based upon a scientific description of the language to be learned, carefully compared with a parallel description of the native language of the learner'. As a result, a series of contrastive theses, dissertations, papers and monographs began to appear.

The approach adopted by the authors of almost all of these works was, as might have been expected, pedagogically oriented. Their aim was to discover and predict learning difficulties by comparing the native language with the foreign language.

The basic assumption underlying these studies, as Lado (1957: 2) put it, was 'that the student who comes in contact with a foreign language will find some features of it quite easy and others extremely difficult. Those elements that are similar to his native language will be simple for him, and those elements that are different will be difficult. The teacher who has made a comparison of a foreign language with the native language of the student will know better what the real learning problems are and can better provide for teaching them.'

This view, that differences are more difficult, prevailed in the United States and elsewhere well into the sixties. However, both similarities and differences may be equally troublesome in learning another language.

Apart from pedagogically motivated contrastive studies, American linguists also contributed to more theoretically oriented contrastive studies, ie to the area of bilingualism and language contact phenomena. The works of U Weinreich (1953) and E Haugen (1953, 1954, 1958) clarified a number of contrastive issues, particularly in phonology, eg the inadequacy of structural phonology for contrastive studies, etc.

As has been rightly pointed out by Sajavaara (1977: 10), however, 'the theoretical objectives were almost entirely forgotten in the wake of Weinreich's (1953) and Lado's (1957) work'. What is even more significant is the fact that works which were not essentially pedagogical were considered to be such, and consequently had to take the blame for the failures of contrastive linguistics, either because they were not designed to attain the goals or because the goals themselves were too ambitious and beyond the reach of even properly constructed contrastive grammars (cf, for example, the works of Gage, 1962; Kufner, 1962; Moulton, 1962; Stockwell and Bowen, 1965; and Agard and DiPietro, 1965). Hence so much misconstrued criticism against contrastive linguistics in general, culminating with the 1968 Georgetown Roundtable (Alatis, 1968) which constitutes a landmark in the development of contrastive linguistics particularly in the United States, where not much has happened in the field ever since (cf DiPietro, 1976).

The situation has been entirely different in Europe (cf the conferences in Zagreb 1968 and 1970 and Mannheim 1970). Apart from the Prague linguists, individual scholars in different countries produced a number of meaningful theoretical contributions in the fifties and early sixties (Valtonen, 1953; Orr, 1953; Kielski, 1957–1960; Glinz, 1957; Krušelnickaja, 1961; and Enkvist, 1963, to name only a few). Pedagogically oriented analyses were produced as well. Some of the confusion characteristic of the American scene was also transferred to Europe, giving rise to discussions reminiscent of the situation across the Atlantic. Yet the European scene followed its traditions more faithfully. Many organized projects came into existence between 1965 and 1975 (German–English, Serbo-Croatian–English, Polish–English, Romanian–English, Hungarian–English, Finnish–English, French–English, Swedish–English, Danish–English, etc) and over 1000 papers and monographs were written within and outside the projects during the period (Sajavaara and Lehtonen, 1975). Interest in contrastive linguistics has not diminished over the last five years, either.

Numerous theoretically oriented works have been written (cf Filipović, 1977). At the same time, applied contrastive linguistics seems to have found its proper perspective and a well-deserved place in applied linguistics. All this took place amidst vigorous discussions concerning the status, validity, applications, etc, of contrastive linguistics. The voices of critics have often been louder than either those of the supporters of contrastive linguistics, who expected something positive to result from contrastive research, or those of contrastivists themselves, who have worked on various theoretical or applied aspects.

Most of the criticism has come from those quarters which consider contrastive linguistics *in toto* as part of applied linguistics. This is a misunderstanding which stems partly from developments in the United States in the fifties and early sixties (cf Alatis, 1968) as well as from the lack of awareness of the history of contrastive linguistics and developments in this field both in West and East Europe (cf Corder, 1975; Dirven, 1976; Sanders, 1976; and Lieb 1978).

The aim of this brief history of Contrastive Linguistics is to point to its duality, ie to the existence of a theoretical branch and an applied branch which have to be kept separate if further progress is to be made, and meaningless controversies avoided. The distinction is important, and a clear understanding of it against the background of contrastive tradition and current research is the only guarantee of a proper assessment of the place of contrastive linguistics in modern linguistics as a whole.

As regards the application of contrastive studies, many linguists and language teachers have gone so far as to reject validity and usefulness altogether. This attitude results from a number of misinterpretations and misunderstandings created by such factors as the peculiar methodological status of contrastive studies, and from the lack of a clear-cut distinction in the past between the theoretical and applied branches (Stockwell, 1968; Fisiak, 1971) and of a precise formulation of their different aims. This has been aggravated by a confusion of the relationship between contrastive studies, the psycholinguistic theory of interference and errors, and the theory of second language learning. Some confusion stems from the misunderstanding of the relationship between contrastive studies and linguistic theory.

One of the arguments raised (without distinction between theoretical and applied) is the issue of predictability of interference.

Theoretical contrastive studies as part of comparative linguistics, are totally neutral with respect to this problem, since their aim is to provide linguistic information concerning two grammars, ie to discover what underlies language competence, and not to predict what will happen when competence is converted into performance. It is the theory of interference, using the necessary amount of information provided by contrastive studies as well as psychological and other extralinguistic factors, that will have to account for errors.

The criticism that applied contrastive studies fail to predict interference and errors, and that their usefulness can be judged only on the basis that their claim to do so is not substantiated, seems ill-conceived. It has never been claimed that predictability of interference and errors is the sole purpose of contrastive studies or that interference is the only source of errors (James, 1971). The value and importance of contrastive studies lies in its ability to indicate potential areas of interference and errors. Not all errors are the result of interference. Psychological and pedagogical, as well as other extralinguistic factors contribute to the formation of errors; therefore error analysis as part of applied linguistics cannot replace contrastive studies but only supplement them. Contrastive studies predict errors, error analysis verifies contrastive predictions, a posteriori, explaining deviations from the predictions.

The fact that differences in particular areas of language systems cause interference only in some cases and not in all, and that no linguistic solution can be provided, is due not to the weakness of contrastive linguistics but to other factors indicated above.

In view of what has been said, one might suggest that applied contrastive studies, apart from selecting pertinent facts from theoretical studies and presenting them in a form adequate for a given purpose, should also have a psycholinguistic component capable of handling psycholinguistic problems which are outside of the domain of linguistics proper.

The criticism that contrastive studies are of no use, because a hierarchy of difficulty established on such a basis is inappropriate for the sequencing of teaching materials, is only partly valid. Likewise in the area of predictability, contrastive studies may only be one of the factors helping to establish such a hierarchy. Even in Stockwell and Bowen (1965) such factors as functional load, potential mis-hearing and pattern congruity were added to purely contrastive criteria. Again, it has never been claimed that contrastive studies will solve this problem. It is, however, necessary to remember that we have to know which of the contrastive facts contribute to establishing a hierarchy of difficulty. One should know, for instance, when structures existing in two contrasted languages have a different stylistic distribution, thus helping teachers and textbook writers to take care of subtle shades of meaning.

The last major criticism against contrastive studies is that their results have no immediate use in the classroom. This argument contains several misunderstandings. Firstly, nobody wants to use the results of theoretical contrastive studies in the classroom. As Sanders (1976) has aptly put it: 'To use the results of CA (Contrastive Analysis) raw in the classroom is rather like presenting a customer in a restaurant with the ingredients and a recipe.' Secondly, even applied contrastive studies will have to select from a contrastive grammar the minimum that students at a certain age and with a certain educational and linguistic background can digest. When used in the classroom, comparative studies form a useful technique, employing the previous knowledge of the learner, informing him about similarities and differences between his native language and the foreign language he is studying, also warning him about making false analogies and about the potential areas of interference (Marton, 1972, 1973, 1979).

For the teacher, contrastive studies are undoubtedly essential for designing syllabuses and preparing teaching materials. Likewise, the usefulness of contrastive studies cannot be denied for textbook writers.

In this brief review we have tried to survey but a few fundamental issues concerning Contrastive Linguistics emphasizing primarily the applied aspect.

More can be found in the papers included in the present volume as well as in the growing body of contrastive literature which, together with an increasing number of courses offered at universities throughout the world, and numerous international contrastive conferences, gives evidence of the continuing vitality and importance of this branch of theoretical and applied linguistics.

References

Agard, F and DiPietro, R J (1975) *The sounds of English and Italian.* Chicago: University of Chicago Press.

Agard, F and DiPietro, R J (1965) *The structure of English and Italian.* Chicago: University of Chicago Press.

Akhmanova, O and Melenčuk, D (1977) *The principles of linguistic confrontation.* Moscow: University Press.

Alatis, J (ed) (1968) *Contrastive linguistics and its pedagogical implications. GURT* 21. Washington, DC: Georgetown University Press.

Baudouin de Courtenay, J (1912) *Polskij jazyk sravnitelno s russkim i drevnocerkevnoslovjanskim.* St Petersburg.

Bojorodickij, V A (1915) *Fizjologia proiznošenija jazykov francuzkogo, anglijskogo i nemeckogo sravnitelno s russkom.* Kazań.

Corder, S P (1975) 'Error analysis, interlanguage and second language acquisition: survey article'. *Language teaching and linguistics: abstracts* 8, 201–218.

Dirven, R (1976) 'A redefinition of contrastive linguistics' *IRAL* 14, 1–14.

Ellis, J (1966) *Towards a general comparative linguistics.* The Hague: Mouton.

Enkvist, N E (1963) 'The English and Finnish vowel systems: a comparison.' *Suomen Englanninkielen Opettajinen Yhdiste* 3, 44–49.

Filipović, R (1977) 'The value of contrastive analysis to general linguistics.' Paper presented at the 12th International Congress of Linguists, Vienna, 1977.

Firbas, J (1964) 'From comparative word-order studies.' *BSE* 4, 111–128.

Fisiak, J (1971) 'The Poznań Polish–English Contrastive Project.' In Filipović (1971), 87–96.

Fisiak, J (1975) 'The contrastive analysis of phonological systems.' *Kwartalnik Neofilologiczny* 22, 341–351.

Fisiak, J (1976) 'Generative phonology and contrastive studies.' *Canadian Journal of Linguistics* 21, 171–179.

Fisiak, J, Lipińska-Grzegorek, M and Zabrocki, T (1978) *An introductory English–Polish contrastive grammar.* Warszawa: PWN.

Fries, C C (1945) *Teaching and learning English as a foreign language.* Ann Arbor: Wahr.

Gage, W W (1962) The sounds of English and Russian. Unpublished MS.

Glinz, H (1957) 'Wortarten und Satzglieder im Deutschen, Französischen und Lateinischen.' *Der Deutschunterricht* 4,3,12–38.

Grandgent, C H (1892) *German and English sounds.* Boston: Ginn.

Haugen, E (1953) *The Norwegian language in the United States.* Philadelphia: University of Pennsylvania Press.

Haugen, E (1954) 'Problems of bilingual description'. *GURT* 7, 9–19.

Haugen, E (1958) 'Report.' In Sivertsen, E *ed* (1958) *Proceedings of the Eighth International Congress of Linguists.* Oslo: University Press.

Isačenko, A V (1954–60) *Grammatičeskij stroj russkogo jazyka u sopostovlenii s slovackim,* 2 vols. Bratislava.

Jackson, H (1976) 'Contrastive linguistics—what is it?, *ITL* 32, 1–32.

James, C (1971) 'The exculpation of contrastive linguistics.' In Nickel (1971), 53–68.

Kielski, B. (1957–60) *Struktura języków francuskiego i polskiego w w świetle analizy porównawczzej,* Vols 1–2. Łódź: Łódzkie Towarzystwo Naukowe.

Krušlnickaja, K G (1961) *Očerki po sopostovitelnoj grammatikie nemeckogo i russkogo jazyjov.* Moscow: Izdatelstvo literatury na inostranny jazyk.

Krzeszowski, T P (1971) 'Equivalence, congruence and deep structure.' In Nickel (1971), 37–48.

Krzeszowski, T P (1974) *Contrastive generative grammar.* Łódź: Uniwersytet Łódzki.

Kufner, H L (1962) *The structure of English and German.* Chicago: University of Chicago Press.

Lado, R (1957) *Linguistics across cultures.* Ann Arbor: University of Michigan Press.

Leisi, E (1961) 'Deutsch und Englisch. Ein Vergleich zwischen zwei Sprachen.' *Muttersprache,* 1961, 257–264.

Lieb, H-H (1978) 'Integrational linguistics as a basis for contrastive studies.' Unpublished paper.

Lipińska, M (1975) 'Contrastive analysis and the modern theory of language.' *PSiCL* 3, 5–62.

Marton, W (1968) 'Equivalence and congruence in transformational contrastive studies.' *SAP* 1, 53–62.

Marton, W (1972) 'Pedagogical implications of contrastive studies.' *SAP* 4, 115–125.

Marton, W (1979) 'Some more remarks on the pedagogical uses of contrastive studies.' *PSiCL* 9, 35–45.

Mathesius, V (1928) 'On the linguistic characterology of modern English.' *Actes du Premier Congrès International de Linguistes á la Haye.* The Hague, pp. 59–67.

Mathesius, V (1936) 'On some problems of the systematic analysis of grammar.' *TCLP* 6, 95–107.

Moulton, W G (1962) *The sounds of English and German.* Chicago: University of Chicago Press.

Nickel, G *ed* (1971) *Papers in contrastive linguistics.* Cambridge: University Press.

Orr, J (1953) *Words and sounds in English and French.* Oxford: Blackwell.

Passy, P (1912) *Petite Phonétique Comparée des Principales Langues Européen.* Leipzig: Teubner.

Rivers, W (1968) 'Contrastive linguistics in textbook and classroom.' In Alatis (1968), 151–158.

Sajavaara, K (1977) 'Contrastive linguistics past and present and a communicative approach.' *Jyväskylä contrastive studies* 4, 9–30.

Sajavaara, K and Lehtonen, J eds. *A select bibliography of contrastive analysis.* *Jyväskylä contrastive studies* 1.

Sanders, C (1976) 'Recent developments in contrastive analysis and their relevance to language teaching.' *IRAL* 14, 67–73.

Stockwell, R P (1968) 'Contrastive analysis and lapsed time.' In Alatis (1968), 11–26.

Stockwell, R P and Bowen, D (1965) *The sounds of English and Spanish.* Chicago: University of Chicago Press.

Trager, G L (1949) *The field of linguistics.* Norman, Okla.: Battenburg Press.

Trnka, B (1953–5) *Rozbor nynější spisovné angličtiny,* 3 vols. Prague.

Vachek, J (1961) 'Some less familiar aspects of the analytical trend of English'. *BSE* 3, 9–78.

Vachek, J (1980) 'Mathesius as a contrastive linguist'. *PSiCL* 11, 5–16.

Valtonen, T (1953) 'Some notes on syntactical similarities and parallels between English and Finnish.' *Suomen Englanninkielen Opettajien Yhdistyksen Vuosikirja* 1951–52, pp. 88–96.

Viëtor, W (1894³) *Elemente der Phonetik des Deutschen, Englischen und Französischen.* Leipzig: Reisland.

Viëtor, W (1903) *German pronunciation: practice and theory.* Leipzig: Reisland.

Weinreich, U (1953) *Languages in contact.* New York: Linguistic Circle of New York.

Whorf, B L (1941) 'Languages and logic.' *Technological review* 43, 250–252, 266, 268, 272.

Zabrocki, L (1970) 'Grundfragen der konfrontativen Grammatik.' In *Probleme der kontrastiven Grammatik.* Düsseldorf: Schwemm, pp. 31–53.

2. Contrastive Studies in Two Perspectives

Michael Sharwood Smith

University of Utrecht

1.1. The aims of contrastive studies have been much discussed and will doubtless continue to be discussed. The discussion usually centres round two fundamental points of view: the theoretical and the practical. Theoretical aims include the desire to increase present knowledge within the field of linguistics while practical aims mainly relate to teaching and the construction of teaching materials. Most discussions end with the general agreement that contrastive studies shall try to contribute to the fulfilment of both theoretical and practical aims. However, if contrastive studies are to be related to these very different fields of interest, they must be considered in two different ways, that is, in the linguistic perspective and in the perspective proper to language teaching. Furthermore, it must be clearly specified exactly how these two perspectives may best be combined within one organised contrastive studies project. It becomes vital to examine the links—possible and desirable—between linguistics and language teaching as a whole to determine where contrastive studies fit in and in what way an exhaustive comparison of two or more languages can serve both the linguistic and the language teacher alike.

2.1. Linguistics has often been termed the '*scientific*' study of language. Its scientific character was stressed particularly in the earlier days of its growth as an autonomous discipline so as to contrast with the more humanistic and haphazard descriptions of language that had existed before. Also it must be admitted that linguists wished to identify themselves and their studies with the modern technological—*Zeitgeist*. Nowadays a more mature view is prevalent and linguistics is seen as belonging to a kind of midway area between the world of physics and chemistry and other natural sciences on the one hand and the humanities on the other. All the same, linguists adhere as closely as possible to scientific method and try to present their hypotheses, theories and descriptions in as objective and systematic a way as they can. To this extent linguistics is a science.

2.2. Linguistics, as a science, includes both theory and application. Some linguist may evolve a theory of language from which a description of one or more languages may follow. The theory is thus applied to a particular task and the result is a grammar. A modern grammar is then no longer a piecemeal description of some language based on some accepted and vaguely formulated principles but rather a fairly rigorous application of some theory. Any problems encountered in the application will have immediate consequences on the shape of the theory which may then have to be explicitly altered to account for the 'data'.

2.3. The term 'applied linguistics' has been coined, probably on analogy with the applied sciences, to indicate certain applications of linguistics in more practical spheres of activity. However, it is usually understood in the absence of further qualification as the application of linguistics in the field of language teaching. It is an unfortunate term nevertheless due to the generality of the term 'applied' which does not tell us exactly what is applied to what. It is reasonable to argue as, for example S Pit Corder does at Edinburgh, that the first application of linguistics is in fact the description of language. Using the description is a further and separate application which must not be confused with the first which is based on an abstract theory. The term 'applied linguistics', although current, is therefore ambiguous.

2.4. In this paper applications of linguistics will be of two basic types:[1] first-order applications which follow directly from linguistic theory and second-order applications which involve considerations external to linguistics proper. Second-order applications help to constitute a number of 'interdisciplines, that is, areas of interest which occur at the interface[2] between linguistics and some other area. For example, the interface between linguistics and psychology results in the area called 'psycholinguistics'. In the same way we obtain a specification of what concerns among others sociolinguists, neurolinguists, mathematical linguists, computational linguists and, as will be seen later, pedagogical linguists.

2.5. First-order applications of linguistic theory involve very detailed and explicit descriptions of language systems. The theory must be rigorously tested against the realities of language which the theory aims to account for in some way. Thus not only must the application be meticulous. It must also be exhaustive so that facts which the theory cannot account for are not conveniently set aside. A theory must be vulnerable according to scientific method and must be rejected or changed in the face of contradictory evidence. The theory and first-order application of the theory is dealt with in a scientific frame of reference and may be subsumed under the heading of linguistics or 'the linguistic sciences'.[3] The comparison and contrasting of two or more languages may be undertaken within this perspective and the term contrastive linguistics is usually used to characterise it. This term of course denotes a type of linguistics and not an interface between two disciplines.

2.6. Second-order applications, that is, applications of linguistics (theory and first-order applications) combine interests of two disciplines. A psychologist is interested in language behaviour as a part of general human behaviour and he needs the systematic theories and descriptions of the linguist to further his research into this field now called psycholinguistics. Similarly a sociologist is interested in language as a social phenomenon and he too needs linguistics for his work in sociolinguistics. We may reverse the picture by saying that certain linguists, following the general principle that every aspect of language is of interest to the linguist, specialise in psychological or social or other aspects where they need the insights provided by the sister disciplines. It is immediately apparent that psychology and sociology are in no way subordinate to linguistics and even the interdisciplines created at their interface with linguistics may be treated to some extent as independent areas of study. The same may be said of all the other second-order applications and those sister disciplines, like language teaching, which they relate to linguistics.

3.1. Language teaching is less easy to describe in simple terms. It can be both a study in the academic sense and an activity undertaken in the unordered changing context of everyday life. It is not a science in any strict sense although the study of language teaching may have its scientific aspects. In spite of the fact that it must be viewed principally as an activity, however, language teachers nowadays are confronted with a body of theoretical academic knowledge designed to aid them in some way when they come to actually teach in the classroom. This knowledge is often presented during teacher-training or at conferences and courses designed to acquaint them with current trends. We can therefore speak of language teaching in an academic sense and here the term 'language pedagogy' is used to cover this meaning and distinguish it from language teaching in the practical sense. Language pedagogy concerns itself with the total language teaching situation some parts of which may be dealt with in a scientific or quasi-scientific way and other parts of which are more humanistic and view teaching as an art as well as an application of some theory. Language pedagogy is not a science[4] but a conglomerate of knowledge typical of the content of a teacher training course for language teachers. Much has to do with language but there are elements common to all areas of pedagogy like general educational theory, administrative principles and general cultural aspects of the teaching situation. Language pedagogy is more a cover title for the academic study of language teaching than a unified well-defined discipline like linguistics.

4.1. A large and important part of language pedagogy will concern itself with language and the various ways in which language is studied. However, it would be a mistake to imagine that the complex first-order descriptions of language, contrastive or otherwise, are suitable for language teaching. Such descriptions must be processed for pedagogical consumption. This extremely important operation will involve a process of selection, modification and rejection of items according to the demands of language teaching. Such processes must be based on clear principles derived from psychological, social and other considerations and it is clear that this must all be undertaken within a defined field of interest which will here be termed 'pedagogical linguistics'[5] and which has often been called applied linguistics despite the ambiguities of that term. Pedagogical linguistics may be viewed as a second-order application of linguistics and a subject in its own right with theoretical principles and an output of practical material for eventual use in, or adaptation to, particular teaching situations. It will use material not only from linguistics proper but also from other applications of linguistics. Pedagogical linguistics deserves to be seen as a separate and important field with its own principles and not vaguely by some term such as 'methodology' or applied linguistics.

4.2. The most important contribution of pedagogical linguistics is pedagogical grammar, ie language descriptions geared to the demands of teaching. Whereas a linguist attempts to look at all areas of grammar with the same objective eye, the pedagogical linguist will shape his grammars according to the priorities of a given teaching situation or set of teaching situations. Again, his selective principles will not only operate within one particular language description offered by linguistics. It will also operate over the whole range of linguistic theories. Whereas for the linguist it is usually a matter of working within one theory rather than another, for the pedagogical linguist it may well be a matter of selecting from different grammars reflecting different theories since two separate theories may offer equally useful insights into the language, useful, that is, from a teaching point of view. At first sight it may seem that a pedagogical linguist has greater freedom than a linguist proper but it must be remembered a pedagogical grammar will be judged from at least two points of view, ie according to its representation of the language or languages under consideration and also according to its suitability to the particular pedagogical demands which it claims to serve. This makes the pedagogical linguist's task if anything more difficult and this fact should be duly recognised.

4.3. A special type of pedagogical grammar is likely to be of particular value (though this is still disputed) and that is contrastive pedagogical grammar. This is chiefly a processing of the contributions of contrastive linguistics for teaching purposes. It was claimed earlier that a (theoretical) contrastive description would successfully predict all the learner's errors for it was naïvely thought that these arose simply out of differences between the native and target language. This view was proved wrong by an analysis of actual errors and by the observations that contrastive descriptions took no account of the psychological processes involved in language learning. Under the system presented in this paper theoretical contrastive descriptions are undertaken within the field of linguistics with the aim of furthering linguistic knowledge including such questions as the establishing of language universals. A pedagogical contrastive grammar undertaken within a different area of study, ie pedagogical linguistics, seeks to discover contrastive insights that are useful in some way for language teachers. With the newly awakened interest in cognitive psychology and the re-emergence (or persistence) of such teaching techniques as translation and the overt presentation of language differences, it would seem that contrastive pedagogical grammar will be of real value. It may also be linked up with error analysis and attempts at a psychological model of language learning.

4.4. Pedagogical grammar and consequently contrastive pedagogical grammar will use insights from other second-order applications of linguistics, especially from psycholinguistics and sociolinguistics and their various offshoots. Just as it will take into account the psychological processes of learning a second language, it will also take into account the way language is used in society and decisions will have to be made as to what varieties and modes of a given language are to be described and taught. A quick survey of present-day intensive courses and textbooks reveals that a sound theoretical basis which a contrastive pedagogical grammar might provide is frequently lacking.

5.1. Having established the links between linguistics and language teaching and defined some of the interrelating areas we may now specify what a contrastive studies project can seek to achieve within the two perspectives. From a theoretical point of view it can contribute to contrastive linguistics, that is, to the testing of specific linguistic theories, to our detailed knowledge of the contrasted languages and to the establishment of certain language universals. From a practical point of view it can lead to the production of teaching materials and teaching methods. But in order to do the latter the theoretical contrastive analyses must be processed by pedagogical linguists according to the demands of specified teaching situations and decisions must be taken about what areas of the language are relevant. On a more fundamental level decisions must be taken about a given contrastive studies project as to what extent it will function with respect to the theoretical linguistic and the language teaching perspectives.

As has been shown, these perspectives involve very different approaches but with a framework such as the one outlined above the two fields of interest may be coordinated.

Notes

1. These two basic distinctions, which follow from Corder's criticisms at Edinburgh, are broad ones aiming at simplification and do not reflect the complex ways in which each field may relate to both linguistics and other associated fields.
2. Professor Strevens used this term at Essex University. The aim of the present paper is to emphasise the fact that semi-independent studies may be usefully set up at an interface rather than letting it remain a vague disputed no-man's land.
3. We of course include phonetic studies cf Halliday et al (1964).
4. Although the trend is to bring every facet of the classroom situation into the domain of controlled scientific analysis it must be recognised that there will always be some less easily defined aspects of teaching and learning which may yet be seriously discussed and brought to the attention of all teachers be they theoreticians or practicians of what is still called an 'art'. This clarification was prompted by a discussion with Dr W Marton.
5. This term was coined by T P Krzeszowski and discussed in the introduction of Krzeszowski (1970).

References

Crystal, D (1971) *Linguistics*. London: Pelican.

Crystal, D and Davy, D (1969) *Investigating English style*. London: Longmans.

Halliday, M A K, McIntosh, A and Strevens, P (1964) *The linguistic sciences and language teaching*. London: Longmans.

Krzeszowski, T P (1970) *Teaching English to Polish learners*. Warszawa: PWN.

Wilkins, D A (1972) 'Linguistics and the scientific study of language teaching'. *AVLA journal* 10, 23–33.

3. Recent Developments in Contrastive Analysis and Their Relevance to Language Teaching

Carol Sanders
University of Sussex

In view of the current wave of eclecticism in Applied Linguistics, I feel that it is time for Contrastive Analysis to be looked at afresh. It was pulled down from its pedestal as ungracefully and as unnecessarily as it had been hoisted up there following *Linguistics across Cultures*. It is time for people to recognise that it is still widely used without being acknowledged, by language teachers and textbook writers. Attempts in the last few years to see contrastive analysis in the context of generative linguistics to some extent meet the criticisms made of structuralist contrastive analysis, but need looking at closely for their implications for language teaching.

In its hey-day, the value of taxonomic contrastive analysis went virtually unquestioned and was often exaggerated. Many well-quoted claims come to mind: Fries (1945),[1] or Politzer (1968).[2] The reaction which set in gave rise to a plethora of articles, rightly challenging the more extreme claims which had been made on behalf of contrastive analysis, but wrongly overlooking those aspects of contrastive analysis which had not been invalidated by these arguments and which had proved useful to the language teacher. Another group of critics rejected contrastive analysis because of its affinities with Structural Linguistics and Behaviourist Psychology. That there is no need for this has been shown by Di Pietro in *Language Structures in Contrast*[3] who, as Dwight Bolinger says in his introduction, 'keeps the baby and changes the bath'. Di Pietro's reinstatement of contrastive analysis based on generative linguistics is of great theoretical interest, but there is, nevertheless, much that is open to question, and regrettably little in the chapter on contrastive analysis and language teaching

21

which actually relates his theoretical model for contrasting two languages to classroom practice, as I hope to show later in a fuller discussion of this book. In this article, I would like to look first of all at some of the general criticisms which continue to be levelled at contrastive analysis, then in particular at the implications of a generative-based theory of contrastive analysis for language teaching.

I. Criticisms of contrastive analysis

This first part will not be a complete inventory of criticisms of contrastive analysis in language teaching and possible replies to them, since many of these are well known, and are summed up in an excellent paper by James.[4] What I want to do is to criticise the assumptions of the critics, and in doing so perhaps add a few points to James. The first assumption is that extreme claims made at one time for contrastive analysis are its only claims. Jack Richards[5] is at pains to point out that L1 interference is by no means the only source of error: the obvious reply is that it is indeed one of several sources and that contrastive analysis is just a part of the research needed to predict, explain and remedy errors. Secondly, it is too readily forgotten that the immediate findings of contrastive analysis are not for classroom consumption; they are for the textbook writer and the teacher, and many faults attributed to contrastive analysis itself stem from misapplication.

An example of the first assumption is the criticism that contrastive analysis does not have 100% predictive reliability. Lee,[6] for example, complains of this, and other people[7] call attention to the way in which contrastive analysis cannot predict which of several items will be chosen by certain foreigners learning another language. I would go along with James' reply that no one now claims 100% reliability for contrastive analysis; indeed, before better predictions can be made in language teaching in general, more research needs to be done on L1 and L2 interaction, and on psychological phenomena affecting performance. As Lado[8] says, contrastive analyses assumes 'maximum transfer' and refers to 'behaviour that is likely to appear with greater than random frequency'. But there are more points to add. Firstly, the very knowledge that an item is non-existent in a learner's L1 is useful in identifying a problem-area even if it can go no further. Secondly, it is important to remember that if certain items are substituted regularly in the target language, then there is a good chance that the interference is due to the L1, and that what is needed is more contrastive analysis research and not less. It may be that when the languages are seen as wholes, and not isolated parts, the explanation for the error will be apparent[9] (cf my later discussion of Di Pietro's book). Thirdly, there are those who say that contrastive analysis' role is explanatory, prediction being more efficiently left to error-counts—(Lado tells us what a very large sample is needed for enough of the distortions to appear[10])—or the subjective experience of the teacher. Obviously teaching experience and contrastive analysis should complement each other, but given that perception is as misleading as we know it to be (think, for example, of the different reaction to the same voice reading English or French, reported by Gardner and Lambert[11]), to rely only on unscientifically collected data seems unnecessarily risky. Anyway, by the time a large sample of errors has been collected, how many students have made these mistakes repeatedly, instead of being taught with materials which eliminate them as early as possible? What of the teacher going to a new language situation for which he wishes to prepare materials in advance? In such circumstances contrastive analysis is one tool among many, but a very useful one which has the ability to predict potential errors, and helps to explain and remedy those which are actually present.

The next three criticisms that I would like to deal with all show confusion between contrastive analysis and pedagogical presentation based on contrastive analysis. Thus Di Pietro claims that a linguistic item from the target language is not necessarily best taught in contrast with its 'opposite number', quoting the example of English speakers' learning Italian flap 'r' more easily by reference to the articulation of the medial consonant in American English 'matter'. If the teacher is dealing with the articulation of this sound, he should indeed not apply a contrastive analysis of the phonology of the two languages. He should rather find out from the contrastive analysis as a whole that there is a sound in L1 which will facilitate the learning of a certain target language sound.

Secondly, it is said that a hierarchy of difficulties based on contrastive analysis may not be an appropriate basis for the sequencing of teaching materials. That is, a textbook or teacher may devote a lot of time to practising a target language structure for the sole reason that it does not occur in the learner's L1, when it might be more useful to him to have more practice in a structure which has a higher frequency in the foreign language, even if contrast analysis did not foresee his having much difficulty with it. Once again, the first reply is that contrastive analysis is one of several criteria. (Stockwell and Bowen,[12] for example, add functional load, potential mishearing and pattern congruity as three others.) Next, some sort of emphasis must naturally be given to items which have a high frequency in the target language, but deciding which these are is to some extent the business of contrastive analysis. We need to know when a structure which exists in both languages and will, therefore, not cause interference, has a different stylistic distribution in each language. The important part that this plays in making a speaker sound fluent and in making him able to communicate subtle shades of meaning and feeling is apparent from an article by Levenston.[13] A final point: Wilga Rivers[14] makes the observation that hierarchies of difficulty need also to take into account pedagogical considerations (which item is easiest to dramatise, for example) that are too often forgotten.

The third criticism sometimes made is that there are certain juxtapositions which confuse the learner. This point of view is put by Hadlich[15] who takes the example of *ser* and *estar* for English-speaking learners of Spanish, for whom there is no problem if these items are not taught together. One asks oneself what sort of teacher it is that presents points to learners in this way rather than seeing that contrastive analysis points to these items being separated in teaching. To use the results of contrastive analysis 'raw' in the classroom is rather like presenting a customer in a restaurant with the ingredients and a recipe.

II. Generative contrastive analysis and language teaching

In this book *Language Structures in Contrast*, Di Pietro does a good job defending contrastive analysis and of infusing it with new generative blood. A taxonomic contrastive analysis is sometimes useful to the language teacher, but in general, we would agree that it may have the disadvantages that Di Pietro attributes to it: 'The alternative to positing universals in contrastive analysis is a list of contrasting paradigms and autonomous descriptive statements with no interrelating of the languages being contrasted.' The model he presents is theoretically convincing and, aiming as it does at greater 'completeness, accuracy, explicitness and simplicity', it is of obvious long-term interest to the applied linguist concerned with language teaching. There is, however, no indication that an immediate application would be desirable. Rivers' warning[16] against over-hasty extrapolation from theoretical linguistics is not out of place here. Di Pietro's final chapter is called 'Contrastive Analysis and the Foreign Language Teacher'. I shall try to show why his attempts to apply generative contrastive analysis to language teaching are misguided.

According to Di Pietro, the contrastive analyst should be most interested in the levels between deep structure and surface structure. We can appreciate that in his example of 'It's raining' in English, German, Italian and Spanish, there will probably be no grammatical interference between Spanish and Italian since they have the most intermediate structures in common, while English and German differ in sharing the dummy subject but are not so close as Spanish and Italian, as English moreover has the progressive form of the verb. We are obviously keen for the student to realise this and to accept that there will be a similar procedure for 'It's snowing'. Viewed like this, it seems as if this is what some language teachers have been trying to do for some time. Di Pietro, however, does not leave it at this 'intermediate level', but carries his criticism of structuralist contrastive analysis' dealing with only surface structure to its extreme by suggesting that we should try to 'teach' deep structures. It is here that Di Pietro would find dissenters. Rivers, for example, says the child learning his L1 'detects logical relations and begins in a basic fashion to express these relations... which are a part of universal grammar.[17] The mature learner, on the other hand, has developed these: his mistake lies in assuming that the target language surface structures will be the same as in his L1, that is, that the deep to surface structure procedure will be the same. It may be interesting—or even reassuring—to the student to be shown a common deep structure, but in practising the language this will not put an end to his L1 interference errors. Language teaching has always been concerned with getting the student to produce correct surface structures; the 'intermediate level' does not seem to change much of what we actually present to the student. Moulton[18] in advocating generative contrastive analysis says, in fact, that it is the transformational rules and 'grammatical baggage' associated with them which cause most of the interference, and 'most of the grammar' that we traditionally teach to our students is concerned precisely with transformational rules and with the grammatical baggage that they so often introduce'. Di Pietro's suggestions for the classroom, which are supposed to arise from his theoretical model, contain little that is different, as we shall see later.

The next step, which Di Pietro logically takes, is to say that language teaching based on generative contrastive analysis should be rule-orientated. If, however, as Chomsky[19] suggests, 'A person is not generally aware of the rules that govern sentence-interpretation in the language that he knows; nor, in fact, is there any reason to suppose that the rules can be brought to consciousness', then there is again no reason to suppose that it will help the learner with his actual production of the foreign language to see 'similarities' at the deep structure level. It has also been suggested that we should adapt the order of our teaching materials to fit in with an ordered sequence of transformational rules. For this also we should need to know that 'the speaker's brain ... busily scampers and scuttles through the transformationalist's rules of creation',[20] which Di Pietro himself admits is uncertain.[21] Moreover, if we *do* get evidence of this 'scuttling' in the speaker's brain, it would still be questionable whether he learns to do this from an input of rules. This is certainly not the case in L1 learning, and in view of the lack of evidence it is unwise to assume that it might be the case—or that it might be a shortcut—for the foreign language learner.

Even were it to be desirable to present the rules of the deep structure to the learner, a satisfactory suggestion of how this could be done has not been given. Moulton[22] seems merely to suggest drawing a tree diagram on the board; Lado,[23] in suggesting a formula for the rules of the respective positions of the adjective in Spanish and in English, expresses strong reservations about whether these rules would actually *teach* the point. In any case, these suggestions are far from adequate for the teacher, and the problem of getting the learner to internalise the rules remains. Di Pietro, apart from translation, parsing and tree diagrams, suggests 'substitution types' and 'pattern transformations' which add little to existing language teaching methodology. He is right, no doubt, in saying that if a learner does not know the rules of the target language he will fall back on those of L1, but it is not logical to conclude that teaching must therefore be rule-orientated.

III. Contrastive analysis and translation

The rule-orientated teaching envisaged seems necessarily to involve translation, as explained by Moulton.[24] It had previously been affirmed that contrastive analysis did not imply classroom translation.[25] The language teacher needs to look closely at Di Pietro's assumption that in foreign language production, translation is inevitable, and that, therefore, only a partial account of the target language need be given to the learner. Contrastive analysis having shown where the two languages differ, it will be necessary, the theory goes, to practise only these items and leave the learner to transfer others from his L1, which you cannot stop him doing anyway. Such a supposition will cause problems for teacher and learner alike; if you sanction the learner's temptation to fall back on his L1, then you are assuming that good teaching of items which are different will suffice to forestall his doing the same with these. But even then, presumably, the presentation of the target language cannot be partial in this way, since the learner cannot know which items he can base on his L1 unless they are presented to him at some stage. It is, incidentally, interesting to surmise that this may explain the idea put forward by some that more L1 interference is experienced in learning a similar language. If this 'translation' method has been used, then the habit of falling back on L1 will be probably hard to break. Lee,[26] who felt there was little interference when he was learning Chinese, presumably worked on the assumption that there was no common ground on which to fall back.

It is surely this assumption in the learner that is more likely to result in a fluent use of the target language. From the beginning the learner should be encouraged not to fall back on his L1; rather, when not knowing how to say something in the target language he should try to paraphrase and exploit that mastery of the target language that he has acquired so far. In this way, he can gradually increase his knowledge of acceptable target language utterances. If, on the contrary, we encourage the learner to fall back on the L1 for these items which have not been presented to him as 'different', then he will have a great deal of cause to do this in the early stages. We are, moreover, asking of him something unnecessarily complicated: that he operate in two different ways while trying to use the target language, sometimes transferring, sometimes 'thinking in the language'. The alternative is to encourage him to build up a coordinate system. This is what Rivers,[27] following Pike, calls 'emic' description, or seeing the target language as a coherent system from the inside. If, therefore, the learner is to aim at native speaker mastery, he must practise all the elements which are needed to give him a view of the system of the target language as a whole. As is often pointed out, a learner may master the phonemes singled out by contrastive analysis but will sound distinctly foreign if he has not learnt certain phonetic features of the language (which can equally well be the subject of contrastive analysis).

Now Di Pietro maintains that the learner cannot avoid thinking in his L1 while learning to use the target language. This point is by no means sufficiently well proven for Di Pietro to make it so central to his argument. Not enough is yet known about the complex interaction between language and thought. All we can say is that it is possible to put forward a point of view different from Di Pietro's. Lado,[28] for example, does so, giving two examples to illustrate his hypothesis that there is 'metalinguistic' thought which is distinct from language. He maintains that this is shown in the fact that he can perfectly well understand the distinction in the Hopi plural between *ten men* (an aggregate) and *ten days* (a sequence), even though this is not a distinction made in English plural. Also, he asks pertinently, are we to suppose that a coordinate bilingual programmes himself to think in the language he is about to speak in, or are there some cases when he might have a 'metalinguistic' thought and then be capable of encoding it in whichever language was appropriate for his audience? Lado's 'metalinguistic thought' is the sort of hypothesis that underlies the attempts to teach a mature learner to become a coordinate bilingual. He does not 'modify' his L1 rules, as Di Pietro suggests,[29] but learns a *new* set of rules which would coexist with the L1 set. Interference should thus be minimised: when it occurs through a temporary breakdown of the coordinate system, there will in the advanced target language learner be interference both from the L1 to the target language and vice versa. (This can certainly be seen to happen, contrary to what some people have maintained.[30]) Di Pietro argues that when we are at a loss for a structure or word in the target language, it is impossible to behave as if we knew no other language. In the unstructured situation, however, the immigrant or tourist is more likely to be understood if he builds on his existing target language knowledge than if he falls back on what is effectively translation. And in the structured language learning situation, the question does not arise if the learner is at first practising only those items which have been presented to him.

While not wishing to be fanatical about banishing the L1 from the classroom entirely, many teachers will testify to slower target language learning when frequent recourse to the L1 is allowed. To encourage translation from the beginning makes it very difficult for the advanced learner to avoid translating later on. And while translating, it is unlikely that he will be taken for a native speaker. It is hard to find many structures which can, in fact, be transferred from one language to another, and this is especially true at the advanced level. Differences in frequency, distribution, and stylistic connotation bring us back once more to the errors described by Levenston.

There are thus at least three good reasons why 'similarities' as well as 'differences' should be practised (using contrastive analysis as a starting-point): (1) so that learner will not have to guess in the early stages about which forms are 'similar'; (2) so that he can get an 'emic' view of the target language; (3) so that a hierarchy of difficulties may be based on more than differences. Whether or not teaching based on contrastive analysis should deal only with differences was a subject of debate long before a generative model was proposed, and brings us back to the general points we were making at the beginning about contrastive analysis. There may still be more to be learnt about the various substitutes chosen by a learner for items which do not exist in his L1 from as complete a contrastive analysis as possible; but at the very least, contrastive analysis can help to teach him to use native-type non-distinctive features in his speech, and thus to stop sounding 'foreign'.

To conclude, therefore, contrastive analysis is still in use, and of use, in language teaching. The part it can play should be neither exaggerated nor understated, and there is a place for continuing research. Contrastive analysis based on a structuralist view of language has both its advantages and disadvantages in language teaching. Account must be taken of empirical evidence of its usefulness, and the distinction between a linguistic and a pedagogical grammar borne in mind. We must remember, with Hamp,[31] that a 'good theory' may not be of relevance in teaching. Di Pietro's generative model of contrastive analysis is an exciting theoretical development, but the conclusions he draws for language teaching are highly questionable. It is harmful to make premature and simplistic applications of a new theoretical model, especially since trends in linguistics are sometimes polarised in the extreme. There is no reason why applied linguists should not listen to the voices of empiricism and of eclecticism, the latter having been advocated by the wisest from among their number from Henry Sweet to Wilga Rivers.[32]

Notes

1. Fries, C C (1945) *Teaching and Learning English as a Foreign Language*, University of Michigan: 'The most effective materials are those that are based upon a scientific description of the language to be learned, carefully compared with a parallel description of the native language of the learner' (p. 9).
2. Politzer, R (1968) 'Towards psycholinguistic models of language instruction', *TESOL Quarterly*, Vol. 2, No. 3, Sept. 1968: 'Perhaps the least questioned and least questionable application of Linguistics is the contribution of Contrastive Analysis.'
3. Di Pietro, R (1971) *Language Structures in Contrast*, Newbury House.
4. James, C (1971) 'The exculpation of contrastive linguistics', in G Nickel (ed), *Papers in Contrastive Linguistics*, CUP, pp. 53–68.

5. Richards, J (1971) 'A non-contrastive approach to error analysis' *English Language Teaching*, No. 25, pp. 204-219.
6. Lee, W R (1968) 'Thoughts on contrastive linguistics in the context of language teaching', in J Alatis (*ed*), *Report of 19th Annual Round Table Meeting on Linguistics and Language Studies: Contrastive Linguistics and its Pedagogical Implications*, Georgetown.
7. Baird, A (1967) 'Contrastive studies and the language teacher', *English Language Teaching*, No. 21, gives the example of certain Indian speakers who could use either a dental or retroflex 't' for English 't', whereas in fact, there is a majority who use the retroflex.
8. Lado, R (1968) 'Contrastive linguistics in a mentalistic view of language learning', in J. Alatis, *op cit*.
9. One systematic variation to be explained is Wilkins' observation that French speakers substitute /z/ and /s/ and French Canadians substitute /d/ and /t/ for English /ð/ and /θ/ (*Linguistics in Language Teaching*, p. 201).
10. Lado, R (1968) 'Language learning' in J Alatis, *op cit*.
11. Gardner, R and Lambert, W (1972) *Attitudes and Motivation in Second Language Learning*, Newbury House, Rowley, Mass.
12. Stockwell, R and Bowen, J D (1965) *The Sounds of English and Spanish*, University of Chicago Press.
13. Levenston, E A (1971) 'Over-indulgence and under representation—aspects of mother-tongue interference', in G Nickel, *op cit*, pp. 115–121.
14. Rivers, W (1968) 'Contrastive linguistics in textbook and classroom', in J Alatis (*ed*), *op cit*.
15. Hadlich, R (1965) 'Lexical contrastive analysis', *Modern Language Journal*, No. 49, pp. 426–9.
16. Rivers, W (1972) *Speaking in Many Tongues*, Newbury House, Rowley, Mass.
17. *Op cit*, p. 76.
18. Moulton, W (1968) 'The use of models in contrastive linguistics', in J Alatis (*ed*), *op cit*.
19. Chomsky, N (1966) *Topics in the Theory of Generative Grammar*, The Hague, Mouton.
20. Pulgram, E (1967) 'Sciences, humanities, & the place of linguistics' in D E Thackrey (*ed*), *Research: Definitions Reflections*, University of Michigan Press.
21. *Language Structures in Contrast*, p. 28.
22. Moulton, *op cit*.
23. Lado, *op cit*.
24. Moulton, *op cit*.
25. See C James (1969) 'Deeper contrastive study.' *IRAL*, No 7, pp 83–95.
26. Lee, *op cit*.
27. Rivers, in J Alatis (*ed*), p. 154.
28. Lado, *op cit*.

29. *Language Structures in Contrast*, p. 15.
30. See James in G Nickel (*ed*), *op cit*.
31. Hamp, E P (1968) 'What a contrastive grammar is not, if it is' in J Alatis (*ed*).
32. See C Sanders (1975): 'Troubled relations: linguistic theory and language-teaching', *Modern Languages*, Vol. LVI no. 3 pp. 145–150.

4. Contrastive Linguistics Past and Present and a Communicative Approach

Kari Sajavaara

University of Jyväskylä

Introduction

Since the adoption of the term 'contrastive linguistics' to describe a certain type of comparison between two or more languages, this field of linguistic analysis has been subjected to both great expectations and severe criticism.[1] Most of the recent literature concerning contrastive analysis gives the impression that contrastive linguistics is in the grip of a severe crisis after a boom in the early 1960s. Yet the crisis, if there is one, exists at the level of theoretical discussion only, and contrastive linguistics has progressed rapidly at various centres of active research.

The 'crisis' is at least partly due to a paradox between the theoretical basis of contrastive analysis is and its objectives. As an explanation of this paradox, reference can be made to the past history of contrastive analysis. In this paper, an attempt is made to review the history of contrastive analysis against the background of its objectives and its present problems and to present an outline of procedures which seem to be necessary to make the methods meet the objectives of applied contrastive analysis. Pragmatic and communicative criteria will be introduced for this purpose.

Contrastive analysis past and present

The history of contrastive analysis remains to be written. Only a number of highly cursory discussions are available (Di Pietro, 1971: vii–xv, 9–12; Fisiak 1975; Rusiecki, 1976; Jackson, 1976); these sketches give only a pale reflection of the work of the past decade for

33

the reason that these histories mostly stop at the Georgetown Round Table Conference devoted to contrastive analysis (Alatis (*ed*), 1968) and the active research into contrastive analysis in Europe is not given the attention which it deserves. In the same way, the work being done in a number of Eastern European countries is neglected in general summaries and criticisms of contrastive analysis (eg Corder, 1975; Dirven, 1976; Sanders, 1976). Only exceptionally do the writers accomplish more than mere listings of the projects; the material concerning the objectives and results will have to be collected from a number of conference reports (particularly Filipović (*ed*), 1971; Chitoran (*ed*), 1976) or reports on specific contrastive problems in the series published by various projects. Contrastive analysis had a twin starting-point, although this has not always been recognized. This concerns both the contrastive type of linguistic analysis at the turn of the century and in the thirties (see Fisiak, 1975: 341), and the beginnings of modern contrastive analysis in the forties (Fries, 1945; Trager, 1949). The theoretical objectives were almost entirely forgotten in the wake of Weinreich's (1953) and Lado's (1957) work. For a long time their idea that learning difficulties are equal to the difference between the systems of the two languages contrasted remained highly influential in contrastive analysis. In addition, Lado's statement (1957: vii) to the effect that patterns which will, or will not, cause difficulty can be predicted and described 'by comparing systematically the language and culture to be learned with the native language and the culture of the student' (which was later to be called the Strong Hypothesis for contrastive analysis) may be considered as one of the primary causes of the controversy which ensued in the 1960s. Today, twenty years later, it is rather difficult to see the point in Lado's blue-eyed optimism and one can even venture to express the doubt that Lado never intended his remark to be taken as categorically as some critics of contrastive analysis have taken it; it is to be remembered, however, that, in the late fifties, modern sociolinguistics and psycholinguistics did not exist. Lado's emphasis on the comparison of cultures was mostly forgotten; yet it is there that we can find a clue for a modern revision of the contrastive hypothesis. Side by side with cultural contrasts Lado also stressed the importance of the psychological aspects of language learning.

The early stages of modern contrastive linguistics can be connected with the American type of structuralism, which is another obvious cause for later criticism. The culminating point was, on the one hand, the publication of the Contrastive Structure Series in 1962–1965 and, on the other, the Georgetown Round Table Conference in 1968. The Contrastive Structure Series was primarily designed to help the language teacher in his problems. The volumes which were published reflect the transfer in linguistics from pure structuralism over to transformational grammar. It is ominous in a sense that to this day the CSS volumes remain the last 'complete' contrastive presentations of any two languages and that the studies between English and French and between English and Russian were never published.

The Georgetown conference struck the heaviest note of criticism and for many people this note seems to have subsisted as the last word about contrastive analysis; in most cases the criticism has been accepted without further considering the development which led to it. The Georgetown conference also introduced error analysis as a 'contestant' to contrastive analysis. The discussion which follows is unnecessarily garbled by views which see these two types of analysis as opponents. The re-evaluation of contrastive analysis went on at the Pacific Conference on Contrastive Linguistics and Language Universals, which was held in Hawaii in 1971 (see Whitman and Jackson (ed), 1971).

While American contrastive linguistics slowly died out as a result of severe criticism, the interest in this area of linguistic study was revived in Europe. The German–English PAKS in Kiel, later in Stuttgart, the Polish–English project in Poznań, the Serbo-Croatian–English project in Zagreb, the Romanian–English project in Bucharest and the Hungarian–English in Budapest (see Filipović (ed), 1971) were launched in the mid-sixties. All of the projects initially announced pedagogical applications as their major objective; from the very beginning, however, the research carried out under their auspices covered widely different areas. The PAKS project concentrated on the problems of applying transformational-generative grammar to contrastive analysis (König, 1971); after some promising work the project was discontinued due to a lack of funds. The Polish project has been highly productive (see Kawińska (ed), 1976). It has orientated towards the more theoretical aspects of contrastive analysis—for the past five years within the framework of generative semantics. Pedagogical applications are few in number.

The Zagreb project aims at more practical objectives, which is reflected in a separate pedagogical reports series (eg Filipović (ed), 1974). In the beginning, the results—as voluminous as those of the Polish project—were rather conventional as a result of a close adherence to a translation corpus but more recently the analysis has followed developments in linguistic theory more closely (Filipović, 1976). From the very beginning the Romanian–English project sought ways of avoiding the traditional contrasting of structures and has approached error analysis with psycholinguistic starting-points (Slama-Cazacu, 1971a, 1974; Chitoran, 1976).

The Hungarian project has expanded rapidly in the last few years: the approach is eclectic (see Dezsö and Stephanides, 1976). Problems of theory and methodology have attracted quite a lot of attention in Yugoslavia and Romania but so far the results have been fairly traditional.

No 'complete' contrastive grammar has been published. The introductory Polish–English contrastive grammar, which is in press in Poland, is primarily a textbook of contrastive linguistics based on TG (Fisiak et al, 1975). The book by Burgschmidt and Götz (1974) is, despite its name, a general introduction to contrastive analysis, not a German–English grammar (see James, 1976).

Several new projects were started in the 1970s. The Swedish–English contrastive studies project (SECS) in Lund concentrated on error analysis. Analyses with English have also been launched in Jyväskylä (Finnish), Copenhagen (Danish), and Leuven (French). All of these apply eclectic methodology and aim at practical ends. An important centre in the field is the Mannheim Institute of the German language, where German is contrasted with French, Spanish, and Japanese, among others (Stickel, 1976).

Most of the introductory material on CA is available in a number of conference reports (eg Alatis (ed), 1968; Filipović (ed), 1971; Nickel (ed), 1971, 1974; Chitoran (ed), 1976). Di Pietro made an attempt to review contrastive linguistics for pedagogical purposes on the basis of TG (Di Pietro, 1971); for applied purposes the book contains only rather scanty material. Krzeszowski's contrastive generative grammar (1974) is an important landmark in the history of contrastive theory formation; it leads the way towards still deeper contrastive analysis. By the mid-seventies, a clear picture of the influence of transformational grammar on contrastive analysis has developed (see Lipińska, 1975). Several transformational grammar problems have proved fruitful from the theoretical point of view while the number of practical applications has remained small (see van Buren, 1976; Kohn, 1976). For the time being at least, it is too early to tell if a transformational grammar approach to contrastive analysis will be any more fruitful for applied purposes than structuralism. The major reason for this may be the simple fact that applications of linguistics are not really possible unless the study starts from the problems and tries to find out if there is anything in linguistics that might be useful in solving them. Purity of theory is thus secondary.

The literature concerning contrastive analysis is vast. The most recent bibliography (Sajavaara and Lehtonen (ed), 1975) contains some 1000 titles for the period of the past ten years, and the bibliography is by no means exhaustive. There also exists a recent bibliography of error analysis (Palmberg (ed), 1976).

Traditional contrastive analysis is characterized by the methodological principle that the structure of the languages to be contrasted will have to be described first by means of one and the same theoretical model, and these descriptions are then contrasted for the specification of similarities and dissimilarities. In most cases, the procedure is one of the following five (see, for example, Kühlwein, 1975: 85–86): (1) the same categories of the two languages are contrasted; (2) the equivalents for a certain category of the target language are sought in the source language; (3) rules or hierarchies of rules in the two languages are compared; (4) the analysis starts from a semantic category whose surface realizations are sought in the languages to be contrasted; and (5) the analysis starts from various uses of language.

Reasons for the 'crisis' of contrastive analysis

Despite the fact that most of the literature criticizing contrastive analysis derives its information from dated material, it is quite evident today that traditional contrastive analysis has been unable to solve the problems which have been set for applied contrastive analysis. Most of the criticism centres round the papers presented at the Georgetown conference and takes its driving force from the strong hypothesis of contrastive analysis. As late as the mid-seventies, there still appear reviews of contrastive analysis in which post-Georgetown developments have been disregarded (see, for example, Sanders, 1976; Dirven, 1976). James's paper (1971) refutes most of the points taken up in the criticism in the 1960s. More attention should, however, be paid to criticism which starts from the fact that an important part of contrastive analysis has been much too abstract as compared to its objectives (Slama-Cazacu, 1971; Bausch, 1973).

The reasons for criticism can be found in the history of contrastive analysis, in the heterogeneous nature of the criticism itself, in the theoretical and methodological problems of contrastive analysis, and in the general problems of linguistic theory. The areas causing criticism can be classified in the following way:

(1) relevance for language teaching:
    (a) the predictive nature of contrastive analysis;
    (b) language teaching methodology and contrastive analysis;
(2) structuralism and contrastive analysis;
(3) the turmoil in the theory of grammar;
(4) the theory and methodology of contrastive analysis:
    (a) the problem of equivalence;
    (b) the theory of transfer;
    (c) the independence of linguistic descriptions;
    (d) the abstract nature of the analysis;
    (e) the static nature of the analysis;
(5) the nature of the criticism.

It is somehow contradictory that at the same time as contrastive analysis is severely criticized it appeals to more and more research workers all over the world. Each one of the above points will be discussed separately below.

Relative to language teaching

The first phase of contrastive analysis in the United States can be connected with objectives relevant for language teaching, as implied by the first statements by Fries (1945). In most cases, however, traditional contrastive analysis produced results which were either platitudes known to every experienced language teacher or such abstract contrasts that their application for language teaching purposes seemed fruitless. Most of the results were of the type which could be revealed easily by means of error analysis, and it is not surprising that proponents of error analysis were able to gain ground. This resulted in a lengthy discussion about which of the two should be preferred to the other or which of the two should be subordinated to the other— whether contrastive analysis is subsidiary to error analysis or the other way round. To a certain extent, the distinction between the 'strong' and 'weak' hypotheses of contrastive analysis cleared the air (Wardhaugh, 1970), but by the end of the 1970s it has become quite evident that linguistic contrastive analysis cannot solve all the problems of language learning because not all of them are linguistic.

The obvious connection of contrastive analysis with the mother tongue of language learners produced another point of criticism because in this way contrastive analysis was seen to conflict with the audiolingual method of language teaching. The conflict derives from a misconception about the role of contrastive analysis in the service of language teaching: applied contrastive analysis does not necessarily mean that contrastive analysis is taken to the classroom. The idea that a bilingual method automatically means the acceptance of contrastive methodology is also wrong: bilingual teaching does not necessarily imply contrastive analysis; in superficial contrasting it may even be misleading.

Structuralism and contrastive analysis

The early phases of contrastive analysis are closely related to American structuralism, and many of the early contrastive analyses were written under the influence of the Bloomfieldian type of structuralism. Structuralism lays a strong emphasis on differences between languages, and when it became evident that contrastive analysis cannot concentrate on distinctions alone but should pay attention to similarities, structuralism turned out to be a rather odd bedfellow. It is worth pointing out in this context, however, that American structuralism, as advocated by Sapir and Whorf, also sowed the seeds of the research on language universals. Since it was considered essential for successful contrastive analysis that the two languages were first described in terms of one and same model and structuralism, for its successful contrastive analysis that the two languages were first described in terms of one and same model and structuralism, for its part, concentrated on features which were language-specific, it was not surprising that structural contrastive analysis could not succeed in meeting the applied objectives.

The turmoil in the theory of grammar

The history of contrastive linguistics shows that the descriptions of individual languages which have been adopted for contrastive analysis have changed in accordance with the development of linguistic theory. This is, for instance, reflected in the Contrastive Structure Series, where the structuralistic approach of the early analyses is replaced by a transformational grammar model in the later ones. Several of the projects launched in the course of the past ten years have remained eclectic without adhering too closely to any one of the existing theoretical models (e.g. the Romanian–English project and the Serbo–Croatian one). The only one which has taken a firm stand in this respect is the Polish–English project, which is based on generative semantics. For theoretical contrastive analysis it makes no difference which one of the existing models is selected if it fulfils the demands of descriptive adequacy; the best model is obviously the one which explains a wider range of parameters (see Fisiak et al. 1975). This does not necessarily mean, however, that this kind of model serves applied purposes as well.

Today, the problems of syntactic theory are greater than ten years ago, and there are few people today who are willing to predict in which direction syntactic theory will develop in the next few years; there is no generally accepted model for linguistic description, which also implies that there are not (and will not be in the very near future at least) any complete descriptions of any two languages according to one and the same model. Since it is not possible to make use of description of this kind for contrastive analysis, the first task awaiting a contrastivist has been the description of the relevant languages, which has been an obvious cause of problems of various kinds.

One more conflicting ingredient was introduced by the realization towards the end of the 1960s of the fact that a sentence which is separated from its context is not an exhaustive starting-point for linguistic discussion.

The theory and methodology of contrastive analysis

Discrepancies and contradictions in contrastive methodology have been a self-evident instigator for critics.

(a) Contrastive analysis is mostly built upon *translation equivalence* as established by a bilingual informant. At a crude level of analysis, translation equivalence serves as a satisfactory basis of contrasting. but it is not unambiguous as a theoretical concept (see, for example, Bouton, 1976). The interrelationship between form and meaning remains a burning problem despite attempts to solve it (Marton, 1968; Krzeszowski, 1971, 1974: 11–14). There is no safe method for the specification of the surface categories which correspond to certain deep semantic entities (cf James, 1976). What this implies in practice is that contrastive presentations results in parallel descriptions at best of pairs of languages. It does not seem possible to solve these problems before we are able to establish a hierarchy of various grammatical, referential, notional, sociolinguistic and textlinguistic factors necessary for the interpretation of communicative intentions.

(b) Under the influence of Harris (1954), on the one hand, and the psychology of learning, on the other, the *theory of transfer* has played an important role in the development of error analysis and applied contrastive analysis. Negative transfer, i.e. interference, is expected to result in erroneous forms in the language of the learner. Similar to the problems connected with translation equivalence, it has proved rather difficult to tell which kind of units and at which level this transfer takes place (see Slama-Cazacu, 1971; James, 1976). Moreover, it is difficult to draw a boundary between interference proper and various unconscious strategies whose purpose is to make the foreign-language learning task easier (for a thorough discussion of the problems involved see Kellerman, 1977).

(c) The *independence of the descriptions* of structures in two languages, which is considered essential for contrastive analysis, is illusory only. All major grammatical models have been created in close adherence to descriptions of certain individual languages (see James, 1976); describing other languages by using such models already means contrasting of some kind, and the independence of such a description is questionable. How reliable any further contrastive analyses between these languages are remains a serious theoretical problem.

(d) The *abstract nature* of the analysis has always been a fruitful source of criticism. It is obvious that only rarely can a solution to the problems of language teaching be found in contrastive analysis which is purely linguistic: all the problems are not linguistic. Yet contrastive analysis can be blamed for its abstract nature (eg Slama-Cazacu, 1971; Bausch, 1973) only if contrastive linguistics is regarded as a field of applied linguistics, and there is no reason to do so. Theoretical contrastive linguistics is clearly a branch of theoretical linguistics. If the area of applied linguistics is expanded to cover the application of a grammatical model to the description of an individual language, most contrastive work falls within this area. It is rather difficult, however, to draw the boundary between theoretical and applied research unless all research with a definite objective outside purely scholarly interests is considered as applied research (see Barrera-Vidal and Kühlwein, 1976: 7).

Traditional contrastive analysis has also been too abstract in another sense: it has been too far removed from the reality of a language learner. The research has not started from the problems which a teacher or a learner may have had: applications have been expected to result like parasites from theoretical contrasts (see Sharwood Smith, 1975; cf Bausch and Raabe, 1975 and Wilkins, 1972). Despite finely formulated objectives, contrastive analysis has too often become art for art's sake. Contrastive problems have been discussed in a vacuum without any clear link with the problems raised in the statements concerning the objectives, or in many cases theoretical contrastive analysis, which has an autonomous status as a self-sufficient discipline without any consideration of possible applications, has been made for the purposes of language teaching and has then been criticized for not having applications in language teaching: this kind of criticism has been justified if the contrastivists themselves have been unable to see the distinction between theoretical and applied contrastive analysis.

Many theoretical contrastive descriptions are based on models of linguistic competence. Such models have not, however, been designed to predict how this competence is reflected at the performance level of an individual user of the language. For theoretical purposes a descriptive adequacy of the model is necessary: a theoretical analysis can never be eclectic (Fisiak, 1975: 345). For applied purposes no such preconditions are necessary.

In some models the decoding process of the communication theory has been used to describe the problems of foreign language learning and thereby extended to cover contrastive analysis (see Chitoran, 1970; Nickel, 1971). In such models, the contrast between the source language and the target language is seen as a continuous active process which is supposed to be reflected in both the didactic and methodic programming of teaching. This approach does not solve the basic problems connected with the abstract nature of those linguistic descriptions which are not connected to the communicative function.

Applied contrastive linguistics aims at selecting from all the material available the elements which are necesary for a certain specific purpose. In most cases this means that linguistic competence will have to be correlated to performance, the meaningful use of linguistic and other parameters in various communicative tasks. From a contrastive point of view it is important to see what decisions the speaker has to make to produce a foreign-language utterance instead of a native-language one on the basis of one and the same set of concepts and communicative intentions (cf. Marton, 1974).

(e) Traditional contrastive analysis is based on too *static* a view of the interlingual contrasts. It is static in a number of ways: (1) The variation of natural languages is disregarded, mainly because the descriptions of individual languages are based on the scholar's competence or normative descriptions. (2) The source language and target language are considered to be equal as far as the student is concerned (see, however, Fisiak, 1975). (3) The learner's position in relation to the target language (as well as to the source language) is regarded as stable; yet an elementary learner is in a position different from that of an advanced learner (for an interesting discussion of this distinction as regards the lexicon, see Marton, 1977), a child's position is different from that of an adult, etc. While the proficiency in the foreign language increases, the learner's stand in relation to both languages changes radically. (4) Not much attention has been paid to the roles of the speaker and the hearer and the constant shifting of these roles in a communicative situation. The psychological and neurological aspects of the process of production and that of perception remain unknown for the most part; it seems probable that the theories based on the communication theory which regarded these processes as equivalents of encoding and decoding are not correct. Production and reception cannot be considered reverse processes, mirror images of each other. The native speaker seems to rely on a capacity of prediction which is derived from his experience with the language. Perception actually means parallel construction of the sentence by means of all available cues, both linguistic and non-linguistic.

It is quite evident today that much more attention should be paid to the different roles of the speaker/hearer for the purposes of applied contrastive analysis.

The nature of the criticism

Most of the criticism of contrastive analysis has dwelt on the fact that contrastive analysis has been unable to meet the objectives which were set for it in the fifties. Few critics have stopped to question whether contrastive analysis was actually able to pinpoint linguistic structures whose analysis would produce desired results. It is clear today that early contrastive analysis did not meet its objectives, but it is difficult to tell where it really went wrong. What was definitely not wrong was the basic idea of contrasting languages; the evidence of transfer and interference even at a rather superficial level of analysis is so plentiful that it cannot be ignored. If the basic assumption was not wrong, which implies the validity of a contrastive analysis hypothesis, then the source of the problems will have to be sought in the ways and means of carrying out the task of contrasting languages: the only conclusion which can be drawn from a discussion like this is the insufficiency of the study of the linguistic parameters for the solution of the problems which contrastive analysis was expected to untangle.

In many cases, error analysis was offered as aid in the methodological crisis of contrastive analysis (see, for example, Grucza, 1976): it was considered either as a replacement for contrastive analysis or as a primary level of analysis to which contrastive analysis was to be subordinated. Yet many proponents of error analysis failed to see that applied contrastive analysis and error analysis are both methods whose target is one and the same: the problems connected with the learner's language. Several scholars interested in this area have expressed the opinion that contrastive analysis should begin with the investigation of the phenomenon for which it was originally created, i.e. interference (see, for example, Slama-Cazacu, 1971; Bausch, 1973). The Romanian–English contrastive project has successfully applied this principle in its contact analysis (see Slama-Cazacu (ed), 1975).

In the last few years, proponents of error analysis have given up the one-sided description of learners' errors in favour of the study of interlanguage (approximate system). In this way, a rather static basis of analysis has been replaced by an analysis of the processes of language learning; the learner's language is no longer seen as an erroneous form of the language but as an *état de dialecte* (Corder, 1972, 1975).

It is certainly wrong to assume that contrastive analysis and error analysis are subsidiary to each other or that they only complement one another. Rather, they are two fields of inquiry within a vast entity, the research into the problems of learning strategies. The main emphasis should be put on the whole of the learner's language; contrastive analysis and error analysis should be correlated to each other within this framework (they cannot be separated); furthermore, they should be correlated to the general principles of communicative networks.

Communicative competence

In the linguistic discussion of the last few years, the original Chomskyan borderline between competence and performance has been
disintegrating, mainly under the influence of sociolinguistic research.
Linguistic competence—most of the attention has been focused on
grammatical competence—is now seen to be a part of a wider entity;
the entire communicative behaviour of the human being is now under
scrutiny. Emphasis lies on utterances in contexts where they are made
(see Campbell and Wales, 1970). Grammatical competence has been
replaced by communicative competence, which means the ability to
communicate verbally and non-verbally in culturally restricted contexts. Furthermore, communicative competence is an element in a
wider entity, sociocultural competence (see Dirven *et al*, 1976: 2), but
for the purposes of the present discussion this distinction can be
disregarded. The same concerns the distinction between communicative competence and communicative behaviour (Piepho, 1974: 12).
(For various terminological and related problems connected with the
concept of communicative competence, see Östman and Phillips,
1977.)

Communicative competence consists of grammatical competence and
pragmatics. A major part of linguistic research has so far centred
round the problems of grammatical competence involving various
aspects of the interrelationship between form and meaning. Communication is a form of social behaviour which cannot be separated
from the context where it takes place and where the participants in
the communicative act are involved in constant interaction; pragmatics can be considered the set of rules for such an interactional
behaviour. It can be likened to a game; language structures correspond to various pieces and the rules to rules of the game:

> Speech communication is a series of events resembling a game in which
> each time we make a move we have to produce for ourselves the piece we
> intend to move. It is difficult to tell what is more important in the game:
> if we do not know the pieces used in the game (recognize phonemes of a
> foreign language in speech), we cannot interpret the moves of our oppo-
> nent even if we know the rules of the game; if we are not acquainted with
> the rules of the game (for instance, the phonological structure of words in
> the language), the mere skill of recognizing the characteristics of the

pieces is not sufficient; if we are not able to shape our pieces so that the opponent can recognize our moves, it will be difficult for our opponent to grasp the meaning of our intention in the game. Just like the game of chess, speech communication is a game played by two people whose respective moves always take place in response to those of the fellow player. In a speech game it is equally important for us to understand what our fellow speaker means by what he says as it is for the speaker of a foreign language to understand the meaning of our message. The purpose of the speech game is not however to checkmate the opponent. (Lehtonen, Sajavaara and May, 1977: 12.)

In communicative situations, the pragmatics, ie the rules of the game, consist of various parameters related to psycholinguistics (eg the attitudes of the speaker and the hearer and possible third parties towards the speech situation), to social psychology (eg the roles of the participants), and to sociolinguistics (eg various norms involved). In interactional behaviour it is necessary for the participants to recognize and heed each other's communicative intentions. Communicative behaviour is based on a number of rules, 'conversational postulates', which are seldom ignored (see Grice, 1975; Gordon and Lakoff, 1975; Lakoff, 1972). For the time being, we have not yet got enough information about the relevance of all the different parameters which are present at a communicative act (see in particular Golopentia–Eretescu, 1974). The following list is not exhaustive: speaker, hearer, time and place, code (broken down to various components), channel, various prerequisites of the speaker–hearer (knowledge of the world, knowledge of the other parties of the speech event, social relationships and roles, including various rules of politeness and hierarchies, norms, understanding of earlier messages, most of which is normally covered by the concept of presupposition), intentions of the speaker and the hearer, affective states, non-verbal elements of the communicative act, and problem-solving capacity (see Wunderlich, 1971; Dirven and Radden, 1976: 63; Fawcett, 1973: 8; Baur *et al*, 1975; Hening and Huth, 1975). In many cases, the verbal part of the message may be so garbled that it remains unintelligible to persons who are not acquainted with at least the majority of the parameters listed above.

The communicative approach has meant that language is no longer studied as a 'grammar', abstract, divorced from its user, but is approached as a means of human interaction. In this respect, language follows the same rules as other types of behaviour, and the description of how people use language will have to be correlated to our knowledge of man's overall cognitive behaviour and perceptive capacities. For language teaching, the communicative approach has meant the connection of linguistic elements with meaningful speech acts and with contexts where speech acts are made. Today it is also clear that the situational approach to language teaching does not really mean any thorough change in the grammatical and audio-lingual method unless some sort of a notional or functional system is introduced at the same time. The speech acts will have to be connected with contexts, but a lot of research is needed in the ordering of various notional, referential, sociolinguistic and contextual factors.

The communicative behaviour of a speaker of a foreign language could be viewed through the concept of 'fluency', which is often used to describe the high-level performance of a good foreign-language learner and which is often, wrongly, connected with the production of a certain rate of speech. Criteria such as lack of hesitation and pauses, length of sentences, absence of errors, etc, are also often mentioned, but there is no scientific definition of fluency (see, however, Leeson, 1975).

Fluency cannot, however, be approached from the speaker's point of view alone: the communicative situation will have to be observed as an entity in which the hearer has an important function. The speaker's performance is conditioned by the hearer's performance, ie the linguistic and other cues the latter receives from the speaker or independently brings into the communicative act; is also conditioned by the alternation of the roles of speaker and hearer between the participants in the act.

Fluency necessarily implies quality of performance which consists of a multiplicity of factors (this list is not exhaustive and should be considered only as an indication of the complex nature of the problem; see also Lehtonen, Sajavaara and May, 1977: 20–22).

Linguistic factors:
    (1) phonological and phonetic factors: absence of phonetic and

phonological errors, also as concerns suprasegmental features, variations in performance, mastery of optional cues etc;
(2) syntactic factors: absence of syntactic errors: capacity of generating new utterances to fulfil the communicative needs;
(3) semantic factors: awareness of the interrelationship between syntax and semantics and of the influence of extralinguistic factors on language;
(4) lexical factors: mastery of the vocabulary necessary for linguistic behaviour in a given situation (for highly relevant syntagmatic problems see Marton, 1977);
(5) textual factors: sensitivity to cohesion, ellipsis, deixis, etc.

Psychological (neurological) factors:
(1) absence of phonological distortion brought about by increased breathing rate and noise caused by tension;
(2) absence of pauses and hesitation not allowed by native speakers (as a result of insufficient linguistic competence or various psychological factors such as tension or shyness).

Sociolinguistic factors:
(1) awareness of social judgments necessary for the production of acceptable utterances in a given situation;
(2) sensitivity to various sociolinguistic, cultural and environmental features including those which are based on interpersonal relationships;
(3) correct interpretation of the varieties of language and the functional values of utterance;
(4) ability to make the necessary judgments and decisions within the time constraints of the communicative situation; the limits are set by the speaker/hearer interaction, which for its part is conditioned by a complex of internal (personal and non-personal) and external parameters.

Existence or non-existence of fluency cannot be attributed to any single one of these factors or even a combination of them. Hesitation and pauses as well as false starts and rephrasings are quite natural in native-speaker performance; it is wrong to assume that a foreign-language performance would be any different. The length of the sentence is an indication of the fact that the speaker governs the generative and recursive powers of the language, which, however, is only one ingredient of fluency. The phenomena sketched above approach communicative competence: it is impossible to distinguish fluency from communicative competence.

Communicative competence and contrastive analysis

The native language of a speaker and the foreign languages which he may speak can be regarded as parts of his communicative competence: learning a foreign language means expansion of this competence over to the area of another code. We can expand Halliday's (1975) analysis of the learning of L1 and talk about 'learning how to mean' in another code, another language. This implies that many of the parameters which were discussed in the preceding chapter remain more or less unchanged. Contrastive analysis should therefore be directed to elements of communicative competence which will have to be changed as compared to L1 competence to make L2 competence operative (cf Marton, 1974). Since communicative competence includes a wide range of elements which are outside grammatical competence, it is now evident that traditional contrastive analysis failed to serve the purposes of applied linguistics simply for the reason that contrasting grammatical competence is highly insufficient; even if we wanted to devote our analysis to linguistic elements in contrastive analysis, the results of this analysis should be correlated to the other aspects of communicative competence.

The communicative approach necessarily leads to contrastive discourse analysis. Contrasts of structures which are carried out in laboratory conditions will always remain abstractions from the applied point of view, and it is therefore necessary to study all the various factors of communication and the communicative act which make it possible, or impossible, for the participants to understand the messages. Traditional contrastive analysis has been much too simple for this, and it has postulated contrasts which are far from the psycholinguistic reality of bilingual language user. The psycholinguistic contrast takes place in the form of a contact in the 'mind' of the language learner. Moreover, the speaker and the hearer have been considered from one and the same angle: for contrastive communicative purposes, it is to be remembered that the role of the student as a speaker is highly different from his role as a hearer (see Lehtonen, Sajavaara and May, 1977: 16–19).

Contrastive analysis will have to be expanded to the following areas:

(1) *Linguistic research* is needed in various subdisciplines of linguistic analysis (phonetics, syntax, semantics, lexicon, text). It is not sufficient, however, to analyse the systems of the two languages as mere parallels. Instead, these systems will have to be brought side by side in relevant contexts for making observations on parameters which affect the intelligibility of messages in communicative situations. This implies research on the L1 and L2 discourse of the same informants and on their verbal and non-verbal communicative behaviour with native and non-native speakers of the target language concerned. The whole of the discourse must be observed, both correct and erroneous elements.[2] Particular attention should be paid to features which bring about a 'foreign accent' (see Jenner, 1976).

(2) *Psycholinguistic research* (the boundary between this area and the types of research mentioned above is not categorical) will include investigations into the types of hesitation and pauses allowed in L2 discourse without the communication being twisted and into the effects of hesitation and shyness in L1 and L2, particularly as related to insufficient linguistic competence. Contrastive psycholinguistic studies of various attitudinal and emotive factors are also needed.

(3) Contrastive *sociolinguistic studies* are needed of the social decisions which a speaker–hearer is expected to make for his utterances to be acceptable in given social situations. We need contrastive information about the influence of the variation in the two languages on the language contact and about the influence of various functions of language. The roles of the speaker–hearer (including the role of the foreigner) and various norms affecting communication will have to be investigated from a contrastive angle. The time factor referred to above is an important sociolinguistic factor: we will have to investigate how much time the speakers have as conditioned by the situation and the speaker–hearer interaction in order to make decisions as regards the implementation of their communicative intentions.

Conclusion

Language has several ritualistic and conventional elements; such elements are easily overemphasized in foreign language teaching because of their stable character (this was clearly evident in the audiolingual method). Instead of a ritual, language should be seen the way Halliday (1975) sees it, as a potential, and language teaching should aim at a highly efficient use of this potential. This concerns the mother tongue and the foreign/second languages alike. Language was compared above to a game which may be governed differently by different people depending on their different capacities: the rules are the same for everybody but the tactics and strategies applied may differ considerably. The rules vary from language to language, and it is quite evident today that traditional contrastive analysis has only scratched the surface of this complex of rules, the linguistic and communicative behaviour of the human being. Contrastive analysis may be criticized for this, but this does not mean that the contrastive hypothesis had no validity.

Notes

1. A slightly different Finnish version of this paper has appeared in Sajavaara (ed), 1977.
2. For the methodology and practice of contrastive discourse analysis see Lehtonen, Sajavaara and Korpimies, 1977.

References

Alatis, J (ed) (1968) 'Contrastive linguistics and its pedagogical implications.' *Monograph Series on Languages and Linguistics* 21. Washington, DC: Georgetown University Press.

Berrera-Vidal, A and Kühlwein, W (1975) *Angewandte Linguistik für den fremdsprachlichen Unterricht.* Dortmund: Lensing.

Baur, M, Bauer, R S, Bausch, K-R, Brammerts, H, Kleppin, K, Lübbert, E and Moffat, A (1975) *Pragmatik und Fremdsprachenunterricht: eine rollentheoretische Pilotstudie.* Manuscript zur Sprachlehrforschung 8. Bochum: Zentrales Fremdspracheninstitut der Ruhr-Universität Bochum.

Bausch, K-R (1973) 'Kontrastive linguistik.' In W A Koch (ed) (1973 *Perspektiven der Linguistik* 1. Stuttgart: Kröner, 159–182.

Bausch, K-R and Raabe, H (1975) 'Der Filter "Kontrastivität" in einer Lehrer-grammatik: eine Skizze der Probleme und Perspektiven.' In *Beiträge und Materialen zur Ausbildung von Fremdsprachenlehrern* 2. Bochum: Zentrales Fremdspracheninstitut der Ruhr-Universitiät Bochum, 415–439.

Bouton, L F (1976) 'The problem of equivalence in contrastive analysis.' *IRAL* 14, 143–163.

van Buren, P (1976) Review of Krzeszowski (1974) *ISB* 1, 250–329.

Burgschmidt, E and Götz, D (1974) *Kontrastive Linguistik Deutsch/English*. Hueber Hochschulreihe 23. München: Hueber.

Campbell, R and Wales, R (1970) 'The study of language acquisition.' In J Lyons (*ed*) *New horizons in linguistics*. Harmondsworth: Penguin, 242–260.

Chiţoran, D (1971) 'A model for second language acquisition.' In Filipović (*ed*) (1971) 173–180.

Chiţoran, D (1976) 'Report on the Romanian–English contrastive analysis project.' In Chiţoran (*ed*) (1976), 11–34.

Chiţoran, D, (*ed*) (1976) *2nd International Conference of English Contrastive Projects*. Bucharest: University Press.

Cole, P and Morgan, J L (*eds*) (1975) *Syntax and semantics* 3. New York: Academic Press.

Corder, S P (1972) 'Zur Beschreibung der Sprache des Sprachlerners.' In Nickel (*ed*) (1972) 175–184.

Corder, S P (1975) 'Error analysis, interlanguage and second language acquisition: survey article.' *Language teaching and linguistics: Abstracts* 8, 201–218.

Dezsö, L and Stephanides, E (1976) 'Report on the English–Hungarian contrastive linguistics project.' In Chiţoran (*ed*) (1976), 53–58.

Di Pietro, R J (1971) *Language structures in contrast*. Rowley, Mass.: Newbury House.

Dirven, R (1976) 'A redefinition of contrastive linguistics.' *IRAL* 14, 1–14.

Dirven, R and Radden, G (1976) *Semantic syntax of English: a constrastive approach*. Trier: LAUT.

Dirven, R, Hünig, W, Kühlwein, W, Radden, G and Strauss, J (1976) *Die Leistung der Linguistik für den Englischunterricht*. Tübingen: Niemeyer.

Fawcett, R (1973) 'Language functions and language variation in a cognitive model of communication.' Paper presented to the AILA/BAAL seminar on 'The communicative teaching of English' held at Lancaster, March–April 1973.

Filipović, R (1976) 'The Yugoslav Serbo-Croatian–English contrastive project from the Zagreb conference to the present.' In Chiţoran (*ed*) (1976), 35–51.

Filipović, R (*ed*) (1971) *Zagreb conference on English contrastive projects, 7–9 December 1970* The Yugoslav Serbo-Croatian–English contrastive project. B. Studies. Zagreb: Institute of Linguistics.

Filipović, R (*ed*) (1974) *Pedagogical materials* 2. The Yugoslav Serbo-Croatian–English contrastive project. Zagreb: Institute of English.

Fisiak, J (1975) 'The contrastive analysis of phonological systems.' *Kwartalnik Neofilologiczny* 22, 341–351.

Fisiak, J, Lipińska-Grzegorek, M and Zabrocki, T (1978) *An introductory English-Polish contrastive grammar*. Warszawa: PWN.

Fisiak, J (*ed*) (1975) *Papers and studies in contrastive linguistics* 3. Poznań: Adam Mickiewicz University.

Fisiak, J (*ed*) (1976) *Papers and studies in contrastive linguistics* 5. Poznań: Adam Mickiewicz University.

Fries, C C (1945) *Teaching and learning English as a foreign language*. Ann Arbor: University of Michigan Press.

Golopenţia-Eretescu, S (1974) 'Towards a contrastive analysis of conversational strategy.' In *Further developments in contrastive studies*. The Romanian-English contrastive analysis project. Bucharest: University Press, 79–132.

Gordon, D and Lakoff, G (1975) 'Conversational postulates.' In Cole and Morgan (*eds*) (1975) 83–106.

Grice, H P (1975) 'Logic and conversation.' In Cole and Morgan (*eds*) (1975), 41–58.

Grucza, F (1976) 'Fehlerlinguistik, Lapsologie und Kontrastive Forschungen.' *Kwartalnik Neofilologiczny* 23, 237–247.

Halliday, M A K (1975) *Learning how to mean*. London: Arnold.

Harris, Z S (1954) 'Transfer grammar.' *IRAL* 20, 259–270.

Hennig, J and Huth, L (1975) *Kommunikation als Problem der Linguistik*. Göttingen: Vanderhoeck and Ruprecht.

Jackson, H (1976) 'Contrastive linguistics—what is it?' *ITL* 32, 1–32.

James, C (1971) 'The exculpation of contrastive linguistics.' In Nickel (*ed*) (1971), 53–68.

James, C (1976) Review of Burgschmidt and Götz (1974). *IRAL* 14, 203–205.

Jenner, B R A (1976) 'Interlanguage and foreign accent.' *ISB* 1, 166–196.

Kellerman, E (1977) 'Towards a characterization of the strategy of transfer in second language learning.' *ISB* 2, 58–145.

Kohn, K (1976) 'Theoretical aspects of generative contrastive analysis.' *Folia Linguistica* 9, 125–134.

König, E (1971) 'Transformational grammar and contrastive analysis.' In Filipović (*ed*) (1971), 130–145.

Krzeszowski, T P (1971) 'Equivalance, congruence and deep structure.' In Nickel (*ed*) (1971), 37–48.

Krzeszowski, T P (1974) *Contrastive generative grammar: Theoretical foundations*. Łódź: University of Łódź.

Kühlwein, W (1975) 'Grundsatzfragen der kontrastiven Linguistik.' *Neusprachliche Mitteilungen* 28, 80–99.

Lado, R (1957) *Linguistics across cultures*. Ann Arbor: University of Michigan Press.

Lakoff, R (1972) 'Language in context.' *Language* 48, 907–927.

Leeson, R (1975) *Fluency and language teaching*. London: Longman.

Lehtonen, J Sajavaara K and May A (1977) *Spoken English: The perception and* production of spoken English on a Finnish–English contrastive basis. Jyväskylä: Gummerus.

Lehtonen, J, Sajavaara, K and Korpimies, L (1977) 'The methodology and practice of contrastive discourse analysis.' In Sajavaara and Lehtonen (eds) Jyväskylä contrastive studies 5. Jyväskylä: Department of English.

Lipińska, M (1975) 'Contrastive analysis and the modern theory of language.' In Fisiak (ed) (1975), 5–62.

Marton, W (1968) 'Equivalence and congruence in transformational contrastive studies.' Studia Anglica Posnaniensia 1, 62–63.

Marton, W (1974) 'Some remarks on the formal properties of contrastive pedagogical grammars.' In Nickel (ed) (1974), 182–195.

Marton, W (1977) 'Foreign vocabulary learning as problem no. 1 of language teaching at the advanced level.' ISB 2, 33–57.

Mieszek, A (1976) 'Bibliography of English–Polish contrastive studies in Poland.' In Fisiak (ed) (1976) pp. 288–300.

Nickel, G (1971) 'Contrastive linguistics and foreign language teaching.' In Nickel (ed) (1971), 1–16.

Nickel, G (ed) (1971) Papers in contrastive linguistics. Cambridge: Cambridge University Press.

Nickel, G (ed) (1972) Reader zur kontrastiven Linguistik. Frankfurt am Main: Athenäum Fischer.

Nickel, G (ed) (1974) AILA Third congress—Copenhagen 1972. Proceedings 1. Heidelberg: Julius Groos.

Östman, J-O and Philips, G (1977) 'Communicative competence and special issue on teaching and testing communicative competence.' Kielikeskusuutisia (Language Centre News, University of Jyväskylä) 1, 11–23.

Palmberg, R (ed) (1976) 'A select bibliography of error analysis and related topics.' ISB 1, 340–389.

Piepho, H-E (1974) Kommunikative Kompetenz als übergeordnetes Lernziel im Englischunterricht. Dornburg-Frickhofen: Frankonius-Verlag.

Rusiecki, J (1976) 'The development of contrastive linguistics.' ISB 1, 12–44.

Sajavaara, K (ed) (1977) Näkökulmia kieleen. Suomen sovelletun kielitieteen yhdistyksen AFinLA:n julkaisuja. Helsinki: AFinLA.

Sajavaara, K and Lehtonen, J (eds) (1975) 'A select bibliography of contrastive analysis.' Jyväskylä contrastive studies 1. Reports from the Department of English 1. Jyväskylä: Department of English.

Sanders, C (1976) 'Recent developments in contrastive analysis and their relevance to language teaching.' IRAL 14, 67–73.

Sharwood Smith, M (1974) 'Contrastive studies in two perspectives.' In Fisiak (ed) PSiCL 2, 5–10.

Slama-Cazacu, T (1971) 'Psycholinguistics and contrastive studies.' In Filipović (ed) (1971), 188–206.

Slama-Cazacu, T (1974) 'The concepts of "acquisition corpus", "abberrant corpus", and "hierarchical systems of errors" in contrastive analysis.' In Nickel (ed) (1974), 235–251.

Slama-Cazacu, T (ed) (1975) *The psycholinguistic approach in the Romanian–English contrastive analysis project 1*. Bucharest: University Press.

Stickel, G (1976) 'Voraussetzungen und Ziele einer kontrastiven Untersuchung des Deutschen und des Japanischen.' In Stickel (ed) *Deutsch–japanische Kontraste: Vorstudien zu einer kontrastiven Grammatik*. Forschungsberichte des Instituts für deutsche Sprache 29. Tübingen: TBL Verlag Gunter Narr, 3–29.

Trager, G L (1949) 'The field of linguistics.' *Studies in linguistics. Occasional papers* 1. Norman, Okl.: Battenburg.

Wardhaugh, R (1970) 'The contrastive analysis hypothesis.' *TESOL quarterly* 4, 123–130.

Weinreich, U (1953) *Languages in contact*. Publications of the Linguistic Circle of New York 1. New York: The Linguistic Circle.

Whitman, R L and Jackson, K L (eds) (1971) *The PCCLLU Papers. Working papers in linguistics* 3:4. Honolulu: Department of Linguistics, University of Hawaii.

Wilkins, D (1972) *Linguistics in language teaching*. London: Arnold.

Wunderlich, D (1971) 'Pragmatik, Sprechsituation, Deixis.' *Zeitschrift für Literaturwissenschaft und Linguistik* 1, 153–190.

5. The Transfer of Communicative Competence*

Carl James

University College of North Wales, Bangor

Contrastive Analysis is concerned with the notions of 'transfer' and 'interference', and it is for this concern that it has borne the brunt of the discredit meted out in opposition to structure-based theories of language teaching by advocates of the movement for teaching communicative competence. Note the word-play in some early writings from this movement. Newmark (1970) offered interesting and seminal suggestions on 'How not to interfere with language learning', and Newmark and Reibel (1968: 149) attacked contrastive analysis directly as endorsing a teacher-centred rather than learner-centred approach to foreign-language learning, claiming that 'The excessive preoccupation with the contribution of the teacher ... distracted the theorists from considering the role of the learner as anything but a generator of interference'. It is not my purpose here to vindicate contrastive analysis, but to determine whether and to what extent contrastive analysis and teaching for communicative competence are in fact incompatible enterprises. My terms of reference are the classical Ladonian paradigm of contrastive analysis endorsed by James (1971) and the discourse on the nature of Communicative Competence of Hymes (1971): their common date is to be taken as a fortuitous coincidence.

The communicative competence movement seeks to de-emphasise structure in favour of assigning priority to meaning. This is why it has

* Paper read at the 14th International Conference on Polish–English Contrastive Linguistics, Boszkowe, December 7–10, 1977. I wish to express my indebtedness to the British Council for financially supporting my attendance at this conference.

blossomed in the intellectual climate of Generative Semantics, the contributions from ordinary language philosophers like Austin, Searle and Grice, and Halliday's Functionalism. Yet on the other hand, the movement has relied for its endorsement on *structural* information of a particular kind: that pertaining to child language acquisition. With some alacrity it has welcomed indications, albeit couched in structuralist terms (Dulay and Burt, 1974; Ravem, 1974), that second-language learning in a natural setting is not qualitatively, though it may be quantitatively, different from primary-language acquisition. This finding has been taken as a reliable indication that the student's natural language-learning capacity will ensure success, provided he has sufficient *meaningful* exposure to the target language '... if particular, whole instances of the language are modeled for him and if his own particular acts using the language are selectively reinforced' (Newmark and Reibel, 1968: 149). This proposal is vividly realised in the practices described by Allwright (1977) for managing the English learning of university-level students in a 'remedial' programme.

The study of child language has likewise now begun to turn its back on structural accounts of the process. Developing Brown's (1973) call for 'rich' interpretations of acquisition data, those which rely heavily upon situationally-cued meanings, Halliday (1975) has provided a Functionalist interpretation of the process of a child's (Nigel's) acquisition. Here are some representative statements from Halliday's work:

(i) '... language development is much more than the acquisition of structure' (1975: 3).
(ii) 'Early language development may be interpreted as the child's progressive mastery of functional potential' (1975: 5).
(iii) [The child] '... learns to mean long before he adopts the lexical mode for the realisation of meanings' (1975: 9).

Here, then, is one *crucial* difference between L1 and L2 learning: infants, while mastering the formal devices of languages, are simultaneously, and thereby, learning 'how to mean'. Adult learners of an L2, by contrast, enter the experience with a well-developed command *yes but depends on closeness of L^1 & L_2*

of a functional system: their problem is not to learn *how to mean*, but
to learn how to *convey* an already internalised system of meanings
through a different or partially different structural *code*. Obviously
this code will have to be learnt, and the differences between L1 and
L2 codes '... are the chief source of difficulty in learning a second
language' (Lado, 1964: 21).

That at least one category of foreign-language learners need not be
taught 'how to mean', since they can transfer their L1 modes of
meaning to L2, has been conceded by Widdowson (1975b: 6): '... the
language user himself knows how to create and understand discourse
of different kinds expressed in his own language'. The 'meanings' he
refers to, however, are rather specialised ones, since he is writing of
English for Special Purposes: 'fields of enquiry in the physical and
applied sciences, as they are generally understood, are defined by
their communicative systems, which exist as a kind of cognitive deep
structure independently of individual realisations in different languages' (Widdowson, 1975b: 6) and further 'the communicative systems of different scientific disciplines are independent of any particular linguistic realisation' (1975b: 7). These statements are reminiscent
of those in classical contrastive analysis which refer to *meaning* as the
constant in comparison (the 'tertium comparationis'), the difference
being that Widdowson refers to the supposed universality of specialised communicative systems, familiarity with which he regards as
constituting knowledge of 'how to create and understand discourse'.
Although his concern is with ESP one might perhaps make the same
claim, even more legitimately, in respect of a generalist or generalised
communicative competence. It should be borne in mind that Widdowson's claim about the universality of technical and scientific rhetoric is purely conjectural, awaiting empirical validation, but if it is
indeed universal then there can be no talk of 'contrastive scientific
rhetoric' just as there can be no such thing as 'contrastive semantics',
for the simple reason that universality precludes contrastivity. The
same must be said of the generalist analogue to technical rhetoric,
communicative competence, the proper study of which is the province
of Linguistic Pragmatics: as I understand the term, from my reading
of Stalnaker (1972) and of Lakoff (1976) such things as Grice's (1967)
conversational maxims and Lakoff's rules of politeness are very prob-

ably universal, so there will be no 'contrastive pragmatics' to occupy us in the forseeable future.

The relationship that Widdowson sees between specialist and generalist English is one of complementarity. He assumes that if students have a knowledge of the structural properties of generalist English, they will be able to combine this with their L1 knowledge of their scientific discipline to master the rhetoric of scientific English. In that case I take it that structural knowledge of the L2 must be a prerequisite for specialist communicative competence in the L2. If it is the case that generalist structural knowledge can serve specialist communicative competence we are faced with a number of questions. First, would it not be better for ESP students to have specialist structural facility from the start? Widdowson (1975b: 3) dismisses this on the grounds that 'a knowledge of how English is used in scientific and technical communication can ... [not] ... arise as a natural consequence from the learning of the sentence patterns and vocabulary which are manifested most frequently in samples of communication of this kind'. The next question therefore concerns the *order of priorities* for teaching usage and use: should structural knowledge, a sine qua non for communication, be imparted simultaneously with instruction and opportunities for use, or be imparted prior to these opportunities for use? As Allwright (1977: 3) puts the question:

'Are we teaching *language* (for communication)? or
Are we teaching *communication* (via language)?

Yet, as we have already seen, the communication system *per se* 'as a kind of cognitive deep structure' does not need to be taught, since it is already acquired knowledge in adult generalists and in scientists who know how to be scientists in the L1. What do need to be taught therefore are the structural or formal resources that realise communicative acts in the L2. Where some of these formal resources are isomorphic with those of the L1 they will not have to be taught either, since as contrastive analysts have long insisted, they can be transferred from the L1 to L2. The task at hand is to ascertain which formal resources can be allowed to be transferred, and the answer will be: only those which are both isomorphic and have the same semantic, rhetorical and pragmatic values as the L2 form with which they are matched. It seems that the communicative competence teaching movement is irrationally eclectic in recognising learner's right to transfer his underlying systems of communication, but not their formal realisations, to the L2; even though the feasibility of their transfer *within* the L2, from generalist to specialist use, is endorsed by a writer like Widdowson.

The main reason why there is widespread disaffection toward the teaching of structure is that teachers' efforts have been negatively reinforced by their pupils: there is usually a great discrepancy between 'input' (what is taught) and 'intake' (what is learnt). Instead of learning the forms of the target language, learners exhibit an exasperating tendency to 'learn' deviant forms. Moreover, this deviance seems not to be always proportionate to the degree of mismatch between L1 and L2 forms (cf Whitman and Jackson, 1972). As if in despair, foreign-language teaching theorists have chosen to redraw their policies, and have accordingly decided that grammatical deviance can be tolerated provided learners are putting their message across. It has even been suggested that provided the L2 is being put to meaningful use, the incidence of error in fact drops, though I know of no supportive evidence for this speculation.

Now learners' error making has become big business and has engendered the subdiscipline of Error Analysis within Applied Linguistics. Widdowson (1975b) has interpreted the errors learners make as evidence for what Selinker (1969) called 'strategies of communication', and identifies as their common denominator a desire on the learner's part to simplify: they provide 'a partial account of basic simplifying procedures which lie at the heart of communicative competence' (Widdowson, 1975b). This simplification, he contends, can involve either an increase or decrease in complexity, which is not so paradoxical in the light of the spectacular asymmetry that psycholinguists have revealed between linguistically defined complexity of derivation and psychological difficulty. The pedagogic implication that Widdowson sees is one that you have to be courageous to publish: rather than opting for 'remedial teaching through which errors are eradicated' (as is standard practice), Widdowson proposes 'initial teaching through which errors are exploited. That is to say, one might devise syllabuses which actually presented the erroneous forms which particular groups of learners were prone to produce, gradually bringing 'correct' standard forms into focus as the course progressed'. This approach, he adds, '... would be in line with current approaches to the teaching of communicative competence'.

Widdowson's proposal has been made before, both in covert and in overt forms. In covert form, Hymes (1971: 287) suggests '... one should perhaps contrast a 'long' and a 'short' range view of competency, the short range view being interested primarily in understanding innate capacities as unfolded during the first years of life, and the long range view in understanding the continuing socialization and change of competence through life'. Hymes (1971: 287) has particularly in mind disadvantaged children, whether they be American Blacks or speakers of Bernstein's 'restricted code', those '... whose primary language or language variety is different from that of their school'. It is, claims Hymes, part of person's communicative competence to adapt his speech styles as changing social conditions and experience demand. Having communicative competence means having this adaptability in matters of language.

A difference between Widdowson and Hymes is that the former sees his proposal as emanating from 'the findings of error analysis', while Hymes refers explicitly to the founder of Contrastive Analysis, Weinreich (1953) and his notion of *interference*, which Hymes defines as being concerned with 'problems of the interpretation of manifestations of one system in terms of another'. In fact, Widdowson's view is shared by Krzeszowski (1976: 66) who illuminatingly categorises the five processes that Selinker (1972) considers contribute to the form of interlanguage. Three of these (L1 transfer, transfer of L1 training, and overgeneralisation from the target language) Krzeszowski (1976: 61) calls 'horizontal processes' and the other two ('strategies of communication' and 'strategies of target language learning') he calls 'vertical processes' since '... they do not involve any transfer either from the source or from the target language' (1976: 67). On the other hand, Widdowson has claimed, as I have shown, that these procedures, at least those involving simplification, 'lie at the heart of communicative competence' and that this *is* transferable from L1 use.

The more overt support for Widdowson is my paper (James, 1972) on applied contrastive analysis where I likewise proposed that some status as institutionalised communicative codes should be given to the 'deviant' languages of foreign-language learners. I was encouraged in this by the American efforts to what was technically called 'dialect expansion' in the late 1960s, which were associated with such linguists as Labov, Shuy, Baratz Fasold and Stewart. This movement sought to do two things: to recognise as legitimate and so assign linguistic status to the nonstandard dialects of American Blacks, and to create pedagogic materials to facilitate social 'upward mobility' via the standardisation of these dialects. Politzer (1968: 2) pointed out that any variant of a target language that is coloured by the native language of its learners can similarly be labelled a non-standard dialect of that target language. The sentences of these learner-dialects are of two kinds, the idiosyncratic and the non-idiosyncratic, and it is the latter kind which contrastive analysis has traditionally been concerned with: I call them non-idiosyncratic simply because they are common to population of learners with a shared L1. They need not be obvious replicas of the L1, but their deviance will be systematically, if deviously, traceable to the L1. Since the learner's 'dialect' is in a sense a hybrid between L1 and target language I called it an *interlingua*, a term adopted from translation theory.

Any foreign-language learner has a propensity to construct for himself this interlingua, though it has been pedagogic practice to stifle this act of creativity. It is unrealistic to insist that learners should circumvent it to proceed directly to the native speaker's version of the target language. A further justification for tolerating it is that where the class is L1-homogeneous, the individual learners will converge in tacit agreement on the form of this interlingua, and being institutionalised (Corder, 1975) it will become a vehicle for in-class communication. Accepting the interlingua, like accepting the child's or the immigrant's non-standard language, obviates the necessity to halt the communication process in favour of the learning process, which has been the traditional practice.

For the majority of language learners, the interlingua need not be assigned a low status by being viewed as 'transitional'. Being a viable means of communication, it might, for the majority of learners, represent their terminal competence. It is adequate for those whose foreign-language study ends with school and for those who have specialist and sporadic functional communicative needs. The minority, those who will become professional foreign-language communicators and those whose motives are literary, aesthetic, linguistic or pedagogic, will need to proceed beyond the interlingua. Thus 'advanced' language study will aim at naturalising the interlingua and to this end the procedures advocated by Feigenbaum (1969) are appropriate: the student is required to manipulate certain model sentences through repetition, substitution, and even translation. Often in the past such audiolingualist drills were criticised for their artificiality, but it is this artificiality which makes them suited for dialect expansion by the advanced learner, since they involve him in conscious comparison of differences between his interlingua and target competence. So this drilling involves not the mechanical conditioning of verbal responses but makes use of the learner's *cognitive* capacities. As Hymes says, such adaptability lies at the heart of communicative competence.

I have delayed my definition of communicative competence. Of the many available definitions I shall concentrate on those of Dittmar, of Widdowson, and of Corder. Dittmar (1976: 163) sees as central to communicative competence the language user's realisation of two facts:

(a) that two or more speech acts can be carried by the same linguistic pattern, and
(b) that two or more linguistic patterns can convey the same speech act.

Developing communicative competence involves then an increasing *versatility*. For Widdowson (1975b) *simplification* is the key, so he talks of '...basic simplifying procedures which lie at the heart of communicative competence'. For him they involve '...the process whereby a language user adjusts his language behaviour in the interests of communicative effectiveness'. Moreover, they are exhibited by native speakers and are not 'restricted to people engaged in the learning of a second language system'. Corder (1975) places the emphases differently: rather than viewing interlanguage in terms of simplification or reduction, he prefers to study the processes of *elaboration* demonstrated by learners of a second language. It will be obvious that the naturalisation of the interlingua, as I have presented it, is an aspect of Corder's 'elaboration' as well as of Hymes' 'adaptability'.

I will concede that many of the learner's simplification strategies are universal. Váradi (1973) has discussed these under the title 'Strategies in Target-Language learner communication Message Adjustment'. He recognised three strategies: message abandonment (full or partial); formal replacement; and message adjustment. Results of applying the strategy for the communication of the 'balloon' were: 'air ball', 'special toy for children', 'light bowls (balls) to fly', 'filled with gas'. I am sure that there are syntactic counterparts to these lexical ones. I am also sure that, apart from the universal strategies, there will be those that rely heavily on the L1 of the learners: this is where Contrastive Analysis comes back into the picture.

In her Bangor research project, de Echano (1977) set out to investigate the strategies employed by 'authors' of simplified Readers* in making an original text more accessible to foreign learners of English. The procedures recognised by Váradi were in evidence. In addition, de Echano submitted syntactically difficult English sentences to two populations of informants, one English native-speakers, the other Spanish teachers of English, with instructions to simplify each sentence, if possible, so as to make it easier for foreigners to understand. The informants were being invited to indulge in 'foreigner talk' (Ferguson, 1975) of a rather sophisticated type in the written mode. She selected the test sentences on the basis of high English–Spanish contrastivity, as suggested in Stockwell *et al* (1965). Significantly, the Spanish informants tended to suggest simplified versions which were syntactically convergent toward the nearest Spanish pattern. She concluded that Readers, to be truly effective and significantly simplified, should be composed with the native language of the target reader population in mind. The main inference I wish to draw from de Echano's work is that, although, as Widdowson claims, the ability to simplify language is shared by foreign learners and teachers and

---

* Longman's Bridge Series and Simplified Readers.

native speakers, some of the directions of that simplification are determined by the L1. The second point, following from the first, is that the paraphrase relations recognised by a L1-homogeneous group of foreign learners will make communication more possible than when the group does not have a common L1. I feel that Allwright's experiment in Essex would have yielded a functional interlingua even more rapidly if his learners had all been L1 Spanish speakers.

It might be objected that I have overemphasised the structural aspect of communicative competence. As Hymes (1971: 281) says, 'There are several sectors of communicative competence, of which the grammatical is just one'. My apology might be either that I am concerned with the acquisition rather than the possession of communicative competence, or alternatively that it is time to reinstate the grammatical dimension, which is in danger of being lost sight of. Instead of apologies though, I prefer to consider the *four* 'sectors' of communicative competence that Hymes identifies, namely:

1. 'Whether (and to what degree) is formally possible' (1971: 281). This is the grammaticality sector and it is best approached through the linguistic study of error gravities, as in James (1974) and James (1977).
2. 'Whether (and to what degree) something is feasible' (1971: 281). This is the acceptability sector and concerns 'performance' factors such as memory and cognitive factors. It has been studied by Cook (1977).
3. 'Whether (and to what degree) something is appropriate'. (1971: 281) This is defined in relation to contextual features or how sentences match situations.
4. 'Whether (and to what degree) something is in fact done' (1971: 281). This relates to probability of occurrence. An example is F R Palmer's (1965: 63) contentious claim that *will/shall* are not the commonest forms for future reference in English. As Hymes (1971: 282) says: 'A linguistic illustration: a sentence may be grammatical, awkward, tactful and rare'. And so may an interlingual sentence from a second-language learner. The Polish learner of German, for example, might be allowed or even encouraged to use the alternative German way (a) of asking a

question that is structurally close to his L1 (Polish) way rather than the 'more natural' way (b):

Polish (L1)	German (L2)	
Czy pan go zna?	Ob Sie kennen?	(a)
	Kennen Sie ihn?	(b)

His communicative competence at this stage will be deficient in that the (a) version may be too [casual] to be appropriate and may be relatively rare. But basing the interlingua or 'reduced code' on a contrastive study will ensure that his sentence is grammatical and, for him perhaps even more than for a native speaker of German, feasible. It will be during the naturalisation of the interlingua that attention will be paid to appropriacy and to relative frequency.

As I said at the outset, it is not my vocation to vindicate contrastive analysis. But I hope to have shown that the welcome shift of attention to the communicative ambitions of language learners is not a completely new page in history and that structural considerations, while they should not preoccupy us, should, in their *contrastive* aspect, be continually borne in mind.

References

Allwright, R (1976) Language learning through communication practice.' *ELT documents* 76/3, 2–14.

Brown, R (1973) *A first language: the early stages.* London: Allen & Unwin.

Cook, V J (1977) 'Cognitive processes in second language learning'. *IRAL* 15, 1–20.

Corder, S Pit (1975) ' "Simple codes" and the source of the second-language learner's initial heuristic hypothesis.' Paper read at the 4th Neuchâtel Colloquium on Applied Linguistics.

Davidson, D and Harman, G (eds) (1972) *Semantics of natural language.* Dordrecht: D Reidel.

Dittmar, N (1976) *Sociolinguistics: A critical survey of theory and application.* London: Edward Arnold.

Dulay, H and Burt, M (1974) 'You can't learn without goofing. In Ricards, J C (ed) (1974), pp. 95–124.

Echano, A de (1977) *'Simplification of reading matter of EFL learners'.* Unpublished M A dissertation, Bangor.

Feingenbaum, I (1969) 'The use of nonstandard English in teaching standard'. *Florida FL reporter* VII, 116–123.

Ferguson, C A (1975) 'Towards a characterisation of English foreigner talk'. *Anthropological linguistics* 17, 1–13.

Grice, P (1967) *'The logic of conversation'*. Unpublished MS. University of California, Berkeley.

Halliday, M A K (1975) *'Learning how to mean'*. London: Edward Arnold.

Hymes, D (1972) 'On communicative competence.' In J B Pride and J Holmes (*eds*) (1972), pp. 269–294.

James, C (1971) 'The exculpation of contrastive analysis.' In G Nickel (*ed*) (1971), 53–68.

James, C (1972) 'Foreign language learning by dialect expansion.' In G Nickel (*ed*) (1972), pp. 1–11.

James, C (1974) 'Linguistic measures for error gravity.' *Audio-visual journal* 12, 3–9.

James, C (1977) 'Judgements of error gravities.' *English language teaching journal* 31, 116–124.

Krzeszowski, T (1976) 'Interlanguage and contrastive generative grammar.' *ISB* 1/2, 58–79.

Lado, R (1957) *Linguistics across cultures.* Ann Arbor: University of Michigan Press.

Lado, R (1964) *Language teaching.* New York: McGraw Hill.

Lakoff, R 'Language and society.' In R Wardhaugh and H D Brown (*eds*) (1976), 207–228.

Lester, M (*ed*) (1970) *Readings in applied transformational grammar.* New York: Holt, Rinehart & Winston.

Newmark, L. (1966) 'How not to interfere with language learning.' In M Lester (*ed*) (1970), 219–227.

Newmark, L and Reibel, D (1968) 'Necessity and sufficiency in language learning.' *IRAL* 2, 145–164.

Nickel, G (*ed*) (1971) *Papers in contrastive linguistics.* Cambridge: CUP.

Nickel, G (*ed*) (1972) *Papers from the International Symposium on Applied Contrastive Linguistics.* Bielefeld: Cornelsen-Velhagen & Klasing.

Palmer, F R (1965) *A linguistic study of the English verb.* London: Longman.

Politzer, R L (1968) 'Problems in applying foreign language teaching methods to the teaching of standard English as a second dialect.' *Research and development memorandum No. 40.* Stanford University.

Pride, J B and Holmes, J (*eds*) *Sociolinguistics.* Harmondsworth: Penguin.

Ravem, R (1974) 'Language acquisition in a second language environment.' In J C Richards (*ed*) (1974) 124–134.

Richards, J C (*ed*) (1974) *Error analysis.* London: Longman.

Selinker, L (1972) 'Interlanguage.' *IRAL* 10, 219–231.

Stalnaker, R C (1972) 'Pragmatics.' In D Davidson and G Harman (*eds*) (1972) 380–397.

Stockwell, R, Bowen, J D and Martin, J W (1965) *The grammatical structures of English and Spanish.* Chicago: Chicago University Press.

Váradi, T (1973) 'Strategies in target-language learner communication message adjustment.' *Romanian–English Contrastive Analysis Project.*

Wardhaugh, R and Brown, H D (*eds*) (1976) *A survey of applied linguistics.* Ann-Arbor: University of Michigan Press.

Weinreich, U (1953) *Languages in contact.* New York: Linguistic Circle.

Widdowson, H G (1975a) 'EST in theory and practice.' *English for academic study.* ETIC occasional paper. The British Council.

Widdowson, H G (1975b) 'The significance of simplification.' Paper read at the 4th Neuchâtel Colloquium on Applied Linguistics.

Whitman, R L and Jackson, K L (1972) 'The unpredictability of contrastive analysis.' *Language learning* 22, 29–41.

6. Contrastive Analysis in a New Dimension

Tomasz P. Krzeszowski

University of Gdańsk

Traditional contrastive analyses are all conducted along the *horizontal* dimensions necessarily involved in comparing an element or a class of elements in L1 with an equivalent element or a class of elements in L2 and/or vice versa. The traditional luggage of contrastive analysis must, therefore, contain a set of statements motivating the movement from a specific element in L1 to a specific element in L2. These statements must be based on semantic considerations associated with the notion of *equivalence* (Halliday *et al*, 1964; Catford, 1965; Krzeszowski, 1967) and also on structural (syntactic and morphological) considerations associated with the notion of *congruence* (Krzeszowski, 1967; Marton, 1968). The linguistic nature of elements selected for comparison is strictly dependent upon a particular linguistic theory employed in the description of the compared languages. These elements can be systems (phonological, morphological, syntactic, etc) or subsystems (plosives, personal pronouns, non-finite clauses, etc) in L1 and L2. A comparison of systems and subsystems is usually associated with the adoption of structural theories as foundations for contrastive analysis. It is also possible to contrast various types of *constructions* in the compared languages, eg passive constructions, relative constructions, nominal constructions, etc. Such comparisons can be conducted within nearly all types of theoretical frameworks, including traditional approaches to grammar. Finally, it is also possible to conduct research into a comparison of specific *grammatical rules* in L1 and L2. Within the theoretical framework of transformational generative grammar it is thus possible to compare such rules as subject raising, adjective placement, interrogative inversion and many others. A contrastive analysis, in this case, results in statements about the obligatory or optional status of the compared rules, their ordering and their presence or absence in the compared languages.

In all three types of comparison the notion of equivalence is the crucial one. It provides the necessary criterion of comparability: only equivalent systems, constructions and rules are comparable. Since the notion of equivalence has received a thorough treatment in the literature, especially with respect to the equivalence of constructions (Krzeszowski, 1967, 1971, 1974; Marton, 1968) we need not concern ourselves with this problem here.

As was remarked at the outset of the present paper, all contrastive analyses based on the notion of equivalence are conducted along what may be called a horizontal dimension involving movement from L1 to L2 and vice versa. The comparative technique requires isolating a system or a construction or a rule in L1 and matching it for comparative purposes with an equivalent system, construction or rule in L2. One can also start with L2 and look for equivalent systems, constructions and rules in L1.[1]

The horizontally organized contrastive analyses of systems and constructions across languages originated with Lado (1957) and continued to flourish in various theoretical frameworks. They resulted in inventories of differences and similarities between the compared items. Some attempts were also made to quantify these differences and similarities according to what was believed to reflect the amount of difficulty involved in learning these items in the process of second-language acquisition. What resulted from such attempts were *hierarchies of difficulties* correlated in an intricate, though apparently motivated, way with degrees of similarly (or difference) between the compared items. This correlation was based on the assumption that 'differences are the chief source of difficulty in learning a second language' (Lado, 1964: 21). The phenomenon involved in these difficulties was called *interference*, ie 'difficulty in learning a sound, word or construction in a second language as a result of differences with the habits of the native language' (Lado, 1964: 217). Interference was thus believed to be in inverse proportion to the degree of similarity between the compared items. Consequently, attempts were made to relate 'hierarchies of difficulties' to contrastive statements concerning degrees of difference across languages (Stockwell, Bowen and Martin, 1965; Stockwell and Bowen, 1965). Experiments soon invalidated a large portion of such predictions (Brière, 1968; Politzer, 1968) and called in question the relevance of contrastive analysis in designing materials for foreign-language instruction. The scepticism was reinforced by the realization that interference (or negative transfer) is not exclusively related to differences across languages and that the results of contrastive analysis can be used only to a fairly limited extent in the prediction of errors. This situation led some investigators to the belief that error analysis was a more accurate source of information about difficulties in foreign-language learning. Eventually, what was originally intended as 'a method to test the contrastive prediction and extend its power of pedagogical applications' (Banathy and Madarasz 1969) became an autonomous field of study, more useful in syllabus planning and in designing materials for foreign-language instruction than contrastive analysis.

A thorough study of errors led to the formulation of the theory of so-called 'approximative systems', ie deviant linguistic systems 'employed by foreign learners in an attempt to utilize the target language' (Nemser, 1969).[2] According to Nemser, the process of foreign-language acquisition can be seen as a succession of stages of proficiency, ultimately approaching native-like competence in the target language. In principle, each stage can be described independently, without reference to either the source or the target language.

Without going into details concerning the linguistic status of approximative systems, it is possible to say that each such system can be seen as an intermediate stage on the *horizontal* axis, delimited on one extreme by the source language and on the other extreme by the target language. Whether or not it is possible to claim that a synchronic description of such a system is at all possible is a question that need not be discussed here. All the same it is impossible to refrain from observing that an adequate theory of approximative systems would have to account for their fundamentally dynamic nature, manifested in the perpetual motion (very much resembling linguistic change in general) in the direction of the target language. The theory would have to explain the mechanism and the power underlying this motion.

In an influential paper of 1972 Selinker made an attempt to uncover
and describe the nature of this mechanism by isolating a number of
processes vital in accounting for the form of interlanguage (the term
with which Selinker replaces Nemser's 'approximative system'). Thus
Selinker distinguished 'language transfer', 'transfer of training', 'strategies of second language learning', 'strategies of second language communication' and 'overgeneralization of target language linguistic
material' as factors shaping interlanguage.

Using Selinker's ideas as a starting-point for his own interesting
speculations, Widdowson (forthcoming) claimed that 'all of the processes which Selinker refers to are tactical variations of the same
underlying simplification strategy and [...] in general error analysis
is a partial account of basic simplifying procedures which lie at the
heart of communicative competence'.

It appears that the notion of simplification is a crucial one. To that
notion, therefore, I now propose to turn attention. According to Widdowson, simplification is a result of an attempt to adjust the language
behaviour to the interests of communicative effectiveness. Simplification may, therefore, affect any stage of interlanguage and it may
involve 'a movement away from the reference norm of the standard
language (or even a particular interlanguage) so as to arrive at forms
of speaking judged to be dialectally appropriate in certain contexts of
use.'

Simplification presupposes the existence of a non-simplified or more
complex form of the language. 'Simplified' is a property of language
which is by no means restricted to the foreign learner's interlanguages. It also characterizes such types as pidgins and creoles (Valdman, 1975; de Camp, 1968), 'baby-talk', 'lover's talk', and 'foreigner-
talk' (Ferguson, 1964) and various types of 'reduced registers' such as
'telegraphese', technical descriptions and the language of instructions
(Corder: forthcoming). It is interesting to acknowledge some results
of research into the structure of all these 'simplified' codes. It appears
that all of them share some obvious structural similarities such as an
extremely simple, if any, morphological system, a comparatively rigid
word order, a reduced use of the copula, and the absence of articles
(and to a smaller extent of deictic words). According to Valdman
(forthcoming) pidgins 'are derivationally shallower than other natural

languages and reflect more closely cognitively-based deep structure'. In view of the overt similarities between all types of 'simplified' codes, Valdman's contention can be extended to cover them all.

In the paper already referred to, Widdowson states that the learner's linguistic behaviour is controlled by a set of rules which need not correspond to the set of rules which he recognizes as constituting the correct norm and to which he can make reference when required. Widdowson calls these rules *expression rules* and *reference rules*, respectively. It is clear that in the former literature both the notion of error and the notion of interlanguage were connected with the concept of competence alone and were thus static in nature. There is no doubt, however, that interlanguage, in contrast with language, is a very unstable and constantly evolving system. The problems that must be stated and accounted for are the following: Why do interlanguages vary when they do? Under what conditions do they vary? Why is there a discrepancy between what the learner knows and what he does? Answers to these questions may be sought in Widdowson's distinction between expression rules and reference rules. Expression rules are the rules *in presentio* and are actually used to generate a certain linguistic behaviour meeting the communicational needs of the learner. Reference rules are the rules *in absentio*. They constitute the learner's knowledge of the foreign language, ie his linguistic competence. In the classroom there is always a correcting teacher, who in all manner of ways, implicitly or explicitly, directly or indirectly, imposes references rules upon his learners. But when the learner is left alone to face his communicative needs, he usually finds that his communicative needs exceed his linguistic potential. In economic terms his demands are much higher than the supply placed at his disposal. All the same he is usually able to communicate even if his linguistic competence does not seem to be up to the occasion. Therefore, in the majority of cases communication is achieved at the expense of linguistic orthodoxy.

Widdowson (forthcoming) says that communication in a foreign language involves an adjustment of the learner's language behaviour in the interests of communicative effectiveness. He calls this adjustment 'simplification of use', which 'may involve a decrease or increase in complexity of usage'.[3] Errors result from the learner's attempts to use reference rules as expression rules. Since, as was said earlier, there is always a deficit of reference rules, learners have to simplify their expression rules in one of many possible ways in their efforts to communicate effectively. Simplification conceived in this way lies at the heart of Selinker's five processes establishing the learner's knowledge (interlanguage) as well as his language behaviour. Therefore, Widdowson is able to conclude optimistically that 'a learner's errors are evidence of success not of failure' because 'the failure to confirm to given reference rules is the consequence of success in developing expression rules'.

Corder (forthcoming) expresses an unorthodox view on the role of simplification in language learning. He suggests that it might be possible to regard 'standard' codes as 'elaborated' forms of 'basic simple codes such as pidgins, creoles, interlanguages and all types of 'reduced' registers. This proposal assumes the existence of some universal process of elaboration or *complication* involved in all types of language learning. Though universal, the process would of course involve language specific 'complication rules'. The development of a pidgin into a creole would be a case of progressive complication. Another case would be the development of an interlanguage through increasingly complex 'approximative systems' into the target language. All types of 'reduced' registers used in appropriate situations would be viewed as instances of fossilized intermediate approximative systems or institutionalized, stereotyped stages in the process of complication toward the standard version of the language.

Selinker's interlanguage or Nemser's approximative systems, whether 'fossilized' or in the state of flux, have been demonstrated to be relatively independent of 'transfer' from the mother tongue (Burt and Dulay, 1974b). Moreover, recent studies in error analysis reveal that there exists a common body of errors pointing to some universal learning strategies (Richards, 1974). Transfer phenomena seem to be relatively less numerous and significant than was believed before.

Does it all suggest a further regress of relevance of contrastive analysis conducted for pedagogical purposes? If the prediction of negative transfer (interference) and other horizontal phenomena across languages is to be considered as the main object of contrastive analysis, then in view of the recent revelations described above the answer is perhaps 'yes'. Horizontally organized contrastive analyses are certainly limited to predicting and explaining phenomena which seem to occupy but a small area in the linguistic behaviour of foreign-language learners.[4] Some very crucial and significant processes such as simplification (complication) and fossilization connected with errors escape systematic treatment in terms of horizontally organized contrastive analyses. It is likewise obvious that a large number of errors cannot be explained by the interlanguage theory any more than they can be explained by the transfer theory. Of Selinker's five types of processes responsible for the formation of interlanguage, only three are connected with transfer either from the target language (overgeneralization, analogy) or from the source language (interlinguistic interference). It is worth noting that 'transfer of training', if it results in errors, may be looked at as a special case of wrong generalizations from the target language, since drills and exercises providing the basis for 'transfer of training' are nothing else than didactic texts written in the target language. Ideally, therefore, through careful preparation and manipulation of didactic texts, overgeneralizations of this sort can be eliminated and this type of transfer disregarded since, unlike other types of transfer, it is relatively easy to control.

The remaining two types of processes responsible for the formation of interlanguage, ie 'strategy of second language learning' and 'strategies of communication' cannot be related to transfer phenomena.[5] Of the five types of processes the last two are directly responsible for the phenomenon of simplification (complication) in the sense discussed above. The mutual relations between the source language, the target language, the interlanguage, and the processes which are involved in the formation of interlanguage can now be visualized in the form of the following diagram:

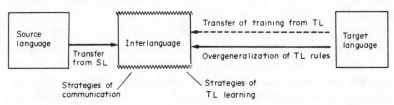

Figure 1

The diagram shows that transfer from the source language, transfer of training from the target language and overgeneralization from the target language are horizontal processes which influence the form of interlanguage. The other two processes cannot be handled in terms of any horizontal description since they do not involve any transfer either from the source or from the target language. In the remainder of this paper I am going to suggest a way of describing the phenomenon of complication which is inseparably connected with strategies of second-language learning and with strategies of communication within the framework of contrastive generative grammar (CGG) (Krzeszowski, 1974).

As was observed earlier, following Corder's argumentation, the development of the learner's language into the target language involves some universal process of complication according to language specific complication rules. The process of complication does not take place along the horizontal dimension but rather along the 'vertical' dimension as the learner moves from some basic language through successive stages of complication toward the target language. This is certainly true of a baby acquiring his native tongue. I wish to hypothesise that the same 'vertical' dimension of movement is involved in the process of second-language learning, even if this process is distorted by other processes including those that can be described horizontally.

The model of second-language learning must include the two types of rules described by Widdowson, ie reference rules and expression rules. It must also account for the mutual traffic between these two types of rules. The model must also account for formal similarities between learners' interlanguages regardless of their native language as well as for the fact that this resemblance tends to be stronger in the case of the most 'basic' forms of interlanguage (cf Dulay and Burt, 1974a).

All these phenomena can be treated only in terms of a theory in which a common conceptual base underlies all forms of more elaborated realizations of the language, with an increasing amount of interlinguistic differences at less 'basic' levels of realizations in various languages. A foreign-language learner, in his attempt to compensate for the deficit in reference rules available to him in the target language, can always resort to the process of *lexicalization* of forms which are less elaborate by being closer to the 'basic' forms. The resulting sentences are deviant. They do not, however, necessarily show symptoms of transfer from the source language, but rather they reflect certain universal properties of underlying representations, simpler in form than the fully elaborated constructions of the target language.

The organization of contrastive grammar suggested by the present author in a number of papers seems to be well fitted for providing a fairly explicit account of the process of complication associated with second-language learning. The 'vertically' organized contrastive grammar is founded upon a universal semantic or conceptual input consisting of configurations of elementary, primitive notions such as Agent, Patient and all sorts of specifications of location in time and space. Such universally structured configurations are assumed to underlie equivalent constructions and sentences across languages. Language specific categorial rules assign major grammatical categories such as 'sentence', 'noun', 'verb', 'adjective' to particular portions of input configurations. The resulting categorized structures are mapped by syntactic transformations onto subsurface representations into which lexical items are inserted by means of rules called lexicalizations. The resulting structures serve as inputs to rules called 'cosmetic' transformations. Syntactic transformations account for surface structures of sentence, ie for hierarchical arrangements of morphemes, constituents of phrases and of phrases, constituents of sentences and of sentences, constituents of sequences.[6] Briefly speaking, syntactic transformations determine the syntactical structure of sentences and their sequences. In addition, they also effect minor lexicalizations by inserting function words into derived constructions. 'Cosmetic' or post-lexical transformations account for linear arrangements of morphemes and word boundaries as well as such phenomena as agreement, concord and government expressed through morphological signals. Cosmetic transformations determine the morphological structure of words.

A grammar organized in this manner involves two kinds of lexicalizations: minor and major. Minor lexicalizations insert function words and belong to syntactic transformations. Major lexicalizations insert content words. In fully elaborated codes all major lexicalizations take place after all syntactic transformations but before cosmetic transformations. In various types of 'simplified' codes, notably also in learners' interlanguages, major lexicalizations may occur at earlier stages of derivation. In extreme cases lexicalizations occur at the level of semantic representations. In such cases cosmetic transformations are either completely ignored or apply only to a limited extent according to poorly investigated rules of complication.[7]

Since major lexicalizations as it were 'fossilize' the syntactic structure of constructions, the degree of syntactic complication of a construction actually uttered by the learner is directly dependent upon the stage of derivation at which the learner lexicalizes his construction. Early lexicalizations result in the syntactically simplest constructions characterized by the absence of function words (inserted by syntactic transformations which in such cases have no chance to apply). Within this framework, complication can be defined as the gradual shift of the place at which major lexicalizations occur from the deepest level of representation, ie the semantic level, to the level of shallow structure, ie the level which constitutes input to cosmetic transformations and where major lexicalizations occur in fully elaborated codes.

One of the observations which can be made on the basis of the theory of contrastive generative grammar is that each language has its specific *pattern of complication* which consists of all possible derivations of all types of constructions derived from semantic representations through syntactic transformations. Since the initial postulate of contrastive generative grammar states that equivalent sentences across languages have identical semantic inputs, equivalent sentences across languages have language specific *complication routes* according for the fact that such sentences exhibit structural and lexical differences (Krzeszowski, 1974: 12). A foreign learner may either lexicalize prematurely, thus producing 'simplified' or 'reduced' constructions which in our terms would merely be constructions that have not been elaborated (complicated) enough, or he may pursue a complication route characteristic of his native language or of some other language which is not L2. In all these cases he will be producing deviant utterances. In the case of premature lexicalizations the resulting 'errors' may be universal in nature. If, however, the learner chooses a complication route of L1 or of some other language different from the target language, the resulting errors may be characteristic of a restricted group of languages or in certain extreme cases (if the complication route is pursued down to its very end) of one particular language. Properly constructed contrastive generative grammar for L1, L2 and other relevant languages should in principle provide explanation for both kinds of errors. If one considers the growing body of knowledge concerning all types of 'reduced' codes, one cannot fail to notice that universal errors can be predicted by contrastive generative grammar with a fair degree of accuracy. Among them are: omission of articles, copulas, tense and aspect markers and of inflectional suffixes as well as a reduction in the vocabulary of function words such as conjunctions and prepositions. These features were originally found to characterize the so-called foreigner-talk as described by Ferguson (1975). The same, however, is also found to be true of pidgins (Valdman, 1975) and other 'reduced' codes such as babytalk, 'telegraphese', 'instructions' (Corder, forthcoming) and the language of Kehaar, a character in *Watership Down*, a story for children (Corder, 1975).

Errors resulting from substituting complication routes of L1 for complication routes of L2 are language specific and can be predicted by contrastive generative grammar on the basis of comparisons of particular languages enumerated by contrastive generative grammar. Such errors may involve word order and faulty uses of various grammatical systems and rules.

Other deviations from L2, those that cannot be recognized either as universal errors or as errors resulting from substituting a complication route of L1 for a complication route of L2, can be viewed as errors of the second order. If one agrees to interpret the foreign learner's 'fossilized' competence as a realization of his learning strategy involving a combination of premature lexicalizations and of complication routes characteristic of some language(s) other than L2, all the remaining errors can be recognized not so much as deviations from L2 but as deviations from the 'fossilized' competence. As such, these errors are no different in nature from the native speaker's deviations from the norms of his own language. Errors of this type are likely to turn out to be mere slips, caused by an assortment of factors of extralinguistic character. They may require no special therapeutic measures, at least no measures which can be derived from a strictly linguistic theory.

Summing up, let us state again that 'vertically' organized contrastive grammar, deriving equivalent sentences across languages from common semantic representations, provides a linguistic framework to deal with the phenomena of simplification and complication. The traditional concepts of negative and positive transfer can be augmented by the more refined concepts of premature lexicalizations and the substitution of complication routes of L1 for complication routes of L2. The two types of processes can be demonstrated to be responsible for a larger body of errors, both universal and language specific, than it has ever been possible to demonstrate by horizontally organized contrastive analyses.

NOTES

1. It must be noted that the notion of equivalence is not the same for each type of comparison. Equivalence of systems expresses a different relation than equivalence of constructions and sentences and equivalence of rules. In horizontally organized contrastive analyses each type of equivalence requires its own independent motivation and explanation. See, for example, an attempt to establish equivalence of phonemes in Milewski (1962) and some amendments suggested by Krzeszowski (1970: 52 ff).

2. The notion but not the term was first introduced by Corder (1967), who referred to it as 'transitional competence'.

3. Widdowson thus explains the apparent contradiction contained in this statement: 'How can one talk of simplification which involves linguistic complexity? One can do so, I suggest, because effectiveness of use in a particular communicative situation might well require explicitness or a conformity to accepted convention which calls for linguistic elaboration' (Widdowson forthcoming). In other words, one often uses linguistically more complicated forms in ignorance of the existing less complicated forms, as in using a definition of a word instead of the word itself, if the word is unknown.

4. See, for example, a study of Spanish–English bilingualism by Lance (1969: 124), who arrives at the following conclusion: 'One of the most important conclusions this writer draws from the research in this project is that interference from Spanish is not a major factor in the way bilinguals construct sentences and use the language.'

5. It remains to be investigated to what extent the particular factors distinguished by Selinker influence each other. For example, it could be so that 'strategies of target language learning' are somehow determined or modified by 'strategies of communication' or by 'transfer from simplified language'. These mutual relations may depend on a specific situation in which interlanguage is used. In the classroom 'transfer of training from target language' and 'strategies of target language learning' may override other factors. In a live communicative situation, however, 'strategies of communication' probably dominate other factors. It would seem that the five factors distinguished by Selinker arrange themselves in a hierarchical order depending on a specific extra-linguistic situation in which interlanguage is used.

6. For the notion of sequence as a linguistic unit consisting of sentences see Krzeszowski (1974: 71 ff).

7. Imitation seems to be an underestimated though very important factor determining the acquisition of 'cosmetic' rules. 'Cosmetic' transformations account for the overt grammatical phenomena such as agreement, concord, government and word boundaries. This area of grammar is probably acquired through the poorly investigated and underestimated process of imitation and analogy, which in spite of Chomsky's claim to the contrary necessarily do play their part in any language acquisition process (cf Chomsky, 1966: 12 ff).

References

Banathy, B H and Madarasz, P H (1969) 'Contrastive analysis and error analysis'. *Journal of English as a foreign language* 4/2, 77–92.

Brière, E J (1968) *A psycholinguistic study of phonological interference.* The Hague: Mouton.

Burt, M and Dulay, H (1974a) 'Natural sequences in child second language acquisition'. *Language learning* 24, 37–53.

Burt, M and Dulay, H (1975b) 'A new perspective on the creative construction process in child second language acquisition'. *OISE working papers in bilingualism* 4.

Catford, J C (1965) *A linguistic theory of translation.* London: Oxford University Press.

Chomsky, N (1960) *Cartesian linguistics.* New York and London: Harper & Row Publishers.

Corder, P (1967) 'The significance of learner's errors' *IRAL* 4, 161–170.

Corder, P (1975) 'The language of Kehaar.' *Work in progress 8.* Department of Linguistics, University of Edinburgh, 41–52.

Corder, P (Forthcoming) '"Simple codes' and the source of the second language learner's initial heuristic hypothesis." Paper read at the 4th Neuchâtel Colloquium on Applied Linguistics. To appear in *Theoretical approaches in applied linguistics.*

DeCamp. D (1968) 'The field of Creole language studies'. *SAP* 1, 29–51.

Ferguson, C A (1964) 'Baby-talk in six languages.' In Gumperz and Hymes, D (eds) (1964), 103–104.

Ferguson, C A (1975) 'Toward a characterization of English foreigner talk.' *Anthropological linguistics* 17, 1–14.

Gumperz, J J and Hymes, D (eds) (1964) *The ethnography of communication.* *American anthropologist* 66 (6), Part 2. Washington: American Anthropological Association.

Halliday, M A K, McIntosh, A, Strevens, P (1964) *The linguistic sciences and language teaching.* London: Longmans.

Krzeszowski, T P (1967) 'Fundamental principles of structural contrastive studies'. *Glottodidactica* (2), 33–40.

Krzeszowski, T P (1970) *Teaching English to Polish learners.* Warszawa: PWN.

Krzeszowski, T P (1971) 'Equivalence, congruence and deep structure'. In Nickel, G (ed) (1971), 37–48.

Krzeszowski, T P (1974) *Contrastive generative grammar: theoretical foundations.* Łódź: Uniwersytet Łódzki.

Lado, R (1957) *Linguistics across cultures.* Ann Arbor: The University of Michigan Press.

Lado, R (1964) *Language teaching: a scientific approach.* New York: McGraw-Hill Inc.

Lance, D (1969) *A brief study of Spanish–English bilingualism.* Final report research project Orr liberal arts 15504. Texas: College Station.

Marton, W (1968) 'Equivalence and congruence in transformational contrastive studies'. *SAP* 1, 53–62.

Milewski, T (1962) 'Założenia językoznawstwa typologicznego.' *BPTJ* 21, 3–40.

Nemser, W (1969) 'Approximative systems of foreign language learners.' *The Jugoslav Serbo-Croatian–English contrastive project* 1, 3–12.

Nickel, G (ed) (1971) *Papers in contrastive linguistics.* Cambridge: Cambridge University Press.

Politzer, R L (1968 'An experiment in the presentation of parallel and contrasting structures.' *Language learning* 18, 1/2, 35–43.

Richards, J C, (ed) (1974) *Error analysis: perspectives on second language acquisition.* London: Longman.

Richards, J C (1974) 'A non-contrastive approach to error analysis.' In J C Richards (ed) (1974), 172–188.

Selinker, L (1972) 'Interlanguage.' *IRAL* 10, 31. Reprinted in J C Richards (ed) (1974), 31–54.

Stockwell, R P, Bowen, J D and Martin, J W (1965) *The grammatical structures of English and Spanish.* Chicago: The University of Chicago Press.

Stockwell, R P and Bowen, J D (1965) *The sounds of English and Spanish.* Chicago: The University of Chicago Press.

Valdman, A and Phillips, J S (Forthcoming) 'Pidgization, creolization and the elaboration of learner systems.' Paper read at the 4th Neuchâtel Colloquium on Applied Linguistics. To appear in *Theoretical approaches in applied linguistics*.

Widdowson, H (Forthcoming) 'The significance of simplification.' Paper read at the 4th Neuchâtel Colloquium on Applied Linguistics. To appear in *Theoretical approaches in applied linguistics*.

7. Psycholinguistic Models, Second-Language Acquisition and Contrastive Analysis

Kari Sajavaara

University of Jyväskylä

'Maybe the things you want are like cards. You don't want them for themselves, really, though you think you do. You don't want a card because you want the card, but because in a perfectly arbitrary system of rules and values and in a special combination of which you already hold a part the card has meaning. But suppose you aren't sitting in a game. Then, even if you know the rules, a card doesn't mean a thing. They all look alike.'

Robert Penn Warren, *All the King's Men*, Harcourt, 1946

General considerations

Jacek Fisiak (1980: 10) points out rightly that doubt concerning the validity and usefulness of contrastive studies 'results from a number of misinterpretations and misunderstandings created by such factors as the peculiar methodological status of CS, the lack of a clearcut distinction in the past between theoretical and applied CS ... and the lack of a precise formulation of the different aims of theoretical CS and applied CS as well as the confusion of the relationship between CS, the psycholinguistic theory of interference and errors, and the theory of second language learning' (see also Sajavaara, 1977). It seems therefore justified to pay more attention than heretofore to the interrelationship between contrastive studies and psycholinguistic processes.

The link between foreign-language teaching methodology and theoretical linguistics has always been very close. Major shifts in linguistic theory have been regularly reflected in language teaching methodology, which implies that linguistic models have been associated with predominant psychological conceptualizations. Audiolingual language-teaching methodology was sponsored by structuralism through its link with behavioural psychology, and cognitive-code approaches became popular in language teaching simultaneously with the hey-day of generative theory. In the last few years, various approaches to communicative competence have been posited alongside grammatical competence (eg Canale and Swain, 1980); this has involved a certain change in the general attitude toward the question of what language is and how it is used.

The teaching of grammar has always been one of the central activities in language teaching. In many cases, knowing a language has been equated with knowing the grammar of the language concerned. It is true that grammatical competence is part of a human being's ability to communicate, but it is totally insufficient to explain the phenomena that are involved in language behaviour. A speaker or a hearer only behaves 'as if he knew the rules' (cf Slobin, 1979: 99). Although it is understandable that the linguist's attention has been focused on elements of the linguistic code, this does not authorize the transfer of categories and phenomena abstracted for a linguistic analysis over to the analysis of human communication. Even the lexicon has been neglected in recent decades as a result of the autonomous status of grammar.

Theoretical linguistic models cannot be sufficient for the description of second-language speech processing. Linguists' descriptions represent final products of language acquisition. For such descriptions, languages have been treated as verbal codes without a link with the dynamism of the contexts where they are used for communication and other purposes (cf Sajavaara and Lehtonen, 1979, 1980). Moreover, the learner is never exposed to the language in its entirety at once (James, 1978).

In primitive conceptualizations of human perception, sensations like vision and hearing were presented as straightforward printouts of the surrounding physical world. What people saw was a picture imprinted on the retina, and what they heard could be directly represented by the acoustic and physiological phenomena involved in the transmission of sounds. In linguistics and in considerations of the production and reception of language, the processes that take place in the speaker and the hearer were seen as mirror-image hierarchical processes in which the speaker's message was turned into a chain of acoustic phenomena, carried across a channel over to the hearer, and decoded through another hierarchical process into a replica of the speaker's message. All such representations involve one serious defect: both the production and the reception are *creative* processes, and the establishment of communication between the two interactants is based only partially on rules which exist in the speech community and are available to its members through socialization and language acquisition. As important as such rules are various negotiation processes which are created *ad hoc* in each individual communicative situation. The linguist's description of the linguistic system functioning in such an interactive process cannot catch the creative aspect, the rules that are made by participants, but even the linguist's representation of the 'established' features of language behaviour may be misleading: the elements of the linguistic and other texture present in a communicative situation obtain their meaning in two ways: the linguist abstracts a function for them through his attempt to 'rulify' language behaviour, which results in also seeing rules where there are none, or language users develop subconsciously a feel for the language system without there being necessarily much overlap between these two.

In the past twenty years we have been presented with a succession of new and 'better' linguistic models. We can agree with Slobin (1979: 31) that 'all these are partial and tentative attempts to map out part of the cognitive configurations underlying verbal behaviour' and that the important thing to remember is that the underlying form is always more detailed than the surface form. Since the linguistic models are replaced continuously by new models, we may tentatively conclude that none of them represents the way in which a human being processes information. An important question remains: What is the status of grammar in the processing of messages?

First of all, the distinction between sentences and utterances should not be forgotten.

> Sentences fall within the domain of competence models, utterances within the domain of performance models. Sentences are abstract objects

which are not tied to a particular context, speaker or time of utterance. Utterances, on the other hand, are datable events, tied to particular grammars, in the sense that a sentence is not grammatical in the absolute, but only with respect to the rules of a certain grammar; utterances, however, may cross the bounds of particular grammars and incorporate words and/or constructions from many different languages, or from no language at all. (Smith and Wilson, 1979).

In many ways the quotation above may repeat something that is a commonplace among linguists and applied linguists but its full relevance has seldom been recognized. It relates to Lyons's distinction between language-system and language-behaviour (Lyons, 1977: 26 ff). In contrastive analysis which aims at applied goals, research based on sentences (the way most of the practice has been) may be totally misleading, when we should direct our attention to utterances. Utterances are expected to reflect what there is in a language-system. Yet grammars are abstract descriptions of system sentences, while for the time being we do not have grammars based on utterances of natural language use. Therefore it may be difficult to work out details of language contrasts for applied purposes.

Speech reception and production can only be approached through reference to interaction; these processes should be related to the exchange 'game' which is going on between two or more interlocutors. All models that neglect the influence of interaction on the processing of speech are bound to be defective. The speaker makes use of several kinds of material for his message: what he thinks the listener knows believes/thinks; the listener's attitudes and feelings as revealed in the situation; mutual agreement or disagreement on attitudes and opinions; shared knowledge; and expected information. A number of universals are always involved here which derive from the general structure of the ways of thinking (Slobin, 1979: 64) and the fact that the interlocutors know that they want or do not want to communicate something and it is in their common interest to build upon this assumption, which, again, results in their willingness or unwillingness to understand each other.

The success of the transmission of messages depends on a multitude of factors. Many things can go wrong, and it is only seldom that it is possible to see for sure that the intended message has been interpreted exactly right by the hearer. Fortunately, approximations are sufficient in most cases without communication being seriously handicapped. Language is typically ambiguous and fuzzy, and the idea that linguistic elements have fixed and universal interpretations within one and the same speech community is an illusion based on normative grammars and other similar aspirations of linguists.

The conceptualization of human speech communication has also been distorted by reference to theoretical models of communication. What has been said above clearly implies that any Shannon-and-Weaver-type models of communication are insufficient as models of human interaction. The acoustic on-line signal bears a certain part of the message only, and many other parameters have to be considered before we can reach a more accurate picture of human language processing. Language serves definite purposes related to the speaker-hearer's intentions in some specific time and environment. Thus, utterances and other behavioural phenomena are necessarily situation-specific (cf Lyons, 1977: 27–29). In a communicative situation, the speaker and the hearer are faced with a problem-solving task, ie reaching agreement on mutual intentions. The speaker is expected to give a sufficient number of cues, verbal and non-verbal, for the hearer to be able to reconstruct the message. The verbal part of the message must be linked with the speaker's 'world' and his expectations as to what takes place in the hearer as an active participant in the situation. The hearer for his part makes use of all the cues available for him—not only in the verbal part of the message—to create the most probable interpretation of how he is expected to reconstruct his knowledge. This reconstruction requires building blocks that come from the outside of the communicative chain as seen traditionally.

The limits of this paper do not allow for an overall discussion of psycholinguistic models or aspects of second-language acquisition, a task which would require a full-length monograph. As far as the models are concerned, this is not really a drawback because much of earlier 'psycholinguistics' deals, despite the name, with rules of transformational grammar or their psycholinguistic relevance, which need not be entered here. The present discussion will be focused on three questions which are considered to be relevant for second-language acquisition and contrastive analysis from a psycholinguistic point of

view: language processing, particularly its dual, data-driven and conceptually-driven, basis, the distinction between hierarchical and heterarchical models, and the role of grammar in language processing. The
paper will be concluded with an overview of some central aspects of
second-language acquisition, and certain conclusions will be drawn
for the purposes of cross language analysis.

Discussion of the problems of second-language acquisition and
second-language acquisition involves a multitude of questions which
relate to the linguistic code, on the one hand, and communication,
human interaction, speech processing as a whole, memory, and perception, on the other. All treatments of the topic without any
recourse to these areas is bound to be defective.

Speech processing: static and dynamic models

When we deal with speech processing, we should aim at a description
of the entire communicative vehicle in which the reverse and shifting
roles of the speaker and the hearer and the perspective of society are
included. A distinction has to be made between a linguistically
oriented and a communicatively oriented approach to the processes
of production and reception (Sajavaara and Lehtonen, 1980): (1) a
linguistically oriented approach aims at explaining how a linguistic
representation results in speech output or is derived from speech
input, and (2) a communicatively oriented approach describes how
the speaker implements his communicative intentions, how the hearer
deciphers the speaker's intentions, and how these interact in particular situations of communication.

The choice of the model to be used in reference to language processing involves a choice between a static view of language and a dynamic one. This choice can also be characterized as one taking place
between a linguistic description and a psycholinguistic one or
between a structural and an operational modelling of the chain of
speech (cf Lehtonen, 1978; see also Davis, 1978; Levelt and Flores
d'Arcais (eds), 1977: xiv). The structural model aims at describing the
language as a set of rules abstracted and idealized from language
data. The dynamic view presupposes that grammatical rules have to
be regarded only as descriptions of certain regular structures of lan-

guage, which function primarily as constraints, and not as models for the mental processes in operation when people are speaking or listening to speech (cf Clark and Clark, 1977: 191 ff).

One of the most misleading features of the static models is their hierarchical construction (see Lee (*ed*), 1980: 236 ff). There are several reasons to assume that linguistic information is not processed hierarchically by proceeding step by step through the levels of grammar, for instance in perception, from a concrete representation to phonology and syntax, and further to more abstract meaning. Instead, the functioning of the perceptual process is to be seen as 'heterarchical': the hearer makes use of all possible knowledge available to him, phonological, syntactic, pragmatic and so on, simultaneously in terms of a time-sharing system. What is particularly important is the fact that the speech signal does not contain all the information necessary for recognition; a great deal is inferred from elements external to the speech input or available in the internal data bank. In message production, similarly, the processes cannot be seen as steps leading from higher linguistic levels to physical speech. In all processing, surface perceptual cues are important because the perceiver uses them to construct 'functional propositional units' (Marslen-Wilson *et al*, 1978: 244). Therefore, more attention should be paid to the role of certain surface features (cf also Flores d'Arcais, 1978; Carroll *et al*, 1978). However, such structures are important as reveal aspects of psychological operations (Carroll and Bever, 1976).

In reception, the primary process is knowledge-driven; it is operating simultaneously with the secondary, input-driven analysis (see Lindsay and Norman, 1977: 278 ff; cf Clark and Clark, 1977: 219–220). An important part of the system is a constant retroactive reworking effect: the interpretation of message units (words or word sequences) is open to later changes on the basis of later information. In most cases, the speaker–hearer is unaware of the process; what he is able to perceive is the single final option. Thus, the recognition of speech does not proceed lineally from phone to phone. There is plenty of experimental evidence of the fact that the information for the successive segments of the speech chain and cues used for the identification of single elements by the listener are spread out over several segments, or cues for several successive segments can be collapsed into a single element. In phonetics, for instance, it is well known that information which occurs later in real time can have an effect on the interpretation of preceding structures; in Finnish, for instance, the phonological status of the first-syllable vowel cannot be established before the second syllable is heard (Lehtonen, 1970). Since perception is not accomplished segment by segment as a linear process, it must be assumed that the processes of segmental perception operate over stretches of speech which are longer than single elements and integrate the cues spread out in real time into a 'Gestalt', a percept skeleton, which is used as a direct input to various indentification processes (see Lehtonen and Sajavaara, 1980).

As with perception, speech production too takes place in units larger than the segmental speech sounds. Production of speech does not require a hierarchical model either (cf Clark and Clark, 1977: 224–225). In ordinary natural speech, where we have exchanges between two or more interlocutors, the units of production are not sentences; the basic unit is much smaller. For instance, the opening of an utterance is usually cued by the previous utterance and the opening element then functions as a grammatical, semantic, and pragmatic constraint for the subsequent part of the utterance. When a 'syntactic' unit is opened, the speaker may not have any idea of how it is supposed to be concluded. It is obvious that we must presuppose an overall intention or goal for the speaker's behaviour to be realized through more specific plans, but it seems doubtful whether the planning goes beyond rather restricted stretches of utterance which can be maintained in short-term memory. Most of this is affected by two of the sets of constraints mentioned by Slobin (1979: 64), the processing constraints, primarily the temporal ordering and rapid fading of the code, and the discourse constraints, the nature and goals of human interaction, which were discussed above. An indirect proof of the fact that, even at the level of phones, speech production is not hierarchical in certain types of transfer from the native language in the speech of second-language speakers; it is often disguised by various dynamic patterns of speech such as stress, rhythm, intonation and pausing.

The processes of perception are more easily accessible to testing. Perception is also more important than production because languages are acquired via perception and the original reason for many errors can be found in perception. In the discussion of second-language acquisition, perception should be given the primary position also from the communicative point of view. The native listener can understand the learner's message, however distorted, because he can apply all of his linguistic and other knowledge to the task, while the student has to learn to understand the 'normal' accent of his foreign interlocutor.

The first stage of the perceptual process is concerned with precategorical or phonetic signal processing (see Lehtonen and Sajavaara, 1980), which has no specific place in the information-processing mechanisms of the central nervous system. Features detected in this process may or may not correlate to categories abstracted in phonological analysis. The information available from this process varies in richness in relation to the clarity of pronunciation but an unambiguous phonological identification can never be reached through this process alone. The second step may consist of the construction of the 'word's' phonological structure on the basis of phonetically analysed cue information, but this step is optional. In normal fluent speech perception, meaningful items, words in a very broad sense, are identified directly on the basis of detected cue information which constitutes the 'Gestalt' of the items. The processes are illustrated by Figure 1 (from Lehtonen and Sajavaara, 1980). If, however, the word is difficult, ie it cannot be immediately recognized from the acoustic cue information, phonological categorization is needed for identification as an auxiliary strategy; it is always available whenever the cue pattern of the input signal finds no matching items in memory. Phonological analysis is also needed when it is necessary to make use of the information available in the affixes of complex derivative forms. Both channels are open all the time, but the budding phonological process simply fades away when a new input chunk arrives, if it is not needed. Thus, the identification of the phonological segment string is possible but not obligatory. Some experimental evidence for the existence of parallel phonological processes can be found in recent work by Foss and his associates (Foss and Blank, 1980; Foss et al, 1980). Lamminmäki's study is also very revealing as regards the dual nature of the interpretation process. It was normal for his subjects to identify the test items on the basis of features other than those which belonged to the

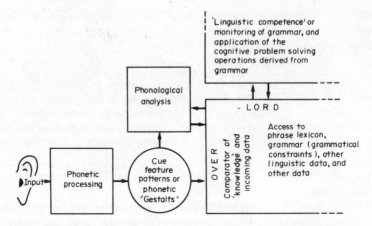

Figure 1. A partial model of speech perception (from Lehtonen and Sajavaara, 1980). Meaningful items, 'words' in a broad sense, are identified directly on the basis of cue features constituting the 'Gestalt' of the items. An optional process of phonological analysis is also fed by the same cue pattern. The two processes are assumed to be simultaneous.

phonological code; whatever the speech signal, the subjects 'heard' lexical items that were familiar to them (Lamminmäki, 1979).

Grammar in speech processing

The communicative approach implies a relocation of grammar. Some recent work by Marslen-Wilson and his colleagues (eg Marslen-Wilson and Tyler, 1980) is an example of research in which various on-line interactive processes are seen in a new light. In a dynamic model, grammar refers to such characteristics of the communicative mechanism as make it possible for a native speaker to produce a 'grammatically acceptable' text and make it possible for a native speaker to interpret the information embedded in a text in a predictable way. Such grammatical rules must be represented in neurobehavioural structures (cf Buckingham and Hollien, 1978: 294), which does not, however, mean that such rules are neurobehavioural structures. In the processing of speech, the function of lexical, syntactic and phonological structures is that of constraints: they reduce the

number of potential guesses available for the identification of the acoustic speech input.
Slobin writes (1979: 59):

> The psycholinguist is concerned with rules of language *use*. He wants to account for such things as how long it takes people to understand certain forms, what happens to them in memory, and so forth. He is not concerned with an elegant description of the language *per se*, but the language user.... Processing strategies employ knowledge organized for use—the particular use of speaking and understanding. A grammar written by a linguist is organized for a different purpose, namely, to effectively and efficiently describe a language for purposes of analysis and study.

For instance, in structural linguistics the description was based on an atomistic method: the language code was divided into subsystems, and for purposes of efficient analysis the variation and fuzziness found in real language communication were annulled by means of a suitable level of abstraction. Obviously there is nothing wrong with this as long as it remains an attempt at linguistic analysis. When, however, such constructs and items are regarded as basic elements, for instance, in language teaching, ie linguistic analysis is considered a solution for a psycholinguistic problem, a grave error is committed. The assumption that constructs of linguistic description, which have changed radically through ages, are relevant units in the production and reception of messages must be considered unfounded (Lehtonen, 1980b).

Lehtonen (1980b) points out that since grammatical rules are formulations of structural regularities, or the speaker's knowledge of such regularities, in the sentences of the language, 'an adequate description of a grammar is important for psycholinguistics, too, because in order to be able to approach the productive mechanism we first have to learn all about the structure of its products'. What we have to forget in this context is the hierarchical constitution of grammar. Lehtonen concludes:

> My point on the concept of grammar and the choice of an appropriate theory of grammar for psycholinguistics could be summarized as follows: the structural grammar (including transformational grammar and other 'generative' approaches) aims at the description of the regularities in the

text or linguistic product (or at the description of the speaker's competence or intuitions of the delivery of the ideal speaker). The object of a dynamic, or psycholinguistic, or communicative, grammar, on the other hand, should be to describe in which way linguistic knowledge participates in the processes of message production and perception. These two grammars are not alternative approaches but both are necessary.

The interrelationship between grammar and lexicon is one of the most interesting and problematic points in the interactive model of message processing. The above discussion of phonological processing implied that lexical elements bear an important function in speech processing. It could be hypothesized accordingly that information is embedded in memory in the form of lexical items, a kind of 'words'. In accordance with Marslen-Wilson and Welsh (1978: 58), such lexical memory items are thus defined as intersections of various procedures operating over a range of cognitive dimensions (cf Morton, 1979; Ellis, 1979). Such a 'word' implies a pretheoretical label for a processing unit; it contains information concerning its use in utterances and its relationships to other words within and outside utterances. A 'word' activates various processing procedures through this information; such procedures reach from prefabricated phrases and frequent word combinations over to grammatical constraints and semantic fields. What comes immediately to mind when this kind of processing model is suggested is a left-to-right probabilistic model, which was criticized as early as 1951 by Lashley (1951), and the Markov process, a language 'automaton' which was given up by Chomsky as a finite state grammar (Chomsky, 1957). A grammatical view of sentence processing obviously makes such models unacceptable; in a dynamic psycholinguistic model, in which 'words' are given a primary status and not understood in a narrow sense, the Markov process becomes an alternative which is worth reconsidering (Lehtonen, 1980b).

Cross-language comparison implies that lexical items may be detected through different processes in different languages (see Karlsson, 1979; Lehtonen, 1980a). In Finnish, a word contains a wealth of syntactic and semantic information for the analysis of the entire message through the suffixes that are attached to it, while in English the same information is found in independent morphemes attached to the word or in the order of such morphemes. When a speaker-hearer is processing the speech input in these two languages, he is bound to look for totally different kind of cues, in Finnish the cue features embedded in single words, in English the data involved in the relevant order of the elements. Moreover, there is some evidence of a non-equal status of different types of lexical elements; in Finnish much of the processing load seems to centre on verbal items, while in English it is the nominal parts of the utterance that bear the major burden. In Finnish the finite verb is relatively easily recognizable in the speech chain (cf Karlsson, 1979).

A model of message processing

In order to integrate human information processing with data from research on cross-language problems and second-language acquisition, the Finnish–English Cross-language Project has developed a tentative model of message processing (see Figure 2).* The leading principle in the model is the description of the phenomena and processes which result in communicative success in accordance with the communicatively oriented approach which was delineated above.

A central position in the model is occupied by a network of different types of knowledge essential for efficient communication. In addition to grammar and lexis, these include discourse history, facts and beliefs, and information about language-world relationships. The network is 'governed' by the Overlord, a decision-maker/problem-solver, which has access to all the sources of information all the time. The functioning of the system is affected by three sets of intervening variables described by the three boxes below the major box, ie will and intention, affective and emotional variables and performance potential. All these are, to a certain extent at least, open to external

---

*I wish to acknowledge my debt to Jaakko Lehtonen, who has participated in the production of the model. The model should be considered as a representation of the problem points in language processing and an attempt to correlate linguistic elements to other elements. It is not meant to be a representation of the flow of data in the processing mechanisms; thus, the arrows indicate relationships and channels for feeding in data (see Lehtonen, 1980a).

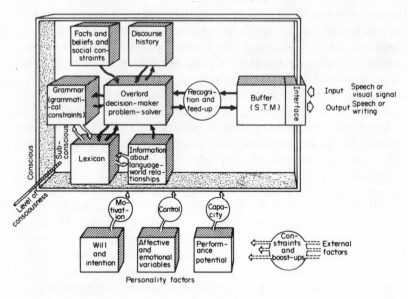

Figure 2. A model of message processing (from Sajavaara and Lehtonen, 1980).

influence (see Sajavaara, 1978a). What this means is that the communicative performance of an individual is never constant but varies under the influence of these factors.

The Overlord makes use of the information heterarchically, which means in practice that it is not possible to predict what the pieces of information are that result in the 'right' interpretation of the message. There are two simultaneous processes—the data-driven process and the conceptually-driven one; both are necessary. The Overlord's major task is to compare both the incoming data and the data stored in memory and make decisions as concerns the most probable interpretation of the message—also as concerns corrections to earlier interpretations made necessary by new information. The functioning of the Overlord is dependent on data available in the data bank, because recognition of new information takes place in reference to previous knowledge.

The model is three-dimensional, the third dimension representing the consciousness axis. The nature of the data available in the data bank varies from fully conscious to totally subconscious: some data which is constantly used for purposes of interpretation never reaches the level of consciousness, some lies at the borderline, and some data is based on explicit formulations of rules and definitions (the borderline is never strict and the whole is to be seen as a continuum).

The 'buffer', which includes short-term memory, and the interface take care of the dosage of the incoming flow of material into chunks which can be processed by the system (see Ellis, 1979). The interface is responsible for the reduction of the incoming data (from sound waves and letter symbols) to the extent that the buffer can handle it. The interface must carry this function out, at least partially, on the basis of certain physical features of the incoming stimulus (see above). A certain number of the cues embedded in this stimulus are language-specific, others are universal (eg the information that a stimulus is human speech). The interface and the buffer are necessary both in the production and in the reception of speech. The processes that are executed here are the reception and actual transmission of linguistic data and the control of the articulatory organs and their motor programmes and the hearing organs and processes.

All the information available in the data bank is of equal value and can be used simultaneously by the cognitive mechanism materializing in the Overlord. The syntactic, morphotactic and pragmatic rules, as well as various semantic networks which have been activated through the identification in the incoming signal of a certain 'key element' together with the earlier results of the progressing analysis, are available at each stage of the process as constraints which open up or restrict potential choices in the construction of message content or in the production of speech. The data-driven analysis is necessarily an on-line process which proceeds word by word but, through the retroactive reworking effect, any interpretation may be changed later in the light of subsequent context. The 'Gestalts' which are an important element in the detection mechanism are used to make predictions as concerns the nature of forthcoming data (see Lehtonen, 1980a; Sajavaara, 1980).

The dual nature of the processing system together with the general functioning principle of the Overlord implies that most of the assumptions concerning interference in various contrastive theorizings have been based on too straightforward an idea of what takes place in the human brain. Yet the same model also indicates that in some respects the contrastivist conjecture have been too complicated in assuming that all the hierarchical 'linguistic' steps are activated all the time in language processing. The partial model in Figure 1 above predicts interference on three levels of message processing in cross-language communication: detection of cue patterns, lexical identification, and reconstruction of phonological target structure. We will return to the contrastive implications of the model later.

The production process is somewhat more complicated to reconstruct than the reception process (here it is not necessary to take any stand as concerns the existence or non-existence of two different systems for production and reception; it is assumed here as a working hypothesis that in a fully developed processing system it is one and the same mechanism which works in both directions; see Tarone, 1974; Ruder and Finch, 1980). An attempt by Lehtonen and Sajavaara to reconstruct the progression of communicative events from a speaker's viewpoint can be found in Lehtonen (1980b) as reproduced in Figure 3. The communicative event is based on the speaker's overt communicative behaviour, both verbal and non-verbal, on the one hand, and on various non-intentional features to be detected in the speaker and/or the situation, on the other. It is here assumed that the motive for communicative behaviour arouses various kinds of communicative plans simultaneously, and it is at the execution stage that certain of these plans are deleted, eg in some cases only verbal behaviour materializes, in some it is non-verbal, in some it is both. (It is also noteworthy that non-verbal behaviour or paralinguistic elements involved in verbal behaviour determine the interpretation of utterances when the verbal and the non-verbal features suggest different interpretations (cf Lyons, 1977: 61–63). Despite the fact that the verbal part is linguistically more central (see Lyons, 1977: 61), the pragmatic interpretation is more highly dependent on the non-verbal part, which is more closely associated with the social and expressive function of language).

It is important to remember that this kind of a model is not meant to be a scientific description of how the human brain functions (similarly the size of each individual box bears no resemblance to the relevant factor's importance in human speech processing). The modelling of the processes and phenomena is valuable for the illustration of what is regarded as important in human speech communication, on the one hand, and also of the structuring of research problems and starting-points for experimental research. It would be misleading to suggest that the 'black box' could be described by means of a model (and in this sense the present model cannot be considered to be any better than all other models that are available), but this fact does not undermine the reasoning behind the building of the model presented here.

Second-language acquisition

Language competence was earlier mostly understood to mean internalized knowledge of the verbal code; this is the inference we can make on the basis of language-teaching materials. Today it is perhaps much more difficult to make statements as to what it means that somebody knows or does not know a language. Despite a pronounced

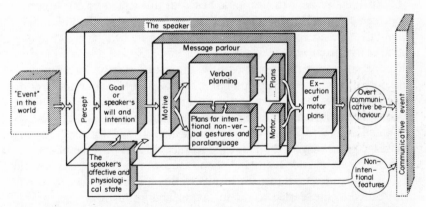

Figure 3. In this model of the progression of communicative events from the speaker's viewpoint (developed by the Finnish–English Cross-language Project, see Lehtonen, 1980b), the communicative event is seen to be based on the speaker's overt communicative behaviour, both verbal and non-verbal, on the one hand, and on various non-intentional features to be detected in the speaker, on the other. In addition, the 'event' in the world also may add its own elements to the communicative event.

emphasis on communication in language teaching, nothing much has changed in actual practice: in many cases 'communicative' language teaching aims at the production of grammatically well-formed *sentences* on the basis of the recognition and segmentation of elements and phenomena abstracted by linguists. If communicative competence means, however, the ability to use the mechanism described above in an acceptable way, the function of linguistic elements changes radically. Formal teaching obviously leads to knowledge about grammatical constraints in the form of generalized rules, which results in what could be termed as 'pseudo-competence', while true communicative competence can be reached through natural communication only (cf Krashen, 1978: 15 ff; Widdowson, 1979: 246).

In language acquisition, the acquirer builds up his language system on the basis of the input of concrete representations that is available to him. The process works from the concrete to the abstract. In language-teaching practices, the case has normally been the reverse. The learner has been provided with a set of abstractions, a number of isolated rules at relatively autonomous levels of description, which he should then be able to use as a basis for the creation of concrete representations. Resulting pseudo-competence may allow for the simulation of acceptable language behaviour in favourable circumstances (see Sajavaara, 1978a: 59–60).

From a cross-language point of view, the major research tasks centre on two primary areas (Sajavaara and Lehtonen, 1980): (1) research on cross-language interaction to find out how learners develop the ability to produce the right kind of cues, linguistic and non-linguistic, and the ability to interpret the cues correctly; and (2) research on message processing in the language learner to deal with the phenomena which are outside the scope of consciousness. For the purposes of foreign-language teaching, the results of this research will have to be correlated to the learner in the formal teaching situation.

Several approaches to the theory of second language acquisition have been developed recently. We have Krashen's Monitor Model (Krashen, 1978), Schumann's and Stauble's Acculturation Model (Schumann, 1978), and Selinker's and Lamendella's (1978) neurofunctional perspective (see also Schumann, 1979). Hatch's work on input (Hatch, 1979) and Seliger's on high-and-low-input generators (Seliger,

1977) have been important contributions as well as Fillmore's findings concerning the relevance of social skills for language acquisition. There is also the model developed by Bialystok (1978) and the work on universal tendencies by Wode and his collaborators (Wode, 1979). ——— Many research programmes concerned with various aspects of bilingualism (eg the Canadian immersion programme, the Heidelberg project, the ZISA project, see Cummins, 1979; Dittmar, 1978; Meisel, 1980, respectively) or with cross-language problems (see Faerch, 1979; Sajavaara and Lehtonen, 1979) have produced data relevant for second-language acquisition theory. At the moment we have a great number of parameters which are known to be present in the second-language acquisition process; there is still, however, a long way to go before we can have an integrated picture where the formal aspects of language fit in with other developmental features.* If it is assumed that everybody, at any age, can internalize languages (cf Krashen, 1978), what is needed is knowledge about why the process does not always result in language proficiency. It seems that many of the intervening variables are social or—in formal teaching situations—pedagogical; there are some indications of the fact that without the influence of such intervening variables the developmental processes might be fairly universal (see Seliger, 1980; Meisel, 1980).

Language acquirers who are successful in natural settings—success meaning rapid progress—are more concerned with communication than with form (see Fillmore, 1976); caretakers tend to pay attention to children's messages and not to their grammar (Snow and Ferguson (eds), 1977; Waterson and Snow (eds), 1978). Learning a second language means an expansion of communicative potential to the area of another code, and therefore the learner's role in communicative interaction requires more attention.

Recent literature on second-language acquisition (see Hatch, 1977; Hakuta and Cancino, 1977) is mainly concerned with learners who are acquiring second languages in natural settings. More data is needed about language acquisition in formal classroom settings (see, however, Wode, 1979). In some recent work on the acquisition of

---

* No attempt will be made here to deal with the rich literature on second language learning strategies (see, for example Faerch and Kasper, 1980).

second languages, a distinction has been made between conscious language learning (memorization of rules) and unconscious acquisition, which results from exposure to the target language (see Krashen, 1978; Bialystok, 1978; d'Anglejan, 1978). Instead of a strict dichotomy we should consider a continuum with two extremes: at one end there is 'total' acquisition, which results in native-like performance, and at the other end a perhaps hypothetical language system which is based entirely on explicit memorization of rules, sufficient for the production of acceptable L2 strings under favourable circumstances (cf Sajavaara, 1978a). In addition to the type of exposure to the target language, the age of the learner, the type of the rule system, the level of acculturation, and the complex of factors involved in the L1–L2 interrelationship also affect the outcome, to mention a few of the most prominent parameters (see Gingras (ed), 1978). Children before the 'critical' age mainly acquire, while older people can both acquire and learn, although explicit memorization of rules and their application to practice obviously becomes more difficult with age. In rule systems which relate to semantics, notional categories, pragmatics and sociolinguistics, learners must rely more on acquisition than on learning, and there are rules which can only be acquired because they cannot be specified (see Krashen, 1978; Gingras, 1978). Optimal acquisition requires a high level of acculturation and integrative motivation, while a total lack of them may block acquisition entirely (Schumann, 1978).

Conscious learning is not necessary for acquisition; acquisition is not necessarily the result of conscious learning. Formal teaching may develop in learners an ability to use overtly formulated rules for various classroom practices, but they are not easily transferred outside the classroom (Lamendella, 1979). Krashen explains the inability of learners to use explicit knowledge about the language for communication as a function of his Monitor (Krashen, 1978); in a more general frame of reference, eg the one given in Figure 2 above, it could however be described in terms of the interplay between the conscious and subconscious strata of the information-processing mechanism.

The two channels of the identification process described in Figure 1 above, ie phonological mediation and direct lexical access on the basis of 'Gestalt' cues, correlate with Lamendella's (1979) notions of Foreign Language Learning based on the cognition hierarchy of neurofunctional systems and Secondary Language Acquisition based on the communication hierarchy and with Krashen's (1978) dichotomy of learned vs acquired rules. In fluent processing, which results from acquisition, the synthetic 'Gestalt' mode is the regular one. Language learning emphasizes an analytical approach and gives preference to processes which are dependent on phonological mediation or similar procedures.

This analytical mode of processing is often reinforced in the available teaching methodologies. If foreign language is approached through detailed acoustic, physiological, and other similar phenomena, the student may be misled to paying attention to factors which are of relatively small importance rather than to more comprehensive units of speech and communication. The processing of individual phonological items hardly causes any serious problems if we find ways of teaching the learners to 'hear' the foreign-language input correctly. But in most cases it is not necessary to pay special attention to phonology.

In language contact, intake is regulated by a 'socioaffective filter' (see Dulay and Burt, 1977), which is controlled by various social and personality factors and knowledge of the world (Sajavaara and Lehtonen, 1980). The filter can be opened by integrating the learner psychologically or socially into the target group or by adding to his knowledge of the world. Increased operationality of the new language also lowers the filter. Conscious or subconscious perception of what makes part of the world and the language is governed by previous experience. In this way a great deal of what is important in communication can be transferred from first language skills.

The teacher's main task in the classroom is the opening of the filter and the provision of a sufficient amount of language input. It is important that the language code is not an end in itself; it should be regarded as product of processes whose goals are non-linguistic. When the code was the main target of teaching, it was not considered necessary to tell pupils anything about why it was necessary for them to carry out certain procedures in the classroom. It was sufficient that the teacher knew. For the pupil to know about the purposes of the tasks was considered hazardous or even destructive for learning (seen as habit-formation—the basic idea was obviously derived from behaviouristic psychology). Now it is understood that a learner's performance may be decisively enhanced by his own view of his own chances of success, and therefore it may be of some importance to tell the learner what is expected of him. He may even be taught to learn. An integral part of this work involves bringing language courses closer to reality as it is experienced by the learner, closer to the world he lives in, and the environment he feels to be his own. This means that it is not necessary for the language teacher to operate in a vacuum without any link with what the learners are and what they do or are planning to do outside the classroom.

Several attempts have been made during the past decade to break away from the grammatical syllabus and to approach language-teaching problems through a closer specification of the aims within a different framework. There are, for instance, Wilkins's (1976) notional syllabuses, further developed in the Threshold Level by van Ek (1980), Munby's (1978) communicative syllabus design, and Freihoff's and Takala's taxonomy of language-use situations (Freihoff and Takala, 1974). Although all of these reveal important parameters of what language is and how it is used, the operationalization of such parameters does not seem to create a break out of the vicious circle of the grammatical code. As has been pointed out above, and also by Widdowson in several contexts (eg in a paper read at the Second Nordic Conference of Applied Linguistics at Hanasaari, Finland, in November 1979), it is possible to divide such parameters further and further into smaller units without really assisting the learner in his task of learning how to communicate in the other code, or, preferably, how to extend his communicative potential over to the area of the other code. The basic skills of communication are already there, and it is exactly these skills that are often specified in the taxonomies. The only way seems to be through using language for various tasks whose implementation requires language skills. It would seem that the objectives of language courses should be specified as tasks to be carried out by the learners, not as notional and situational parameters, which after all are not much different.

The four 'basic skills' have attained an important place in many recent theoretical presentations of language-teaching methodology. In many cases the four skills are strictly separated, which is seldom the case in true language behaviour (plentifully illustrated by Widdowson, 1978). In speech communication the roles of the speaker and the hearer alternate. Reading is also a kind of dialogue between the reader and the writer, which implies that writing should be the same. In the classroom, every time the teacher writes something on the blackboard this constitutes a reading exercise, whether it is the intention or not. At a deeper level, in the light of the model presented in Figure 2 above, the four skills are not much different from each other either; for instance, writing always involves certain receptive processes, listening and reading are interrelated, and perceptual processing entails phenomena which are present in production, etc. Therefore, even if in some cases reading comprehension can be given as a reasonable outcome of a course, it should not be specified as the aim; instead it should be considered a means for some other goal, eg gathering information about a certain concept or discipline in a certain language.

In language teaching the following criteria should be observed: (1) Language and communication should be seen as a means, not as an end. (2) Language input should be offered in contexts where it is relevant for the needs of the learners. (3) Language classes should provide a framework for meaningful communication in the target language geared to the experience of the participants. (4) The teaching should involve tasks of information-processing and problem-solving which are intellectually demanding. (5) The courses should be correlated to other task demands, eg other subjects. (6) Formal aspects of the language code should be taught to the extent they can be supported by the learning objectives (eg formal requirements of written texts). (7) Relevant rules of discourse should be given proper attention in the classroom as regards the extent to which they govern the choice of various language items.

Implications for contrastive analysis

Discussion of cross-language influences based on natural language data is seriously handicapped if too simplistic an approach is adopted by the researcher. It should always be remembered that there may be different kinds of influence at different levels of learning and there is variation between learners. L1 influence on L2 is never a matter of a simple yes/no question. At the same time, a number of global characteristics can be seen to operate in language processing and language acquisition (cf Wode, 1980; Meisel, 1980). Various kinds of L1 influence are known to exist at all levels of analysis—the foreign accent is there—but the tests available at the moment are insufficient to reveal the 'critical' points of the interlanguage speech channel. Even today the best way to approach them is through analysis of the student's speech production, because it also reveals problems in perceptual processing.

As was pointed out earlier, the history of contrastive linguistics implies that cross-language analysis based on a static view of language is insufficient. What is needed in addition is mapping differences and similarities in various processes taking place in and between the speaker and the hearer in acts of communication (Sajavaara and Lehtonen, 1979). Since many interference problems can be expected to derive from the clash of the two dynamic information-processing systems, rather than two static rule patterns, it is impossible to predict interference phenomena without reference to speech processing systems. This does not mean that classical contrastive analyses are useless; on the contrary, what is implied by the above discussion of message processing is that such analyses are valuable for the explanation of many phenomena involved, but they can only seldom be sufficient alone for the purposes of foreign language learning. For a 'contrastive' analysis of the linguistic codes, the codes should be located in their proper places in the speech communication processes across the languages, which requires the mapping of the various parameters delineated in the message-processing model above. In this way, contrastive analysis expands to cover the entire chains of communication in two or more languages (see Sajavaara, 1977; Sajavaara and Lehtonen, 1980).

If there is no evidence for the psychological relevance of existing grammars, ie they do not represent structures and processes embedded in the brain, it cannot be expected that structures that form part of descriptions of grammar are necessarily structures that are transferred from L1 to L2. Transfer is a psychological process and only what is psychologically real can be transferred, as is rightly pointed out by Meisel (1980). Thus, for transfer the main problem is that of the psychological reality of grammatical structures. If abstract grammars are 'just convenient fictions for representing certain processing strategies' (Lakoff and Thompson, 1975: 285), how do we then explain the fact that numerous analyses of foreign language learners' errors have proved that grammatical structures are transferred from language to language? It should also be possible to explain the discrepancy (not so surprising as such for foreign-language teachers) that exists between second-language acquirers in natural settings (eg, Dulay and Burt, 1977; Meisel, 1980) and foreign-language learners who have access to L2 data in formal classroom situations. Slobin (1979: 61) asks whether 'grammars are—universally—constrained to take certain forms because of the ways in which language must be used' and whether constraints of perception shape grammar. Some studies concerned with second-language acquisition in natural situations (eg Keller-Cohen, 1979) have indicated that learners' perceptions of L2 are based on previous knowledge. The same is also evident in other types of language learning such as L1, L3, foreign-language teaching, and relearning (Wode, 1980). Now the main issue is the nature of such previous knowledge. What are the structures and processes like which are embedded in long-term memory and which guide perceptions. Here most foreign language learners and most natural language acquirers are in different positions (for some major differences see Ringbom, 1980) because of the differences in the nature of relevant linguistic representations. Natural language acquirers who are uninitiated in the metalanguage of abstract grammars do not transfer categories that make part of linguistic representations, while it can be predicted that problems inherent in L2 can be found. Most foreign learners are exposed to L2 through syllabi which are—explicitly or implicitly—grammatically structured, or explanations of how the languages (L1 or L2) 'function' are given in the form of abstract theoretical representations (it makes no difference which one of the existing models is used). After the learners have been exposed—perhaps only in the 'teaching' of the mother tongue—to such grammatical descriptions, they are able to 'perceive' such categories. In this way, the interference from L1 must be, to great extent, teaching-induced and at least partially related to what Krashen (1978) calls the Monitor. For example, one of the most persistent errors by advanced Finnish learners of English is the wrong use of the passive (of the type *In this paper it is tried to show that . . .)*, which seems to be mainly due to the fact that what is called the passive in Finnish grammars is not really a passive in the same sense as the same term is applied in the grammars of Indo-European languages. A wrong equation between the two codes results in an overgeneralization process in the target language.

Learning a new language means not only the acquisition of new categories but also the reorganization of the criteria which are applied as cues for the identification process of those new categories. The consequences which the model of message processing sketched above has for a description of the data-processing problems which the language learner encounters in foreign language communication can be outlined only tentatively (cf Lehtonen and Sajavaara, 1980).

The model allows for the following cross-language observations:

(1) Processing is based on the learner's previous linguistic knowledge, ie the idiomacy of his L1 pronunciation and the corresponding receptive idiomacy. Successful detection of L2 phenomena is possible only if the speaker has had a sufficient amount of contact with spoken L2. Because of the universal nature of many features in speech, the cueing system seldom fails totally in the case of a foreign-language learner, but if the system resorts to cues which are irrelevant in the target-language system, incorrect identification alternatives may hamper the functioning of the entire mechanism.

(2) Interference in various paradigms and corresponding errors in identification and production have been the object of most contrastive studies. Interpretation of this data is still problematic and it is possible that the significance of this interference has been exaggerated.

(3) Even if appropriate cue patterns are available for the word-identification mechanism, the Overlord may fail to recognize the item because there is a gap in the lexicon. No lexical memory item can be activated on the basis of the incoming cue pattern. It is also possible that the lexical item is stored in a different form (as a graphemic

representation without any corresponding phonetic shape or as a disguised morphological stem which does not open all the necessary derivatives).

According to Krashen (1978), speech performance is always initiated by means of the acquired system, while the learned system is available as a Monitor to edit the output. In acquisition-poor environments, a speaker obviously relies on his L1 competence as performance initiator. The L1 string is then 'translated' into an L2 string, whose grammaticality and acceptability depend on the availability of 'rules' and on the nature of the constraints present. Under optimal circumstances, the L2 string is initiated and processed entirely on the basis of the acquired L2 system without the Monitor being activated. Most L2 speakers are obviously located somewhere between the two extremes; at least occasionally they have to rely on L1 systems for speech processing. This is the case when an L2 unit has not been acquired—when there is a gap—and the Monitor fails to give the right answer. L1 influence on surface strings may be due to the fact that (1) the string has been initiated by the acquired L1 system and the Monitor has not been able to correct the string, (2) the Monitor lacks the correct 'rule' and an L1 rule is used as a repair, or (3) strings originally initiated by the correct L2 system are mutilated by the learned system (Sajavaara, 1978b). The L1 and L2 acquired and learned systems are closely interlinked in the light of the model presented above, and both systems are referred to several times during speech production, which may be one of the reasons for the variable performance by the same speakers in different situations.

Second-language acquirers may experience problems for several reasons (see Sajavaara, 1980): (1) A rule cannot be retrieved. (2) A rule is inaccurate or wrong. (3) The speaker refuses to apply the rule entirely or in some situations (Krashen's (1978: 10–11). Monitor under-users are characterized by not applying the rules even if they know them, and Faerch's and Kasper's (1980) strategy of formal reduction relates to instances where the insufficiency of the linguistic system makes it necessary for the speaker to make do with 'less of their interlanguage repertoire than is in fact at their disposal') or he wants to avoid errors or facilitate speech production to reach higher levels of fluency without distorting the message. (4) The rule has not been acquired at all (the learner has not reached the stage where the rule is acquired, the rule has not been taught, the rule cannot be taught because its exact formulation is not possible or is so complicated that it is functionally unwieldy, or the learner is unable to internalize explicitly formulated rules). (5) The language user exaggerates the importance of monitoring, ie the control of the processing mechanism (Krashen's (1978: 10–11) Monitor over-users), and makes an attempt to apply explicit rules all the time. In L2, the problems are the greater the further away we move from L1-type language acquisition in naturalistic situations, because the system can be expected to be more and more defective and based on more explicit formal properties. It also becomes more delicate and more liable to malfunction due to external factors, since more performance potential is normally required for second-language processing.

In early contrastivist hypotheses, the distance between languages was seen to be indicative of the degree of learning difficulty. The distance is important in an indirect way: a learner's reactions to problems in L2 processing may reflect his mental image of the potential correlation between L1 and L2 structures. This results in the speaker's judgments on what is transferable or not (see Ringbom, 1979; Sharwood Smith, 1979: 350).

In contrastive analysis aiming at applied goals, too much attention may have been paid to the transfer of individual structures. According to Felix (1978: 224), L1 interference seems to occur in the form of sporadic erroneous performance; he concludes that the interrelationship between L1 and L2 lies at a much deeper level than surface or even near-surface categories. He also calls attention to a more global look at the role of previous L1 knowledge in the acquisition of L2, which is well founded in the light of what is known of human information processing, perceptual mechanisms, and memory. Keller-Cohen (1979) points out that learners seek global properties of language, ie large analytic chunks which are linked with clear contexts. Various kinds of surface features may be in different positions depending on the degree of optionality of the items; the persistent problems experienced in pronunciation may be due to the fact that phonetic choices are seldom optional.

Conclusion

One of the most important observations based on what has been said above concerns the high degree of task dependency of speech production and reception. There are few factors that remain constant under all circumstances, from speaker to speaker, and with the same speaker. The whole system aims at efficiency, which does not however mean the economy of surface features (cf Sajavaara, 1978a: 57–59).

At the onset of the second-language-learning process, the learner's cue detection mechanism is tuned to the phenomena and processes of his first language. He tends to hear the target-language utterances in terms of categories and structures of his native language, and it is not surprising at all that he also substitutes elements of his first language for the target structures. Unless various plans and programmes are 'acquired', to use Krashen's dichotomy, the speech-processing mechanism has to resort to 'learned' items. This obviously requires more processing capacity. Insufficient acquisition can be compensated by increased capacity or low task demands. Other simultaneous tasks, emotional states, and high loads on problem-solving capacity may also affect the processing system.

One of the most important parts of the foreign-language learning process involves a continuous reorganization and completion of the cueing mechanism, a 'new deal' of the cards of the communication game. When acquiring the correct 'Gestalts' of target-language items, the learner also tunes the perceptual mechanism to pick up such 'Gestalts'. The whole process is subconscious for the most part and it is impossible to see how it could be directly interfered with. It might seem that the only way to this reorganization is through the right kind of input, by exposing the learner to the kind of L2 material which brings about the shift as a gradual process.

At the present moment, we lack adequate tests to cope with the problems in second-language communication. To a certain extent, this inadequacy results from the fact that there has not been an integrated picture of the mechanisms functioning in first-language communication or language acquisition. The whole problem boils down to the major issue taken up at the beginning of this paper, the distinction between static and dynamic modelling of communicative skills. An integrated picture—whether in L1 or in L2—is possible only if we remember the distinction between the student's knowledge of linguistic structures and his capacity to communicate in the mother tongue or in a foreign language. Most of the previous research has dealt with the final product, the surface string. There is an urgent need to develop methodologies to study the stages before the actual utterance. More information is also needed of discourse planning such as it is revealed, for instance, by speech errors in L1 and L2. Phenomena which will have to be studied include language behaviour in various interactional settings, ability to use different channels of communication to convey messages and intentions, and ability to understand and interpret messages transmitted by other interactants.

References

d'Anglejan, A (1978) 'Language learning in and out of classrooms.' In Richards, J C (ed) *Understanding second and foreign language learning*. Rowley, Mass.: Newbury House, pp 218–236.

Bialystok, E (1978) 'A theoretical model of second language learning.' *Language learning* 28, 69–83.

Buckingham, H and Hollien, H (1978) 'A neural model for language and speech.' *Journal of phonetics* 6, 283–297.

Canale, M and Swain, M (1980) 'Theoretical bases of communicative approaches to second language teaching and testing.' *Applied linguistics* 1, 1–47.

Carroll, J M and Bever, T G (1976) 'Sentence comprehension.' In E C Carterette and M P Friedman (eds) *Handbook of perception 7: Language and speech*. New York: Academic Press, pp 300–344.

Carroll, J M, Tanenhaus, M K and Bever, T G (1978) 'The perception of relations: the interaction of structural, functional, and contextual factors in the segmentation of sentences.' In Levelt and Flores d'Arcais (eds) (1978), pp 187–218.

Chomsky, N (1957) *Syntactic structures*. The Hague: Mouton.

Clark, H H and Clark, E V (1977) *Psychology and language*. New York: Harcourt.

Cummings, J (1979) 'Linguistic interdependence and the educational development of bilingual children.' *Review of educational research* 49, 222–251.

Davis, S M (1978) 'Audition and speech perception.' In R L Schiefelbusch, (ed) *Bases of language intervention*. Baltimore, Md: University Park Press.

Dittmar, N (1978) 'Ordering adult learners according to language abilities.' In N Dittmar, H Haberland, T Skuttnabb-Kangas and U Teleman, (eds) *Papers from the first Scandinavian–German symposium on the language of immigrant workers and their Children.* Roskilde: Universitetscenter, pp 119–147.

Dulay, H and Burt, M (1977) 'Remarks on creativity in language acquisition.' In M Burt, H Dulay and M Finocchiaro, *(eds) Viewpoints on English as a second language.* New York: Regents, 95–126.

van Ek, J (1980) *Threshold level English.* London: Pergamon.

Ellis, A W (1979) 'Speech production and short-term memory.' *Structures and processes.* Psycholinguistic series 2. London: Paul Elek, pp 157–187.

Faerch, C (1979) *Research in foreign language pedagogy: the PIF project.* Anglica et Americana 7. Copenhagen: University of Copenhagen.

Faerch, C and Kasper, G (1980) 'Processes and strategies in foreign language learning and communication.' Manuscript.

Felix, S W (1978) *Linguistische Untersuchungen zum natürlichen Zweitsprachenerwerb.* München: Fink.

Fillmore, L W (1976) *The second time around: cognitive and social strategies in second language acquisition.* PhD dissertation, Stanford University.

Fisiak, J (1980) 'Some notes concerning contrastive linguistics.' *AILA Bulletin* 27:1, 1–17.

Flores d'Arcais, G B (1978) 'The perception of complex sentences.' In Levelt and Flores d'Arcais *(eds)* (1978), 155–186.

Foss, D J and Blank, M A (1980). 'Identifying the speech code.' *Cognitive psychology* 12, 1–31.

Foss, D J, Harwood, D A and Blank, M A (1980) 'Deciphering decoding decisions: data and devices.' In R A Cole *(ed) Perception and production of fluent speech.* Hillsdale, N J: Lawrence Erlbaum.

Freihoff, R and Takala, S (1974) *A systematic description of language teaching objectives based on the specification of language use situations.* Abridged version. Reports from the Language Centre 3/1974. Jyväskylä: Language Centre for Finnish Universities.

Gingras, R C (1978) 'Second language acquisition and foreign language teaching.' In R C Gingras *(ed)* (1978), 88–97.

Gingras, R C *(ed)* (1978) *Second language acquisition and foreign-language teaching.* Arlington, Va: Center for Applied Linguistics.

Hakuta, K and Cancino, H (1977) 'Trends in second language acquisition research.' *Harvard Educational Review* 47, 294–316.

Hatch, E (1977) 'Second language learning.' In *Bilingual education: current perspectives/Linguistics.* Arlington, Va: Center for Applied Linguistics, 60–86.

Hatch, E (1979) 'Input studies.' Paper read at the First Nordic Interlanguage Symposium at Hanasaari, Finland, August 1979.

James, C (1978) 'Quo vadis, psycholinguistics?' *International journal of psycholinguistics* 5, 73–81.

Karlsson, F (1979) 'Automatic morphological segmentation of Finnish word forms.' In K Häkkinen and F Karlsson *(eds) Papers from the conference on general linguistics, Seili, 29–30.8.1979.* Publications of the Linguistic Association of Finland 3. Turku: The Linguistic Association of Finland, pp 51–64.

Keller-Cohen, D (1979) 'Systematicity and variation in the non-native child's acquisition of conversational skills.' *Language learning* 29, 27–44.

Krashen, S D (1978) 'The Monitor Model for second language acquisition.' In Gingras (*ed*) (1978), 1–26.

Lakoff, G and Thompson, H (1975) 'Introducing cognitive grammar.' In C Cogen *et al* (*eds*) *Proceedings of the first annual meeting of the Berkeley Linguistic Society, February 15–17, 1975.* Berkeley, Ca: Berkeley Linguistic Society, 295–309.

Lamendella, J (1979) 'The neurofunctional basis of pattern practice.' *TESOL quarterly* 13, 5–19.

Lamminmäki, R (1979) 'The discrimination and identification of English vowels, consonants, junctures and sentence stress by Finnish comprehensive school pupils.' In J Lehtonen and K Sajavaara (*eds*) *Papers in contrastive phonetics.* Jyväskylä Corss-Language Studies 7. Jyväskylä: Department of English, 165–231.

Lashley, K S (1951) 'The problem of serial order in behavior.' In L A Jeffress (*ed*) *Cerebral mechanisms in behavior.* New York, Wiley, 112–136.

Lee, W A (*ed*) (1980) *Trends in speech recognition.* Englewood Cliffs, NJ: Prentice-Hall.

Lehtonen, J (1970) 'Aspects of quantity in Standard Finnish.' *Studia Philologica Jyväskyläensia* 6. Jyväskylä: University of Jyväskylä.

Lehtonen, J (1978) 'How can the theory and methods of speech sciences contribute to contrastive analysis?' Paper read at the 16th International Conference on Polish–English Contractive Linguistics, Boszkowo, Poland, December 1978. (Forthcoming).

Lehtonen, J (1980a) 'Psykolingvistika aspekter pa en finnes förmaga att första skandinaviska spark.' Paper read at the symposium Internordisk sprakförstaelse, Rungstedgaard, Copenhagen, March 1980. (Forthcoming.)

Lehtonen, J (1980b) 'The communicative approaches to speech and language and the study of grammar.' A comment paper read at the International Workshop on Psycholinguistic Models of Production, University of Kassel, July 1980. (Forthcoming.)

Lehtonen, J and Sajavaara, K (1980) 'Phonology and speech processing: in cross-language communication.' In Eliasson, S (*ed*) *Theoretical issues in contrastive phonology.* Heidelberg: Julius Groos.

Levelt, W J M and Flores d'Arcais, G B (*eds*) (1978) *Studies in the perception of language.* New York: Wiley.

Lindsay, P H and Norman, D A (1977) *Human information processing.* New York: Academic Press.

Lyons, J (1977) *Semantics 1–2.* Cambridge: Cambridge University Press.

Marslen-Wilson, W D and Welsh, A (1978) 'Processing interaction and lexical access during word recognition in continuous speech.' *Cognitive psychology* 10, 29–63.

Marslen-Wilson, W D and Tyler, L K (1980) 'The temporal structure of spoken language understanding.' *Cognition* 8, 1–71.

Marslen-Wilson, W D, Tyler, L K and Seidenberg, M (1978) 'Sentence processing and the clause boundary.' In Levelt and Flores d'Arcais (*eds*) (1978), 219–246.

Meisel, J (1980) 'Strategies of second language acquisition.' *Wuppertaler Arbeitspapiere zur Sprachwissenschaft* 3. Wuppertal: Gesamthochschule Wuppertal, 1–53.

Morton, J (1979) 'Word recognition.' In Morton, J and Marshall, J C (*eds*) *Structures and processes.* Psycholinguistic series 2. London: Paul Elek, 107–156.

Munby, J (1978) *Communicative syllabus design.* Cambridge: Cambridge University Press.

Ringbom, H (1979) 'The English of Finns, Swedes, and Swedish Finns: some concluding remarks.' In Palmberg, R (*ed*) *The perception and production of English: papers on interlanguage*, AFTIL 6. Åbo: Department of English, Åbo Akademi, 77–85.

Ringbom, H (1980) 'Second language acquisition and foreign language learning.' In Sajavaara *et al* (*eds*), 1980.

Ruder K and Finch, A (1980) 'Toward a cognitive-based model of language production.' Paper read at the Workshop on Psycholinguistic Models of Production, University of Kassel, July 1980. (Forthcoming.)

Sajavaara, K (1977) 'Contrastive linguistics past and present and a communicative approach.' In Sajavaara, K and Lehtonen, J (*eds*) *Contrastive papers.* Jyväskylä Contrastive Studies 4. Jyväskylä: Department of English, 9–30.

Sajavaara, K (1978a) 'The monitor model and monitoring in foreign-language speech communication.' In Gingras (*ed*) (1978), 51–67.

Sajavaara, K (1978b) 'The monitor model and contrastive analysis.' Paper read at the 16th International Conference on Polish–English Contrastive Linguistics, Boszkowo, Poland, December 1978. (Forthcoming.)

Sajavaara, K (1980) 'Second language speech production: factors affecting fluency.' Paper read at the International Workshop on Psycholinguistic Models of Production, University of Kassel, July 1980. (Forthcoming.)

Sajavaara, K and Lehtonen, J (1979) 'Prisoners of code-centred privacy: reflections on contrastive linguistics and related disciplines.' In Sajavaara, K and Lehtonen, J (*eds*) *Papers in discourse and contrastive discourse analysis.* Jyväskylä Contrastive Studies 5. Jyväskylä: Department of English.

Sajavaara, K and Lehtonen, J (1980) 'Language teaching and acquisition of communication.' In Sajavaara *et al* (*eds*) (1980).

Sajavaara, K, Räsänen, A and Hirvonen, T (*eds*) (1980) *AFinLA yearbook.* Publications of the Finnish Association of Applied Linguistics AFinLA 28. Jyväskylä: AFinLA.

Schumann, J H (1978) 'The acculturation model for second language acquisition.' In Gingras (ed) (1978), 27–50.

Schumann, J H (1979) 'Three theoretical perspectives on second language acquisition.' Paper presented at the First Nordic Symposium on Interlanguage, Hanasaari, Finland. August 1980.

Seliger, H W (1977) 'Does practice make perfect?: a study of interaction patterns and L2 competence.' Language learning 27, 263–278.

Seliger, H W (1980) 'Strategy and tactic in second language acquisition.' Manuscript.

Selinker, L and Lamendella, J (1978) 'Two perspectives on fossilization in interlanguage learning.' ISB 3, 143–191.

Sharwood Smith, M (1979) 'Strategies, language transfer and the simulation of the second language learner's mental operations.' Language learning 29, 345–361.

Slobin, D I (1979) Psycholinguistics, 2nd edition. Glenview, Ill: Scott, Foresman & Co.

Smith, N and Wilson, D (1979) Modern linguistics: the results of Chomsky's revolution. Harmondsworth: Penguin.

Snow, C and Ferguson, C A (eds) (1977) Talking to children. Cambridge: Cambridge University Press.

Tarone, E (1974) 'Speech perception in second language acquisition: a suggested model.' Language learning 24, 223–233.

Waterson, N and Snow, C (eds) (1978) The development of communication. New York: Wiley.

Widdowson, H (1978) Teaching language as communication. London: Oxford University Press.

Widdowson, H (1979) Explorations in applied linguistics. London: Oxford University Press.

Wilkins, D A (1976) Notional syllabuses. London: Oxford University Press.

Wode, H (1979) Studies in second language acquisition. Occasional papers 11. Singapore: SEAMEO Regional Language Centre.

Wode, H (1980) 'Language acquisitional universals—L1, L2, pidgins and foreign language teaching.' In Sajavaara et al (eds) (1980).

8. Towards a Contrastive Pragmalinguistics

Philip Riley

University of Nancy II

Introduction

There are a number of important aspects of language behaviour which are not amenable to the theories and procedures of classical Contrastive Analysis. In particular Contrastive Analysis has failed to deal with problems of meaning, language use and the various linguistic aspects of interaction. One reaction to this state of affairs is the attempt being made to develop the semantic component of contrastive generative grammars (cf Krzeszowski, 1972, 1976), and it does indeed seem that valuable insights may be gained thereby.

Another reaction, though, has been to turn away from meaning as represented by deep structures 'inside' sentences and to investigate it instead as it is manifested in social acts 'outside' sentences. The focus of such an approach is not on the theories, models and data of linguistic structures but on the social patterning of discourse and interaction. For the pragmalinguist, then, it is language functions rather than linguistic structures—discourse, not grammar, the communicative act in context, not the sentence in isolation—which are central to his investigation.

Can the contrastive analyst benefit from such an approach? Is the work being done in Pragmatics (as well as in related fields such as Discourse Analysis, Social Psychology, Sociology) of value to him? This paper suggests that it is; indeed, it is based on the 'strong hypothesis' that contrastive analysis without a pragmalinguistic dimension is inadequate.

This suggestion is not a new one (Gleason, 1968; Hartmann, 1977) and a valuable programmatic statement of aims and objects has been made (Sajavaara, 1971). But when we come down to the nitty-gritty we find that, in fact, very little has been done, since no suitable model of pragmalinguistic or interactive structure has been available for the contrastive analyst to use even if he wanted to.

So this paper is a first, tentative step in that direction. It is possibly also overambitious, and wrong-headed: but it does try, through the analysis of concrete examples (however inadequate), to make a practical and not just a theoretical contribution to the field.

I. Outline of a model of pragmalinguistics

In this section, we will be considering very briefly a model of pragmalinguistics which has been developed at the CRAPEL over the last four years. Obviously, this is not the place for a detailed discussion of the status and scope of pragmalinguistics (see Stalnaker, 1972) but one or two points need to be made if the relevance and perspective of what follows is not to be distorted.

1. Meaning as a construct of behaviour

We would like first to draw attention to the meaning of *meaning* as it is used here. For the pragmalinguist and the student of interaction, the traditional philosophical and semantic accounts of meaning are of little use or validity; isolated, de-contextualised objects or concepts are unsuitable tools for the description of the dynamics of communication. Rather, he sees meaning as a construct of interaction, and he studies the ways in which participants in a communicative event create, relate, organise and realise meaning in behaviour.

(As will probably be immediately obvious to the reader, the term *pragmalinguistics* is not used here in the sense in which it is used by some philosophers of language, whose main interest is restricted to the referential operations of the verbal code. (Deictics, pronouns, negations, etc.) Such an approach offers little more to the understanding of interactive meaning than does traditional semantics.)

The pragmalinguist regards attempts to define *the* meaning of meaning as a will o' the wisp: meaning for him resides in and is conveyed by the combinations and the relationship between a number of semiotic channels, and it is these operations which form the primary object of his study. He studies and attempts to account for all contributions to communicative interaction, whether verbal, paralinguistic (ie vocal non-verbal) or non-verbal. Semantics, with its traditional focus on the verbal component alone, is of little help in the description and analysis of communicative behaviours involving the whole spectrum of sensory categories—paraphonology, key, intonation, gaze, facial expression, gesture, touch, smell, orientation, proxemics, as well as a myriad of social and situational features.[2]

A fundamental concept for the pragmalinguist, then, is that of the *act of communication*, of which the *speech act* is simply one possible realisation. A nod of the head can communicate agreement just as efficiently as the word 'yes': so, too, can a smile and gesture, acquiescence or the right choice of intonation or key. And this is a crude, over-simplified example, since the meaning of an act of communication is often the sum total of words plus facial expression, plus key, etc—plus all the situationally relevant features. Meaning is the relationship specified by these phenomena in combination.

This objection applies just as strongly to even the most sophisticated kind of contrastive generative semantics, which still has as its object the meaning of the isolated sentence. To put it another way, a bilingual informant's intuitions about equivalence (the sort of thing one might 'get at' via the deep structures and semantic component of a contrastive TGG) will *not* be enough to satisfy the criteria for meaning discussed here: they will still only provide information about a range of possible interpretations in context. No matter how much the grammarians manage to reduce semantic vagueness, isolated sentences will always remain pragmatically vague since they lack the interactive dimension. Again, no amount of cobbling with context-sensitive rules or whatever can repair the basic premise of semantics, namely, that all meaning is internal and verbal. The meaning of face-to-face interaction is an amalgam of information from many channels and, in particular, the discourse structure is mainly marked non-verbally. No account of meaning is adequate which fails to take into consideration such vital questions as who is speaking to who? When? Where? What is the nature of their relationship? Of the circumstances? What activity are they involved in? What is its purpose and that of the communication?

At the double risk of labouring the point and of caricaturing alternative approaches, let us consider an example:

There is an oak-tree in the middle of the meadow.

This, you will agree, is the sort of sentence that often gets taken for semantic analysis. Traditional semantics has been limited to the study of propositions ('sense'). Essentially, this has meant the elaboration of rules for testing the truth of propositions: with relative ease, the semanticist can set up and define classes of referent, to which he can attribute such objects as 'oak-tree' and 'meadow.' He can describe the relationship which is predicated between them, whether oak-trees are the sorts of things one finds in meadows, and so on.

But when a sentence occurs in discourse, as one of a series of utterances, it derives contextual meaning from them (or they select meanings for it). Some of these meanings *may* be connected with the constituent elements of the sentence in isolation (oak-tree, meadow, etc) but a whole new interactive dimension is also added whose meanings cannot be predicted from the sentence in isolation. The reader is invited to imagine that he is the Sheriff-hero of a Western, who has just been captured by the Villain and a band of henchmen. The henchmen are urging their leader to hang the Hero. 'Aha!' says the Villain, with a twirl of his black moustaches, 'there is an oak-tree in the middle of the meadow.'

However inveterate a semanticist, it is unlikely that the reader would start examining the truth of this utterance. Both he and the henchmen would be interested in it as a *reply* and as a *suggestion*—major meanings which it could only have in context, its meanings as a communicative act.

2. Illocution[3]

Within Pragmalinguistics, the study of communicative acts rests on the theory of Illocution (Austin, 1971; Holec, 1975; Searle, 1969). Communicative acts may be realised verbally, paralinguistically or non-verbally. That is, the *speech acts* to which most writers on the subject limit their attention are only one type or realisation of the wider class, communicative acts.

Communicative acts include inviting, accepting, agreeing, disagreeing, explaining, denying, suggesting, hypothesising, promising, offering, etc. The illocutionary value (or *function*) of each acts reflects directly the use which the actor ('speaker') wishes to put it to: loosely, it can often be regarded as an exteriorisation of his intention in carrying out that particular act rather than another.

The illocutionary value of communicative acts has no direct link with their formal realisation. In different contexts, a given grammatical structure may realise a wide range of functions: and, vice versa, the same function may be realised by a wide range of different grammatical structures. Structures and functions are not in a one-to-one relationship: the point is not a new one, but it is worth exemplifying as it is the distinguishing feature of pragmatic as opposed to grammatical descriptions.

(i) *Same form, different functions:*
   You're not going out
   (a) *Prohibiting*—father to a child with a cold: it is raining.
   (b) *Confirming*—I am reacting to the statement of a friend with a cold: he says he's staying in all day.
   (c) *Threatening*—kidnappers to victim.
   (d) *Expressing surprise*—but I thought we were going to see this afternoon's game together!
   (e) '*Stating*'—if anyone calls you'll be here to answer the door.

(ii) *Same function, different forms:*
   Agreeing
   (a) Yes, sure, right, fine, O.K., Bob's your uncle, etc.
   (b) Repetition (You're leaving? I'm leaving).
   (c) Nod of the head.
   (d) I agree, I accept your point, I see what you mean, etc.
   (e) No, I suppose not (You say you can't do it now . . .).

When we talk about the 'same' form or realisation in group (i), it should be clear that we are referring to identity at one level of description only, the morpho-syntactic level. It is precisely because there will be many differences at other levels (paralinguistic, non-verbal, situational) and because these differences will result in differences of meaning, that we must go beyond the semantico-grammatical into the pragmalinguistic. To put it more bluntly, whatever the differences between the items in group (i) they are important, and they are not grammatical.

The second important point which needs to be made is that non-verbal behaviours which realise communicative acts must necessarily be regarded as having an illocutionary function. In group (ii) above, we included the head-nod as a realisation of *agreeing*: other examples are not difficult to find—

(a) *disagreeing* with a shake of the head,
(b) *greeting* (wave and/or eyebrow flash),
(c) *declining* (e.g. by placing one's hand over a cup or glass when offered more to drink),
(d) *insulting* (e.g. giving someone the obscene V-sign),
(e) *commanding* (e.g. by beckoning to someone).

3. Some remarks on non-verbal communication behaviour

Obviously, not all non-verbal behaviours have illocutionary force: those we have classed as *indices*, for example, may carry information about the participants in an interaction which is of general pragmatic interest but which is so low on the scale of linguisticness as to be usually irrelevant to the discourse analyst (see Riley, 1975). The remaining non-verbal behaviours have been categorised as follows:

(i)   Those having *illocutionary force* (see above).
(ii)   *Kinematopoeias* ('illustrators').
(iii) *Deictics*.
(iv)   Regulators of *interactional tactics*:
       —turn-taking signals,
       —attention signals,
       —address signals.

For present purposes we would like to concentrate on the non-verbal behaviours in group (iv), the regulators of interactional tactics. These behaviours are the regulative mechanisms of interaction: they govern the distribution of utterances and the transitions from speaker-state to listener-state and to addressee. They are sets of rule-governed behaviours which control the sequential structure, timing and distribution of utterances: who speaks when, and to whom. We have claimed that meaning in face-to-face interaction is a construct of behaviour: it is these behaviours and the rules which govern them which permit the negotiation between participants which is necessary if their individual contributions are to mesh at all levels, as it must do if any sort of communication is to take place.

Work by Duncan (1972, 1973) and by Kendon (1964, 1967) has described the mechanisms involved in *turn-taking*, and *attention*, particularly those concerning gaze. For example, a speaker who wishes to yield the floor will make eye-contact with his interlocutor immediately before the end of his utterance. Other NV behaviours which may accompany or replace gaze here have also been identified and described: they include a number of postural and gestural behaviours, creaky voice, low key and cessation of body movement.

By *address* we mean that rule-governed set of verbal or non-verbal behaviours by means of which a 'speaker' selects and indicates his addressee(s) in groups above the dyad.[4] When we interact in a group, we do not usually speak to all the group all the time, we speak to individuals or subgroups. We have identified the following non-verbal behaviours as operating in the address system: eye-contact, head direction, orientation, posture and gesture. (Of course, address may also be realised verbally—'Would you like some tea, *Mary*?'—and indeed the choice of verbal address is proving to be a surprisingly useful marker for certain types of discourse.)

Address is a very simple behavioural system: it is also an extremely powerful descriptive tool. By observing address behaviour we are able to state accurately which participant(s) a speaker is 'speaking to' for any given utterance. This means that we now have a way of coding utterances, or, rather *turns*, in all types of interaction. By distinguishing for each turn (1, 2, 3 . . .) which participant (W, X, Y, Z . . .) is the Speaker (S), the Addressee(s) (A), the Listener(s) (L), we are able to code each turn in terms of *participant* states.

Since address (though not necessarily the behavioural mechanism which realises it) *is a universal* the contrastive analyst is now in a position to compare many important aspects of the discourse structure of different languages (an example is given below). Patterns of consecutive codings, expressed in terms of (1) the codings themselves, (2) change of address and (3) change of first speaker, give us discourse units of varying types, corresponding to exchanges/transactions etc. As we try to demonstrate below, such descriptions provide us with valuable formalisations of social role, participant states, formality and situation, ie with information concerning precisely those non-semantic parameters of meaning which, it is the pragmalinguist's contention, are essential to a description of interactive discourse.

4. Outline of a model of discourse

The considerations discussed above concerning
  (i) meaning as a construct of interaction,
  (ii) illocution
  (iii) non-verbal communication.

lead us towards a model of discourse (and eventually to a model of interaction) which differs radically from most others which have been put forward.[5] In very general terms, our work on the structures of written and spoken discourse has led us to the conclusion that, as one passes from discourse which is written, prepared and non-interactive to discourse which is spoken, spontaneous and interactive, structuration depends less and less on the ordering of the propositional content and more and more on the nature of the transaction (Riley, 1975; Abe *et al*, 1975; Duda, 1974; Abe, Duda and Gremmo, 1977).

The investigator of authentic, spontaneous, spoken discourse who tries to base his analysis on a logical approach to propositional content is in for a rough time. Rather, we believe that the only practical approach is via the two other features of spoken discourse which we have already looked at briefly, namely

  (i) illocution,
  (ii) non-verbal behaviours.

We can, that is, describe such discourse as a sequence of illocutionary acts and as a series of interactive acts. Such a distinction is all the more necessary when we consider that much non-verbal behaviour has *no* illocutionary value, its function being the regulation and marking of discourse structure. This gives us *illocutionary structure* (or 'communicative' structure) and an *interactive structure* (or 'discursive' structure). Since elements of the two structures are not in a one-to-one relationship, we may treat them as simultaneous but parallel.

Such an approach to discourse structure might be diagrammed in the following way:

SITUATION

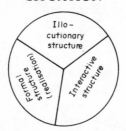

By *Formal Structure* here we mean *realisation*: the set of message-bearing elements (verbal, paralinguistic, non-verbal) in a situation. These elements have substance and are realisations of various systems and structures whose organisation can be described in terms such as class, units, structure and distribution. The textual function of such elements is described in terms of their internal relations (and without reference to the meaning they carry). *Illocutionary Structure*: here we deal with sequences of illocutionary acts (eg Inviting, Accepting, Confirming, Thanking). There is no one-to-one relationship between these acts and units of formal structure, ie they are *not* related at different levels of delicacy.

Interactive Structure: here we describe linguistic organisation in terms of interactional tactics: turns (opening, reply, closing) address, relative distribution of utterances (exchange, transaction). There is no one-to-one relationship between interactive acts and illocutionary acts.

It may help clarify this set of distinctions if we take an example: let us imagine that Mr and Mrs A wish to ask the way in London: they approach a stranger, Mr B, and the following dialogue ensues:

(1) Mr A: Sorry, but can you tell us the way to St James' Park, please?

(2) Mr B: Are you on foot?

(3) Mrs A: Yes, we are. Is it far?
(4) Mr B: Then you just go down those steps there and turn right.
(5) Mr A: Thank you very much.

The *Illocutionary Structure* here is
(1) Requesting information
(2) Requesting information
(3) Informing, Requesting information
(4) Informing
(5) Thanking

The *Interactive Structure* is

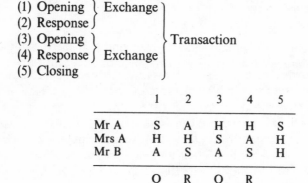

(1) Opening ⎱ Exchange ⎫
(2) Response ⎰   ⎪
(3) Opening ⎱   ⎬ Transaction
(4) Response ⎰ Exchange ⎪
(5) Closing   ⎭

	1	2	3	4	5
Mr A	S	A	H	H	S
Mrs A	H	H	S	A	H
Mr B	A	S	A	S	H
	O	R	O	R	

An important theoretical point can be made here:
By distinguishing between these two types of act, the difficulty of handling the discursive embedding exemplified here is greatly reduced, since we do not need to define illocutionary acts by their place in structure. If that were the case, we would need, for example, a different definition of Requesting information for each of the first three places in the structure of this dialogue.

II Contrastive applications

What use is this type of approach to the contrastive analyst? We can only hope to give hints, suggestions here, but we will make them as concrete as possible:

1. (a) We can compare the range of functions which a structure in one language can realise with the range of functions a similar structure in another language can realise.

Let us take an example: in French, English and Swedish there is a structure If (si, om) + 'conditional' clause. Observation leads us to the conclusion that the French structure can be used to realise at least three different functions:

(i) *Hypothesising*
    S'il arrive, je le lui dirai.
(ii) *Requesting confirmation*
    Si je suis prêt? (C'est bien ce que tu viens de me demander?)
(iii) *Suggesting*
    Et si on allait au cinéma ce soir!

If we turn to colloquial Finnish–Swedish, we find that there too, the 'om and conditional' structure can realise these three functions:

(a) Om han kommer, ska jag berätta det för honom.
(b) Om jag är färdig? (Jo, jo!)
(c) Om vi sku' gå på bio i kväll!

However, when we turn to English, we find a very different kettle of fish!

(a)   If he comes, I'll tell him.
(b)* If I am ready?
(c)* If we go the cinema this evening.

Note what the asterisk means here: these perfectly correct grammatical constructions can not (= do not) function as *requests for confirmation* or *suggestions*.

The implications for contrastive analysis are considerable: any syllabus aiming at communicative competence will have to take such correspondences into account.

One could argue that contrastive analysis could start at an even more primitive level, that of *ethno-discourse*, ie those sets of presuppositions which speakers impose upon the reality their language dissects. However, although some extremely interesting work has been done by the ethnolinguists, anthropologists and socio-linguists (Fishman, 1971;

Gumperz and Hymes, 1972; Labov, 1972 a and b; Sudnow, 1972)
to the best of our knowledge, no directly contrastive studies have
been made on such a basis. Simply as an illustration of the lines such
a contrast might take, let us examine the following exchange:

Child: Dad, I want to go to the match.
Parent: I'm busy this afternoon in the garden.

Now it is quite clear (to anyone who shares the presuppositions of
these speakers' culture) that the Child is *Requesting*—'Please will you
take me to the match' and the Parent is *Refusing*—'No, I can't'. Yet if
we took these two utterances separately, we would have no reason for
labelling or interpreting them thus. It is their juxtaposition, their
relationship in context which enables us to interpret them as acts of
communication by bringing to bear on them the presuppositions of
our ethno-discourse. Even for such a brief example it is difficult to list
the presuppositions exhaustively: a whole society is reflected in the
word 'match' alone. Some of the presuppositions are startlingly
obvious—which is just why we need them:

  (i) The child cannot or does not wish to go alone.
 (ii) The parent can be expected to take the child.
(iii) The parent is responsible for the child in some way.
 (iv) The parent has priority of choice.
  (v) The parent cannot be in two places simultaneously.
 (vi) It is possible for non-players to attend, etc.

It is important to remember, though, that there are societies where (ii)
and (iii) would by no means seem obvious, for example. And why did
the reader probably interpret this as a father/son exchange, not a
mother/daughter one? And why might the author be thinking of a
cricket match, but probably not the reader?

Child: Maman, tu m'achètes un nouveau sous-pull?
Parent: Ton pere dit que ça coûte trop cher.

Here again, we have Requesting–Refusing exchange, but a number of
the presuppositions which enable us to identify it as such are different
(eg Mother buys, Father pays: one cannot buy items which are too
expensive, etc). By accumulating and analysing a large corpus of such

exchanges, one would hope to define the elements of the ethnodiscourse and a cross-cultural comparison would then be possible.

It is important to distinguish between two types of presupposition: the *knowledge of events* which individuals have, and may share, and which enables us to account for certain logico-semantic aspects of discourse structure in terms of A, B and A/B events, and the *knowledge of the universe* which is shared by all members of a speech community by virtue of their speaking the same language. This is not the place to discuss the Whorf–Sapir–Bernstein hypothesis that the language we use segments reality and our perception of the world: but the applied work by perceptual psychologists is beginning to reveal ways in which such problems can be studied objectively. In Berlin and Kay (1969) colour terms and perceptions in a wide range of languages were compared and contrasted and Strömnes (1977) has carried out a contrastive study of the spatial relationships in Finnish and Swedish. There seems no reason why such techniques should not be applied to certain other notions such as time, size, order and growth.

(b) Let us now reverse the process: this time let us take one particular function—*Suggesting*—and look at some of the various realisations which can occur (in the same three languages):

French   Et si on allait au cinéma ce soir.
          On pourrait peut-être aller au cinéma ce soir.
          Vous n'auriez pas envie d'aller au cinéma ce soir.
          Une possibilité serait d'aller au cinéma ca soir.

Swedish   Jag tänkte att vi kunde gå på bio i kvåll.
          Hor skulle det vara att gå på bio i kväll?
          Vi kunde gå på bio i kväll, eller hur?
          Om vi skulle gå på bio i kväll!

English   How about us going to the cinema this evening?
          I tell you what, let's go to the cinema this evening.
          Why don't we go to the cinema this evening.
          I wouldn't mind going to the cinema this evening.

This list is by no means exhaustive, of course, but it fully confirms the logical points that a communicative syllabus cannot be based on a structural progression and that comparisons of this type will provide immediately useful data.

An extremely interesting and important question will be to see whether there are functions which may be realised in, say, the verbal component of language A, but which are realised in the paralinguistic or non-verbal components of language B. Work on intonation and key seems to indicate strongly that this is indeed the case, as does our own work on non-verbal communication. However, to the best of our knowledge, little specifically contrastive work has been done on this problem.

(c) This time, instead of taking sentences/functions in isolation let us consider them in sequence; that is, we are going to look at illocutionary structure. Obviously an enormous amount of descriptive work still remains to be done before such comparisons influence syllabus design: only after corpora of authentic recordings have been analysed can we hope to have the accurate data essential to a valid contrast. But, in principle, there seems to be nothing to stop us proceeding as follows:

English dialogue:
    (1) That's a very pretty dress you're wearing.
    (2) Oh, thank you very much.
    Illocutionary structure: compliment + thanks.

Swedish dialogue:
    (1) En så vacker klänning du har!
    (2) Tack så mycket.
    Illocutionary structure: compliment + thanks.

French dialogue:
    (1) Que c'est jolie, la robe que tu portes!
    (2)   ?
    Illocutionary structure: compliment +?

Further examination would show that a French Compliment is never followed by an expression of thanks (a form such as *Merci beaucoup* occurring in this context would not be interpreted as thanks but might be as ironic commentary).

Such variations in illocutionary structure can, of course, be spread over much larger stretches of time. A hostess in Finland, for example, will expect to have to invite her guests to take their places at table at least three times: to all concerned, anything less would be an unseemly rush! Again, she would expect her guests, when they next met, to begin their conversation by thanking her for her entertainment (Tack för senast/Kiitos viimesestä) even if several *months* had elapsed between the two encounters. Neither in French nor English society is this usually the case. Examples of this sort abound; eg when entering a shop the Frenchman usually greets the other customers (Bonjour Messieurs–Dames): so does a German entering a railway compartment. But anyone who entered an English railway compartment or shop and proclaimed 'Good morning, ladies and gentlemen' would get a distinctly frosty reception (unless he happened to be the ticket-collector). Again, a Frenchman attending a seminar or committee meeting with English speakers almost always manages to give the impression that he is slightly aggressive, over-categorical, 'pushy': in fact, entry strategies in such situations differ considerably between the two languages, both in realisation and *modalisation*. Indeed, the whole structure of such meetings clearly differs from one side of the Channel to the other—but we will only know *how* exactly when the necessary detailed analyses have been carried out, and this is true of dozens of other situations including business negotiations, telephone calls, casual encounters, etc.

By identifying foreign-language learning needs and objectives in terms of the uses to which the learners will wish to put their language, it is hoped that more motivating and effective language programmes will be developed. At least, this is the rationale behind the Council of Europe-sponsored research into the Threshold Level/Le Niveau Seuil (Council of Europe, 1975, 1976) and indeed behind the whole movement towards 'Communicative' or 'Functional' syllabuses. However, it is our contention that little of contrastive value will be produced as long as the confusion between *notions* and *illocutionary forces*, and between *illocutionary acts* and *interactional acts* continues.

2. An example

Let us now try our hands at a bit of contrastive pragmalinguistics. For analysis, we have chosen two passages of approximately the same length. In Passage A, an English teacher is preparing two French students, Mme X and M Z, to practice a dialogue. In Passage B, a French teacher is preparing a group of immigrant workers to do the same sort of thing. Intuitively, we regard these passages (which are both authentic) as 'similar' in some way that is not just related to the content, but to deeper patterns of interaction and role.

PASSAGE A:
(The target discourse dialogue being prepared was:
'Can you tell me the way to Victoria Station, please.'
'Certainly, it's down there on the right.')

1. Teacher	Right ... the bottom of the page, then ... whose turn is it? Mme X.
2. Mme X	Is my turn? What—
3. Teacher	Is it my turn?
4. Mme? X	Is it my turn?
5. Teacher	Good. Yes, I think it was.
6. Mme X	What means 'the way'?
7. Teacher	Anyone?
8. M Y	Le chemin, montrer le chemin.
9. Teacher	le chemin, right, good.
10. Mme X	'Can you tell me the way to Victoria Station, please?'
11/12. Teacher	Fine ... M Z?
13. M Z	'Certainly, it's down there, on the right.'

If we analyse this passage from the point of view of its *illocutionary structure*, we get the following:

INTERACTIONAL STRUCTURE OF PASSAGE A

1. *Framing   Directing   Requesting information   Nominating*
   Right   bottom of the page then   whose turn is it   Mme X?
2. *Requesting confirmation*
   Is my turn?   What—
3. *Correcting*
   Is it my turn?
4. *Practicing*
   Is it my turn?
5. *Evaluating   Confirming*
   Good   Yes, I think it was

6. *Requesting information*
   What means 'the way'?
7. *Performative*
   Anyone?
8. *Informing*
   Le chemin, montrer le chemin
9. *Confirming,   evaluating*
   le chemin,   right, good.
10. *Practicing*
    Can you tell me the way to Victoria Station, please?
11. *Evaluating*   12. *Nominating*
    Fine...   MZ?
13. *Practicing*
    Certainly, it's down there on the right.

The same passage analysed in terms of its *interactional structure* (in accordance with the system described above, p. 136) gives us the following profile:

ILLOCUTIONARY STRUCTURE OF PASSAGE A

	Turn												
Participant	1	2	3	4	5	6	7	8	9	10	11	12	13
Teacher	S	A	S	A	S	A	S	A	S	A	S	S	A
Mme X	A	S	A	S	A	S	H	H	A	S	H	H	H
M Y	H	H	H	H	H	H	A	S	H	H	H	H	H
M Z	H	H	H	H	H	H	A	H	H	H	H	A	S

Legend: 1, 2, 3, etc—turns ('interactional acts') in serial order (each turn may contain several *illocutionary* acts).

        S—Speaker
        A—Addressee (s)
        H—Hearer (s)

1 2	3 4	5 6	7 8	9 10	11	12 13
O R	O R	O R	O R	O R	C	O R
Exchange	Exchange	Exchange	Exchange	Exchange		Exchange

transaction

O = Opening, R = Reply, C = Closing (No *duty to reply* is imposed by the speaker on any other participant, ie there is no address.)

Turning to passage B, we carry out the same analysis. (The target discourse being prepared was: 'Tiens, bonjour Bashir'

'Bonjour Iovan'

Bashir and *Iovan* are names of characters in the textbook.)

PASSAGE B:

1. Teacher	Ca va. Je commence maintenant. 'Tiens, bonjour Bashir.' Tu es Iovan, Ali.
2. Student (Ali)	'Tiens, bonjour Bashir.'
3/4. Teacher	Très bien. Maintenant Bashir dit à Iovan: 'Bonjour Iovan.' Tu es Bashir.
5. Student 2	'Bonjour, tiens bonjour Iovan.'
6. Teacher	Il ne dit pas 'tiens', c'est Iovan qui dit 'tiens bonjour Bashir.' Maintenant Bashir dit simplement 'bonjour.'
7. Student 2	'Bonjour.'
8. Teacher	Il s'appelle comment?
9. Student 3	Iovan.
10. Teacher	(Gesture to student 2 to try again.)
11. Student 2	'Bonjour Iovan.'
12/13. Teacher	Tres bien. Alors, tu es Iovan, tu es Bashir, Allez-là.
14. Student 4	'Tiens, bonjour Bashir.'
15. Teacher	Bashir.
16. Student 5	'Bonjour, Iovan.'
17. Teacher	Tres bien.

ILLOCUTIONARY STRUCTURE OF PASSAGE B

1. *Framing*	*Performative*	*Modelling*	*Nominating*
Ca va?	Je commence maintenant.	'Tiens, bonjour Bashir.'	Tu es Iovan Ali.

2. *Practicing*
'Tiens, bonjour Bashir.'

3. *Evaluating* 4.		*Modelling*	*Nominating*
Trés bien Maintenant Bashir dit à Iovan,		'bonjour Iovan'.	Tu es Bashir.

5. *Practicing*
   'Bonjour, tiens, bonjour Iovan.
6. *Correcting*
   Il ne dit pas 'tiens', c'est Iovan qui dit 'tiens, bonjour Bashir'.
   Maintenant Bashir dit simplement—bonjour ...
7. *Practicing*
   'Bonjour'.
8. *Correcting*
   Il s'appelle comment?
9. *Informing*
   Iovan.
10. [NVC: address and gesture—*Nominating* 2.]
11. *Practicing*
    'Bonjour Iovan'.

12. *Evaluating*	13. *Nominating*	*Directing*
Trés bien	Alors tu es Iovan, tu es Bashir.	Allez-là.

14. *Practicing*	15. *Nominating*	16. *Practicing*
'Tiens bonjour Bashir' Bashir.		'Bonjour Iovan'.

17. *Evaluating*
    Trés bien.

INTERACTIONAL STRUCTURE OF PASSAGE B

	Turn																
Participant	1	2	3	4	5	6	7	8	9	10	11	12	13	14	15	16	17
Teacher	S	A	S	S	A	S	A	S	A	S	A	S	S	A	S	A	S
Student 1	A	S	H	H	H	H	H	H	H	H	H	H	H	H	H	H	H
Student 2	H	H	H	A	S	A	S	H	H	A	S	H	H	H	H	H	H
Student 3	H	H	H	H	H	H	H	A	S	H	H	H	H	H	H	H	H
Student 4	H	H	H	H	H	H	H	H	H	H	H	H	A	S	H	H	H
Student 5	H	H	H	H	H	H	H	H	H	H	H	H	A	H	A	S	H

O R C O R O R O R O R C O R O R C

Ex. Ex. Ex. Ex. Ex. Ex. Ex.

Trans   Transaction   Transaction

O = Opening (A Speaker turn in which (a) participant(s) is addressed, ie the duty to reply is imposed on him).

R = Reply

C = Closing (A Speaker turn performed by the same participant as the 'O', but in which no duty to reply is imposed).

How are we to interpret and contrast these two sets of data?[6] If the claims we have made earlier have any justification, our analyses would provide us with insights into the illocutionary repertoire and structure, the nature of the interaction and discourse, and the presuppositions and social roles of the participants.

For what it is worth, let us first look at a few statistics:

(i) *Types of Illocutionary Act occurring in*

	Passage A			Passage B	
Occurring only in A	(Requesting information	2	Occurring only in B	(Modelling	1
	(Requesting confirmation	1		Framing	1
	(Confirming	2		Directing	2
	Framing	1		Nominating	5
	Directing	1		Correcting	2
	Nominating	2		Practicing	6
	Correcting	1		Evaluating	3
	Practicing	3		Per-	
	Evaluating	1		formative	1
	Performative	1		Informing	1
	Informing	1			22
	Total	16			

(ii) *Distributions*

performed by Teacher:	12	Teacher:	15
performed by Students:	6	Students:	7
Types:	10	Types:	9

Total types A + B: 12

Teacher Acts:

Only in A:	(Framing: 1	Only in B	
	(Directing: 1	(Only in B)	(Modelling: 1
	(Confirming: 2		Framing: 1
	Requesting information: 1		Directing: 2
	Nominating: 2		Nomin-
	Correcting: 1		ating: 5
	Evaluating: 3		Correcting: 2
	Performative: 1		Evaluating: 3
			Per-
			formative: 1

Student Acts:

Practicing: 3	Practicing: 6
Informing: 1	Informing: 1
Requesting confirmation: 1	
Requesting information: 1	

What does all this tell us? Firstly, that our intuition that these two passages were similar was a reasonable one: 8 types of act are common to both passages, out of a total of 12 types, accounting for 32 acts out of the 40 acts occurring in the two passages together.

Secondly, the observer is struck by the very clear preponderance of Teacher Acts in both passages: a ratio of almost exactly 2:1. This confirms what we already know about the proportion of teacher-talk in the classroom, but the familiarity of the observation should not blind us to the important implications in terms of discourse structure and social roles. This is strongly underlined by the very clear distinction between the *types* of acts performed by the teachers and the *types* of acts performed by the students: there is only *one* example of a 'common' act ('Requesting information' in Passage A). All other acts are exclusively part of the teacher's role or the students' role. The teachers are the only participants who can Frame, Direct, Nominate, Correct, Evaluate, Confirm (A), Model (B), or Perform. We believe that 'role' is to be defined in terms of (i) *acts performed* by a participant, (ii) the discourse rights to produce a particular set of acts (cf. Gremmo, Holec and Riley, forthcoming).

What we have here, then, is a clear acceptance by all participants of the traditional roles of Teacher and Student. The event is teacher-centred in every possible sense: his role and status are clearly reflected in his discourse rights. The reader can easily check for himself just how deeply engrained our understanding of this behaviour is, by trying to imagine what would happen if one of the students performed a Teacher Act, such as Directing or Evaluating or even Framing. It would be perceived as a challenge to the Teacher (or as humour, perhaps).

The teacher is model, judge and organiser of the discourse. The teaching–learning process is seen as his to control, and it is something which occurs strictly between him and the students, never between the students themselves.

At the level of Illocutionary Structure (ie sequences of illocutionary acts) we can make the following generalisations: both the passages are characterised by patterns of acts which can be summarized as follows:

		A	B
1.	Teacher.	Framing, Directing, Requesting Information, Nominating, Performative	Framing, Performing, Modelling, Nominating, Directing
2.	Student	Requesting confirmation/information, Practicing, Informing	Practicing, Informing
3.	Teacher	Correcting, Evaluating, Confirming	Evaluating, Correcting

This is, in fact very clear confirmation of the 'Three-part exchange' described by Sinclair and Coulthard (1975). There is no need to labour the point that there is considerable congruence between the two analyses: in both cases the teacher presents material and then solicits a response, which he then judges satisfactory/unsatisfactory. If it is satisfactory he solicits a new response; if unsatisfactory, he corrects it and the student produces a new response which is judged in turn.

Let us now turn to the interpretation of our analyses of these same two passages in terms of interactional acts (cf pp 137–9). Easily the most striking characteristic of both discourse networks (as we call these series of codings) is the teacher's *centrality*. This is a characteristic of his role (as seen by all participants). He is the Paris of centralised France—wherever you want to go, you go via Paris. Whether he likes it or not, the teacher is continually being forced to reply because he is addressed by his students. This is a characteristic of *status* (as seen by his students). Getting them to address one another will be a prerequisite, then, to a reduction of teacher-talk, which in turn will mean a change in the role and status of the teacher, since, in traditional classes such as this, students are discouraged from speaking amongst themselves.

In interactive terms, the teacher has the *right of address* (conferred on him by his status and role). That is, he—and he alone—chooses who is to speak next. It follows, logically enough, that the teacher will have alternative turns (clearly seen in the top line of each network) so that there is a superficial resemblance to dyadic interaction. The relative degree of *freedom of address* in a classroom is a function of social *directivity*: both teachers here may be said to be highly directive, since they allow no freedom at all.

Another crucial teacher-privilege is his right to organise the discourse through interactive *performatives*, ie acts which structure the discourse itself, usually explicitly. Centrality, Address and structuring privileges (realised by acts such as Framing, Directing, Nominating, Performing, Requesting information) all combine to give the Teacher a high degree of discursive *control*.

In A 3, the Teacher interrupts Mme X: now interruptions can be classified in discourse terms according to (i) whether they are in- or between—terms, exchanges, etc, and (ii) whether the Addressee of the Interruptor was the previous turn's S, A or H. Here we have an in-turn interruption—Mme X is not allowed to finish what she was saying. This is perfectly acceptable in the classroom: it is part of the teacher's discursive privileges, a concomitant of his right to correct (a characteristic of role, again) but one which would be unacceptable in many other types of discourse. Indeed, the characteristic of *formality* can usefully be described by (*inter alia*) the types and frequencies of interruptions occurring in a given discourse (although this point is illustrated only once in our examples).

The fact that very little difference is to be discovered between these two passages should not detract from the point that a valid contrast, based on objectively observable behaviours, has been made.

We would claim, then, that we have here a series of extremely useful formalisations: aspects of (i) Role, (ii) Status, (iii) Directivity, (iv) Formality have all been formalised in terms of interactional behaviour, and the discourse privileges of the participants. Moreover, the structure of the interaction into hierarchically ordered units (act, exchange, transaction) is also clearly demonstrated. Since these descriptions are applicable to any face-to-face oral discourse, they add an interesting new weapon to the contrastive analyst's armoury.

Notes

1. Much of the work described in this paper has been carried out with two colleagues in the CRAPEL— M J Gremmo and H Holec. I value this opportunity of expressing to them my affection and gratitude whilst in no way trying to share the blame for any mistakes and over-generalization.
2. For a discussion of the integration of non-verbal communication into discourse analysis, see Riley (1975, 1976); the discursive role of intonation ('key') is the subject of Brazil (1976).
3. The term is taken from Austin (1962).
4. By Addressee we mean the participant(s) upon whom the Speaker imposes the duty/right to reply.
5. With the exception of Widdowson (1977), where a tripartite division very similar to the one suggested here, is also posited.
6. We ask the reader to accept the fictions that it is possible to generalize on the basis of such a small corpus and in particular that the labels for illocutionary acts (eg 'Directing') have been validly defined, whereas in reality that can only be done after far more analyses of this type have been carried out.

References

Abe, D, Billant, J, Duda, R, Gremmo, M-J, Moulden, H and Regent, O (1975) 'Vers une redéfinition de la compréhension en langue étrangere.' In *Mélanges Pédagogiques*. Universite de Nancy II, CRAPEL (1975) 33–44.

Alatis, J E (ed) (1968) *Report of 19th Annual Round Table Meeting on linguistics and language studies*. Washington, DC: Georgetown University Press.

Austin, J L (1962) *How to do things with words*. Oxford University Press.

Berlin, B and Kay, P (1969) *Basic colour terms*. California: University of California Press.

Brazil, D (1976) 'Discourse intonation.' Discourse analysis monographs 1. Birmingham. English language research, Birmingham University.

Coste, D, Courillon, J Ferenczi, V, Martins-Baltar, M and Papo, E (1976) *Un niveau seuil*. Strasbourg: Council of Europe.

Davidson, D and Harman, G (eds) (1972) *Semantics of natural language*. Dordrecht: D Reidel Publishing Company.

Duda, R (1974) 'Functions discursives et communication écrite.' In *Mélanges Pédagogiques*. Université de Nancy II, CRAPEL (1974) 65–76.

Duncan, S (1971) 'Some signals and rules for taking speaking turns in conversation.' *Journal of personality and social psychology* 23, 283–292.

Duncan, S (1973) 'Toward a grammar of dyadic conversations.' *Semiotica* 9, 29–46.

van Ek, J A (1975) *The threshold level*. Strasbourg Council of Europe; 1980 Pergamon, Oxford.

Fishman, J A (*ed*) (1971) *Advances in the sociology of language*. Vol. 1. The Hague: Mouton.

Gleason, H A (1968) 'Contrastive analysis in discourse structure.' In Alatis, J E (*ed*) (1968), 39–63.

Gremmo, M-J (1977) 'Reading as communication.' In *Mélanges Pédagogiques*. Université de Nancy II, CRAPEL (1977), 17–40.

Gremmo, M-J, Holec, H and Riley, P (1977) 'Interactive structure: the role of role.' In *Mélanges Pédagogiques*. Universite de Nancy II, CRAPEL (1977), 41–56.

Gumperz, J J and Hymes, D (*eds*) (1972) *Directions in sociolinguistics: the ethnography of communication*. New York: Holt, Rinehart and Winston, Inc.

Gutknecht, C (*ed*) (1977) *Grundbegriffe und Hauptströmungen der Linguisik*. Hamburg: Hoffmann & Campe.

Hartmann, R (1977) 'Contrastive textology and some of its applications.' Paper delivered to the Annual Meeting of the British Association for Applied Linguistics, University of Essex.

Holec, H (1973) 'L'illocution: problematique et methodologie.' In *Mélanges Pédagogiques*. Université de Nancy II, CRAPEL (1973), 1–20.

Kendon, A (1964) 'The distribution of visual attention in two-person encounters.' *Report to Department of Scientific and Industrial Research*, London.

Kendon, A (1967) 'Some functions of gaze direction in social interaction.' *Acta psychologica* 26, 22–63.

Kendon, A (1972) 'The role of visible behaviour in the organisation of social interaction.' In Seigmann, A and Pope, B (*eds*) (1972), 177–210.

Krzeszowski, T P (1972) Contrastive generative grammar.' *SAP* 5, 105–112.

Krzeszowski, T P (1976) 'On some linguistic limitations of classical contrastive analysis.' *PSiCl* 4, 88–97.

Labov, W (1972a) *Sociolinguistic patterns*. Philadelphia: University of Pennsylvania Press.

Labov, W (1972b) 'Rules for ritual insults.' In Sudnow, D (*ed*) (1972), 120–169.

Munby, J (1977) 'Applying socio-cultural variables in the specification of communicative competence.' Paper delivered to the Annual Meeting of the British Association for Applied Linguistics.

Riley, P (1976a) 'An experiment in teaching communicative competence within a restricted discourse.' In Roulet, E and Holec, H (*eds*) (1976), 129–162.

Riley, P (1976b) 'Discoursive and communicative functions of non-verbal communication.' In *Mélanges Pédagogiques*. Université de Nancy II, CRAPEL (1976), 1–18.

Riley, P (1977) 'Discourse networks in classroom interaction: some problems in communicative language teaching.' In *Mélanges Pédagogiques*. Université de Nancy II, CRAPEL (1977), 109–120.

Roulet, E and Holec, H (*eds*) (1976) *L'enseignement de la compétence de communication en languages secondes*. CILA.

Sajavaara, K (1977) 'Contrastive linguistics past and present, and a communicative approach' *JyCs* 4, 9–30.

Searle, J R (1969) *Speech acts*. Cambridge: CUP.

Seigmann, A and Pope, B (*eds*) (1972) *Studies in dyadic communication*. New York: Pergamon.

Sinclair, J and Coulthard, M (1976) *Towards an analysis of discourse: the language of the classroom*. Cambridge: CUP.

Stalnaker, R C (1972) 'Pragmatics.' In Davidson, D and Harman, G (*eds*) (1972), 380–396.

Stromnes, E J (1976) *A new physics of inner worlds*. University of Tromsø, Institute of Social Science.

Sudnow, D (*ed*) (1972) *Studies in social interaction*. New York: Free Press.

Widdowson, H (1977) 'Approaches to discourse.' In Gutknecht, C (*ed*) (1977).

9. Contrastive Analysis in the Classroom

Waldemar Marton

Adam Mickiewicz University, Poznań

The paper which I presented at the conference in Karpacz last year dealt with various pedagogical implications and applications of contrastive studies in connection with the designing of syllabuses for language courses and the preparation of teaching materials. Lately a number of articles and papers have appeared which envisage the pedagogical application of contrastive studies in essentially the same way, ie for designing syllabuses and preparing teaching materials, usually emphasizing at the same time that it is impossible and contrary to sound pedagogical knowledge to think of a deliberate and systematic use of contrastive analysis in the classroom. Now my contention is that contrastive analysis has great pedagogical value precisely in day-to-day teaching in the classroom, as a useful technique for presenting language materials to the learner and as one of the characteristic aspects of a method of teaching. This paper is a justification of my point of view. Certainly the pedagogical usefulness of this particular application of contrastive analysis which I have in mind is only a hypothesis, but to justify it I shall adopt a procedure characteristic of pedagogical methodology, ie first I shall show that my proposal does not contradict the findings of source such as the psychology of learning and psycho-linguistics and that, on the contrary, it is supported by many facts discovered by these disciplines. Then, I shall show that some of the statements which run counter to my claim have no validity from the point of view of contemporary knowledge. Finally, I shall say a few more words about how I imagine the use of contrastive studies in the classroom. Let me make one more point at the beginning concerning the present confusion in the

147

field of language-teaching methodology. I am of the opinion that a lot of this confusion is unnecessary, because, although second-language learning has its specific aspects, it has many features in common with other kinds of learning, especially in what concerns concept formation, acquisition of habits and skills, and the working of memory. Any psychologist will tell us that quite a lot is known today about these and other aspects of learning and, actually, many ideas have been lying around for quite some time without language teachers making any use of them. I am, therefore, totally in opposition to the 'new orthodoxy' in language learning and teaching, represented by such scholars as Leon Jakobovits, Leonard Newmark, David Reibel, and others, who claim that both first and second-language learning is some mysterious process following its course independently of the intentions of the teacher and learner, and that all we can do is not to interfere with it.

One of the main assumptions of my approach is that the native language of the learner is a very powerful factor in second-language acquisition and one which cannot be eliminated from the process of learning. I am referring here to the situation of language teaching in our schools and various language courses, which, from a psychological point of view, is completely different from the situation of learning a language in the country where it is spoken, or learning it in a very intensive course of total immersion. In the two cases of learning a language in the country where it is spoken or in an intensive course, there are plenty of opportunities for observation and testing one's detailed hypotheses concerning various aspects of the language. But even in these conditions it is very dubious that language habits are formed automatically and by mere exposure to language data, especially in an adult learner.

In our schools, one of the most important language-learning problems is remembering the various features of foreign language learnt in class or during home study. In this respect the crucial problem is that of retroactive inhibition. Certainly the use of the native language between the foreign-language classes, or between a foreign-language class and an occasional use of the foreign language in some other situation, is an interpolated activity strengthening retroactive inhibition. Reasoning in terms of stimuli and responses, we can assume that meanings which an individual wants to express are stimuli, and their encodings into signs of a particular language are responses. It is probably safe to say that no one would deny the existence of the powerful influence of retroactive inhibition, regarded by linguists as 'linguistic interference', on second-language learning. It is also becoming clearer and clearer how strong and persistent the habits of expressing meanings in the native language are, so that they even manifest themselves in individuals who have spent long years in a foreign country functioning primarily in the language spoken in that country. A A Leontiew, one of the top contemporary Soviet psycholinguists and methodologists, writes about this problem (1970: 19):

> 'The phenomenon of transferring skills and habits of the mother-tongue onto a second language takes place independently of our efforts to limit it by a special method, eg, by a direct method. This kind of transfer is deeply rooted in some general principles of the transfer of knowledge, or, rather, the transfer of corrective measures, as it is more economical to be aware of and to automatize some corrections concerning the already existing knowledge than to start building a system of knowledge from scratch.'

The question then suggests itself whether it isn't better to use this habitual transfer in some way rather than desperately trying to fight it and eradicate it, or even to deny its existence. I think that using contrastive analysis in the classroom would go a long way towards controlling this powerful tendency and making an ally of what has long been considered our greatest enemy. The persistence and strength of language interference is readily explained by the well-established fact that retroactive inhibition is greatest where the stimuli for the learned task and the stimuli for the interpolated activity are the same, but the required responses are different. This is exactly the case with second language learning in school situations, where the meanings we want to express in the native and second language are usually the same, but call for different encodings. As Borger and Seaborne (1966: 156) put it: 'Confusion is greatest when on separate occasions people are called upon to behave in different ways under similar circumstances.' What is known about the working of memory also suggests that the process of remembering things and storing them in long-term memory cannot be likened to faithful recording on tape. There seem to be receptive processes involved here which take in and store new information in terms of previously organized material and which result in progressive distortion of the learned material over a period of time (Borger and Seaborne, 1966: 165). The same idea has been stressed by the Gestalt school in their concept of cognitive structure, into which all new bits and pieces of knowledge are fitted in. This particular aspect of memory change has been emphasized by Bartlett (1932). Actually, the results of his experimental studies imply more than simply that learned material is distorted during learning; the distortion, or, in other words, assimilation to pre-existing structures, continues after removal of the original material. This points to a more dynamic aspect of language interference, which is often neglected by linguists dealing with the problem. Taking a psychological point of view, we can say that there is never peaceful coexistence between the two language systems in the learner, but rather constant warfare, and that this warfare is not limited to the moment of cognition, but continues during the period of storing newly learnt items in memory. Accordingly, every Polish sentence I hear, speak, read, or write impairs my English. The reverse is also true, but the so-called 'backlash interference' is not really dangerous in the learning conditions which I have in mind, so I shall not deal with it in the present paper. Taking all of this into consideration, we might conclude that as the process of comparison is going to take place anyway, it is better to make it conscious and channel it to profitable uses, at the same time preventing distortion resulting from uncontrolled assimilation.

Another interesting psychological fact is how much the amount of retroactive inhibition depends on the method of learning used for the task material as compared to the method of learning used for the interpolated material. Experiments by Jenkins and Postman (1949) and by Budohoska (1966) clearly indicate that if the method for learning the interpolated material is essentially the same as the method for learning the task material, retroactive inhibition is markedly increased. Conversely, if the methods are essentially different, retroactive inhibition is decreased. If we assume that the use of the first language can be regarded as the practicing and learning of the interpolated activity, it becomes obvious that the claim made by numerous methodologists that second-language learning should copy the processes characteristic of first-language learning is not as psychologically sound as it seems to be at first sight. From this point of view, then, it is perhaps desirable that a method for second-language learning should be characterized by cognitive elements which would differentiate it from first-language acquisition.

Another important factor lessening the amount of retroactive inhibition is the set or readiness of a learner to prevent its interfering influence. A classical experiment carried out by Lester (1932) with four groups of subjects differently instructed and made aware of the existence of interference from interpolated activities demonstrated very clearly that the subjects who were warned and shown where the interference would appear and who were also instructed how to fight it did incomparably better on the retesting of the learned material than the subjects who were not so instructed. It follows that warning the learner of language interference, showing him clearly and in advance where it may appear and what he should keep in mind to curb it, may greatly facilitate second language learning.

These are only a few of the psychological facts which might be cited to support the idea of using contrastive analysis in the classroom, in the stage of the presentation of language material. Various objections, however, have been raised to this kind of cognitive approach.

It has been clear by now that this approach is also characterized by the use of grammatical explanations and rules and their conscious application in language teaching and learning. Most of the scholars and teachers voicing objections to this method would treat any contrastive statements presented to the learner as increasing the amount of verbalization and rules and, hence, detrimental to the acquisition of competence in the foreign language. The essence of these objections is that any conscious application of verbalized rules makes speech and aural comprehension in the foreign language reflective and slow, and thus renders the acquisition of oral–aural skills impossible. This sort of attitude is well expressed by Sol Saporta (1966: 86), who writes:

> 'Language is rule-governed behaviour, and learning a language involves internalizing the rules. But the ability or inclination to formulate the

rules apparently interferes with the performance which is supposed to lead to making the application of the rules automatic.'

A very serious and persistent misunderstanding underlies all such statements and objections. The misunderstanding consists in treating all applications of rules and comparative statements as static and unchangeable in character. It seems that Saporta and other theoreticians like him think that if a learner has learnt something about the target language via rules and verbalizations, he will have forever to recall all the appropriate rules and verbalizations in exactly the same form in which he learnt them whenever he wants to say something in the language. But the psychological fact is that all these rules and verbalizations, if not studied for their own sake, help mainly to gain insight and understanding about the functioning of some element of the target language and form a helpful crutch mainly in the initial stages of language use. Then the rules are reduced through practice and probably, to a large extent, wear out completely and are not consulted at all in actual use of the language, although they may be stored, ready to be recalled, at some higher level of the conscious knowledge about the language. It seems that the more often the given rule or verbalization has been applied in real or simulated communication by the learner, the less need he has to recall it consciously. In this aspect John B Carrol (1971) is of the opinion that the opposition between 'rule-governed behavior' and 'habits' is false, because language rules are descriptions of language habits and we may proceed from the conscious application of rules to habits. A A Leontiev expresses the same view when he writes (1970):

'A habit may be formed in a bottom-to-top way, as a result of imitation, or in a top-to-bottom way, as a result of automatization and reduction of knowledge.'

These statements can be borne out by the experience of many foreign-language learners, including myself, who have learnt their language through the conscious application of rules, but whose language performance is not marked by any conscious or reflective processes. (This is just like the acquisition of any skill where, in any stage of learning, we have a number of fully automatized activities and at least one being consciously acquired, which becomes automatic in turn.)

All the objections like the one given above ignore one of the fundamental psychological laws of learning, which says that the way in which we learn something does not forever determine the way in which we put this knowledge to use later on. It follows then that the gains from contrastive analysis in the better understanding and retention of the target language material do not have to be offset by slowing down the processes of habit formation. Another widespread objection to the approach I am suggesting here is that it leads to compound bilingualism in which the native language of the learner is used as a matrix of reference for the use of his second language. But today the classical division of learners into compound and coordinate bilinguals is becoming more and more dubious from a psychological point of view. Among psycholinguists and sociolinguists concerned with the issue, the opinion prevails that we can talk not so much about types of bilinguals, but rather about types of bilingual functioning (Fishman: 1966). Some psycholinguists give also evidence for the fact that even the dominance of a particular type of bilingual functioning in an individual is a very unstable thing and changes according to circumstances (E Ingram, personal communication). Be that as it may, it is difficult to conceive of a learner keeping his two languages separate in a situation comparable to the situation in which the Polish secondary-school pupil finds himself. The concept of thinking in a foreign language, stressed to such a degree by Byelyayev (1964), is also quite irrelevant to our considerations, as it confuses thinking in general and particularly operational thinking—which is never completely verbal—with inner speech or inner monologue. Granted, practicing inner speech in second language may very effectively help to master it, but it is something that cannot be taught; it can be only recommended.

Another objection is that the experience with the grammar-translation method has shown that the approach based on grammatical analysis and translation is ineffective. But it is ineffective from the point of view of today's objectives set up for the language learner, ie the acquisition of aural–oral skills. Experimental studies by scholars such as Scherer and Wertheimer (1964) and Smith (1970) have proved that there is no marked advantage in employing strictly audio–lingual techniques even if speaking and aural comprehension are the essential objectives. If anything, these studies have shown, as Carroll (1971) puts it, that '... students learn precisely what they are taught, or at least that transfer of learning is a two-way street between aural–oral and reading–writing skills.'

The reasoning I have just presented is supported by some empirical evidence. As the scope of this paper is strictly limited, let me only mention the experimental data described by Lambert, Gardner, Barik, and Tunstall (Lambert: 1967), who found that in a very intensive language course taught by a direct method, those students who kept their two languages functionally separated throughout the course did not do as well in their work as those who permitted the semantic features of their two languages to interact.

And now, finally, a few words about how I envisage the use of contrastive studies in the classroom. First of all, I think it should be based on semantics; that is, the teacher should show how certain meanings, eg—expressing futurity, are realized syntactically in Polish and in English, and not merely point out differences between language forms. In introducing the use of the Present Tense for expressing futurity in English, the teacher should (1) point out that in Polish the Present Tense is also used for the same purpose, then (2) show the similarities and differences in usage in the two languages, (3) set up the limits for drawing analogies and (4) warn about the areas of possible negative transfer and confusion. All of this should be done before the practising of the given structure so that the habits are formed on a conscious, cognitive basis. Frequent use of translation as a perfect contrastive technique for learning grammatical structures would be one of the characteristics of this approach, although it would not become the only or even the main technique. Such an application of contrastive analysis should be carried out on all levels of grammatical description, ie on the phonological, lexical and syntactic levels.

The hypothesis presented here requires verification by an experiment or rather by putting it to a test by a large number of teachers in a large number of courses. This again involves the necessity of writing a good pedagogical contrastive grammar which is the first and most important task in the area of the pedagogical application of contrastive studies. Language teachers should also be prepared for the use of contrastive analysis in the classroom through a systematic study of contrastive analysis of the two languages involved in the process of learning. This is why a course in contrastive analysis should become a part of the syllabus in all philological departments of our universities and in all in-service teacher training courses.

If the approach outlined above is confirmed by experience in learning and teaching under certain specifiable circumstances, contrastive studies will be demonstrated to have greater pedagogical value than was ever claimed before.

References

Bartlett, F C (1932) *Remembering: a study in experimental and social psychology.* London: Cambridge University Press.

Borger, R and Seaborne, A E M (1967) *The psychology of learning.* Harmondsworth: Penguin.

Budohoska, W (1966) 'Zależność retroakcji od sposobu uczenia się materiału początkowego i interpolowanego.' *Studia Psychologiczne* 7, 137–145.

Carrol, John B (1971) 'Current issues in psycholinguistics and second language teaching.' *TESOL Quarterly* 5, 101–114.

Fishman, J (1966) 'The implications of bilingualisms for language teaching and language learning.' *Trends in language teaching ed* by A Valdman, 121–131. New York: McGraw-Hill.

Jenkins, W O and Postman L (1949) 'An experimental analysis of set in learning: retroactive inhibition as a function of changing set.' *Journal of experimental psychology* 39, 69–73.

Lambert, W E (1967) 'Psychological approaches to the study of language.' *Foreign language teaching: an anthology, ed* by P Michel, 215–250. London: Macmillian.

Leontiev A A (1970) *Nekotorye problemy obuczenija russkomu jazyku kak inostrannomu.* Moskva: Izd. Moskowskogo Universiteta.

Lester, O P (1932) 'Mental set in relation to retroactive inhibition.' *Journal of experimental psychology* 15, 681–689.

Saporta, S (1966) 'Applied linguistics and generative grammar.' *Trends in language teaching, ed* by A Valdman, 81–92. New York: McGraw-Hill.

Scherer, G A and Wertheimer M (1964) *A psycholinguistic experiment in foreign-language teaching.* New York: McGraw-Hill.

Smith, P D Jr (1970) *A comparison of the cognitive and audiolingual approaches to foreign language instruction.* Philadelphia: Center for Curriculum Development.

10. Pedagogical Implications of Contrastive Studies

Waldemar Marton

Adam Mickiewicz University, Poznań

Current views on pedagogical applications of contrastive studies are marked by disappointment and pessimism. The pendulum has swung to the other extreme, which has always been so characteristic of developments in language teaching methods, so that contrastive studies, originally regarded as a panacea for all the problems in language teaching, are now treated by some educators as of no pedagogical use at all. A typical representative of the latter attitude is Leonard Newmark (1970: 225–226), who says, '...the cure for interference is simply the cure for ignorance: learning. There is no particular need to combat the intrusion of the learner's native language—the explicit or implicit justification for the contrastive analysis that applied linguists have been claiming to be necessary for planning language teaching courses.'

According to these opponents of contrastive analysis, its application to the construction of teaching materials may be even harmful, because it may lead to overemphasizing certain elements in the target language, and, consequently, to learning some fragments of that language only, instead of the whole system.

Even attitudes favourable towards contrastive studies lack the enthusiasm so characteristic of the earlier approaches. Ronald Wardhaugh, in his paper at the TESOL Convention in San Francisco in March 1970, stressed that contrastive studies can be of only very limited use for language teaching and learning. The same opinion is given by William E Norris (1970) in his 'state of the art' paper, as characteristic of most language teachers and educators today. Similarly, the conclusions of the contrastive studies Section at the 10th

FIPLV Congress in Zagreb (5–9 April 1968) state that contrastive analysis certainly is not a panacea, but only one of the factors contributing to the preparation of better teaching materials.

The advocates of error analysis have also become more militant lately. One of them is Peter Strevens (1970), who argues that contrastive studies are of no use for language teaching, because, in the first place, a complete analysis involving only two languages is already an extremely difficult and painstaking task, and, in the second, all of this is not worth that much effort, as any experienced language teacher knows where errors mostly occur, anyway.

We might mention here, in passing, that the value of error analysis has always been more emphasized in the European tradition, while contrastive studies have attracted particularly much hope and attention in the United States.

It may be interesting to consider some of the possible causes of this disappointment concerning the pedagogical application of contrastive studies. There are at least two objective causes, namely,

(a) contrastive studies involving more and more languages of the world have proliferated recently, but they constitute most often only fragmentary descriptions of two language systems; there have been very few synthetic descriptions. Besides, most of these studies are of a highly theoretical nature, and, as such, not readily applicable to language teaching;

(b) experience has shown that predicting errors on the basis of contrastive studies is not so simple and easy as it seemed to be, and that in actual learning errors often occur where they are not expected and do not occur in areas of extreme interference as pinpointed by contrastive studies.

This limited predictability of errors has engendered a lot of disappointment and distrust towards contrastive studies on the part of language teachers, but the fact is that contrastive studies were expected to achieve what they are impossible of achieving by their very nature. This misunderstanding was caused by a great oversimplification of psychological processes essential for language learning, and this oversimplification, in turn, was caused by the linguists who first introduced the idea of using contrastive studies for language teaching. The point is that those linguists, having only a very super-ficial knowledge of psychology, based their expectations on the phenomenon of transfer, which, as any psychologist realizes, is still very puzzling and very little understood. Among the psychological authorities who readily admit this are such well-known scholars as the French psychologist Geneviève Oléron (1964: 115–178) and the American psycholinguist Leon A Jakobovits (1970: 189–192), who also warns against too literal extrapolation from experimental find-ings concerning transfer to real-life learning situations.

According to those oversimplified notions, linguistic interference or, in other words, negative transfer occurring in second-language learn-ing and use was believed to be the function of structural differences (in the broad meaning of the term) holding between the native and the target language. But the real problem is much more complex, as is illustrated by Jakobovits (1970: 192) in the following formula:

$$P_{l_2} = f(P_{l_1}, t_{l_1}, t_{l_2}, R_{l_1 - l_2}).$$

This formula says that attained proficiency in l_2 (i.e. the target lan-guage) will be some joint function of attained proficiency in l_1 (i.e. the native language), training in l_1, training in l_2, and the structural re-lationship between l_1 and l_2.

In fact, the overall situation is even more complex owing to the fact that the operation of transfer effects is largely influenced by the so-called attitudinal factors, which are part of the individual's contribu-tion to the process of learning and speaking a foreign language. Some of these factors are already discussed in Weinreich's (1968) classic work on linguistic interference, but particularly in fairly recent publi-cations they have received a lot of attention. One type of attitudinal factor relates to certain social and cultural attitudes shared by the given community, such as loyalty to the mother tongue and emotion-al feelings towards the society and culture represented by the target language. Another type of attitudinal factor and an extremely impor-tant one relates to the individual's learning strategy. One possible kind of approach in language learning is to make the native language a matrix of reference for the acquisition of elements and relations in the target language (this is called 'compound setting'). Another kind of approach is to try to keep the two languages as separate as possible in the process of learning and using the target language ('coordinate setting').

Sometimes conclusions drawn from the consideration of all these nonstructural factors are quite unexpected to language-teaching specialists, who often discuss their problems in a kind of psychological vacuum. For instance, Jakobovits (1970: 196) sets up an interesting hypothesis based on certain principles of transfer operation, and particularly on Osgood's three laws of interlist similarity. The hypothesis predicts that with unrelated languages a coordinate setting will yield less negative transfer than a compound setting, but that with related languages a compound setting will yield more positive transfer than a coordinate setting. If this hypothesis is borne out by the facts, it will be necessary to work out different learning strategies for related and unrelated languages.

The importance of the non-structural factors for the operation of transfer effects has led some experts in the field of language teaching to the conviction that what is needed is not so much a linguistic contrastive analysis but rather a psycholinguistic one. This opinion is held, for instance, by Tatiana Slama-Cazacu, of the University of Bucharest, who in her recent paper given at the Zagreb Conference on English Contrastive Projects (7–9 December 1970) claims the necessity of developing what she calls 'contact analysis in discenti', dealing with the prediction and description of interference as taking place in the learner, and not *in abstracto*. A very similar approach is also represented by William Nemser, of the Center for Applied Linguistics in Washington, DC (1970: 101–128).

What conclusions could be drawn from this somewhat confusing picture sketched above? Are we justified in the pessimistic belief that contrastive studies have nothing to offer to language teaching methodology and procedures and that they are only valuable for theoretical linguistics? My answer to this question is a very emphatic *no*. To present my argument, let me, first of all, point out some of the misunderstandings that seem to confuse a lot of the issues raised in connection with the pedagogical application of contrastive studies.

(a) The first misunderstanding concerns the fear that basing teaching materials on contrastive analysis may result in the learner's being presented not with the whole system of the target language but only with its parts and fragments, which, as many authorities point out (Rivers, 1970: 7–10), may be harmful to the process of learning. Yet it is clear that this incomplete presentation is not a necessary consequence of contrastive studies and is connected more with a certain possible misuse or abuse of these studies than with their reasonable application. Using contrastive analysis as a basis for the construction of a pedagogical grammar, we are by no means limited by this fact to the presentation of not the whole system but only those items which constitute learning problems, although it is reasonable to expect that the latter will receive more emphasis, especially in terms of more intensive drilling.

(b) The second misunderstanding concerns the significance of non-structural factors, brought recently to general attention by psychologists and psycholinguists. The fact that those factors are important or even very important cannot be interpreted as denying the significance of purely structural factors. In fact, the latter are certainly more important, because it is common knowledge that for people of certain language background some foreign languages are more difficult to learn than others, as is generally observed in schools and universities all over the world. There is even some more compelling evidence for this; Cleveland, Mangone, and Adams (1960: 250–251) present a table which specifies the time requirements for attaining specified levels of proficiency for individuals enrolled in intensive language courses. Their table shows that Americans with average language aptitude can attain proficiency in speaking Italian, French, Spanish, Romanian, or German (among others) in two-thirds of the time it takes them to achieve the same proficiency in Russian, Greek, or Finnish (among others), and in only half the time it takes them to learn Chinese, Japanese, or Vietnamese (among others). So it seems that the description of structural differences holding between languages is a worthwhile task for the linguist and one whose results may have great significance for language teaching.

(c) The third misunderstanding concerns the complaints that currently produced contrastive analyses are often so complex and full of technical detail that they cannot be of any use to anyone but a trained linguist. But, again, we have to distinguish between scientific and pedagogical contrastive grammars.

The latter must be presented in such a way that they could be used and understood by the foreign language teacher and even by the interested student. This requirement also determines to a certain degree the length of such analysis; it cannot be a very thick volume describing every item as fully as possible, as, first of all, we would probably have to wait for years for the appearance of such a grammar, and, on the other hand, it might by its very size discourage its potential user. These pragmatic reasons opt for a grammar as complete as possible as far as the presentation of the whole language system is concerned, but treating only the most essential similarities and differences in detail, and others rather cursorily. Ideally, the pedagogical contrastive grammar should be based on scientific study, but, again, as such theoretical treatises are long in the making, it is both advisable and possible to produce a pedagogical grammar without waiting for a complete theoretical analysis.

(d) The fourth misunderstanding consists in presenting error analysis and contrastive studies as two propositions of an alternative choice, while, in fact, they complement each other. Error analysis shows what the most frequent mistakes really are and where they occur. These mistakes should be analysed and those probably caused by structural differences should be separated from the others. Getting data of this kind will be a natural testing procedure verifying hypothetical predictions of contrastive studies. This approach has already been used with good results for phonological interference by Brière (1968). When we know what types of error result from structural differences and when we know exactly why they are made, it is fairly easy to work out a set of pedagogical procedures offsetting the operation of linguistic interference.

These are, then, the basic misunderstandings which so much confuse the whole issue of the applicability of contrastive studies. But besides them there are some controversial points concerning pedagogical uses of contrastive studies, which are solved differently by different authors. Let me discuss briefly three of these problems.

(1) The first is a methodological one, namely, which of the available

linguistic models should be used as the theoretical framework for contrastive studies. It is obvious that the best model, offering the most adequate linguistic descriptions, should be chosen, but it is not always clear which one is really the best. In my opinion, it is transformational generative grammar that is the best model for any linguistic description, in spite of the current lack of uniformity among its followers. But as soon as we decide in favour of transformational grammar, we face another problem that is, whether contrastive studies should be concerned, first of all, with differences and similarities in deep structures of the two languages analysed or in their surface structures. If we assume, as most transformationalists do, that base components of most natural languages are very similar to one another, and that most structural differences reside in surface structures, the conclusion that the latter ought to be the primary concern of contrastive studies is inevitable. This attitude is also strengthened by the fact that in the newest versions of transformational grammar deep structure has either a semantic character or is so abstract that only surface differences and similarities are of any pedagogical consequence.

(2) Another problem concerns the establishing of a hierarchy of difficulty as a result of contrastive analysis. This hierarchy will show which of the target language structures present the most and which the least difficulty to the learner. Several such hierarchies have already been suggested, the best known of them being those worked out by Brière (1966: 768–796) for phonology and by Stockwell (1965: 282–291) for syntactic structures, the latter being in fact the adaptation of the former. These hierarchies are of a very general character, and they do not take particular structures in particular languages into consideration, but rather types of interference depending on relations of correspondence between structures in two languages under analysis. In this way they are a sort of blueprint onto which different structures in particular languages may be mapped. Such hierarchies are useful to a certain extent and may give us some insights into the nature of linguistic interference and language learning, but the discussion whether those suggested by Brière or Stockwell or others are correct or not, is largely academic. They should be confirmed not so

much by one test or experiment but by teaching and learning experience, and it well may be that they will be different for related and unrelated languages, and that they will also depend upon teaching method or learning strategy. From my own experience as a teacher, I am convinced that as far as syntax is concerned, the number one difficulty and major source of interference is what Stockwell calls 'split type' negative correspondence in the native language, which means that there is an obligatory choice between two categories in the target language and no choice, ie only one possible category, in the native language.

(3) Still another problem concerns the use of the results of contrastive studies for the optimal gradation of the target language structures in a pedagogical grammar or textbook. It has often been expected that the above discussed hierarchy of difficulty will automatically provide the best solution concerning the arrangement of teaching materials. The controversy has centered around the question whether it is more advisable to start from the structures similar to certain structures in the native language, or whether to start from those that are different. Again, the whole problem is not properly approached. As far as the starting-point is concerned, both solutions may be harmful from a psychological point of view. If we start from what is similar to the native language, the learner may be established in the belief that everything else in the target language is also similar. If we start from what is different from the native language, the learner may develop an attitude precluding any possibilities of positive transfer. The point is, however, that a lot of other factors have to be taken into consideration for the proper arrangement of the target language items, and not only their degree of similarity to the corresponding native language structures. These other factors include communicative usefulness, ease of presentation in accordance with the principles of the given method, their relation to other structures with which they can be most economically presented, their frequency of occurrence within the given style or register taught in the course, etc. Here also the relatedness or unrelatedness of the languages involved may be another very important consideration. It seems, then, that neither an adequate description of the target language nor the results of a con-

trastive analysis can determine the selection and arrangement of the structures to be taught. They can only provide some raw materials and some basis for a decision for the materials writer, but neither of them can become an overriding determinant. So, as we see, while we cannot expect contrastive studies and the hierarchy of difficulty to select and arrange teaching materials for us, they will nevertheless be helpful in this task and will certainly pinpoint certain areas of difficulty which we must know in order to locate them in the proper place in the pedagogical grammar and in order to provide enough exercises for teaching them.

After this critical discussion of some misunderstandings and problems, let us now try to arrive at the conclusions which could be drawn from the above remarks and which will be a kind of synthesis concerning the role and function of contrastive studies in language teaching. As we have established above, the pedagogical use of contrastive studies does not primarily lie in their predicting errors and pinpointing the learning problems. Many other factors influence the operation of transfer effects in language learning and the structural differences between the target and the native language are only one of them, although, possibly, the most important one. Likewise, contrastive studies do not determine the selection and gradation of the target language structures in any absolute and unique way, because here we also have to take a lot of other things into consideration. What is their use, then?

Their pedagogical use is still very essential, because, complemented by error analysis, they explain and systematize our teaching experience. Error analysis itself does not explain anything explicitly, it only shows what types of error occur but not why they occur, so that when we have data provided by error analysis, we are still in need of their linguistic interpretation, which is not the complete explanation, but, at least, its very essential part. Contrastive studies also provide necessary data, although not the only data, for the authors of textbooks and pedagogical grammars with respect to the selection and arrangement of the target language items, as well as the emphasis and special attention that should be given to particular structures. The future of contrastive studies is also closely linked with the newest trends in language pedagogy, which emphasize the importance of the analysis of the learning processes that take place in the student. The emphasis is now more on the learner and how to learn than on the teacher and how to teach. In order to know what is going on in the learner's mind, we need a psychological and psycholinguistic analysis and not a linguistic one. That is why a psycholinguistic analysis of the operation of transfer effects seems to be a very promising line of development in contrastive studies. In this domain, William Nemser's (1969: 3–12) and T Slama–Cazacu's (1970) suggestions are certainly very interesting and worth being put to test in our contrastive projects. These suggestions postulate analysing the so-called 'approximative systems' which are developed in the learner in his successive approximations to the complete system of the target language as represented by the linguistic performance of the native speaker. There is already some evidence to the effect that these approximations form a series of steps and stages, and each of them is characterized by certain typical errors and deviations. These errors and deviations differ from stage to stage not only quantitatively, but, first of all, qualitatively, so that the learner's progress is not only marked by fewer mistakes but also by mistakes of a successively different sort. It is clear that the analysis and the description of these stages will have a great importance for our understanding of the learning processes and strategies employed by the student, which, in turn, will enable us to control these processes, or, at least, to conform to them for the student's benefit.

Our first aim should be the construction of pedagogical contrastive grammars that could be used by the largest possible number of people interested in language teaching and learning. Accordingly, such grammars must be simple and easily readable and should not contain too many technicalities or irrelevant detail. While being fairly comprehensive, they should, nevertheless, be focused on the greatest difficulties in the target language which should be established partly empirically on the basis of our teaching experience and error analysis.

As to the theoretical framework for the pedagogical contrastive grammars, a non-formalized version of transformational grammar should be used. Only this framework will make it possible for us to take advantage of the most recent insights and discoveries achieved by theoretical linguistics. The transformational approach will help the learner to arrive at a conceptual, integrated knowledge of the whole system of the target language, which is a very important thing if we assume that second-language learning is also an intellectual, cognitive process and not only habit formation. The learner will be better able to see relationships between sentences, and how simple sentences can be joined to form more complex ones, he will be better to learn a number of optional choices which will give him flexibility and creativity in the use of the language. As it seems that whether we use the native or the target language, we always start from some common and general semantic plan, Fillmore's version of transformational grammar might be adopted for contrastive studies. This kind of grammar starts from certain basic semantic relationships, probably common to most natural languages, and shows us how they are realized on the surface, with the assumption that languages mostly differ in the ways of realizing those universal underlying semantic configurations. This is only a suggestion and not an assertion, as certainly only actual work on a contrastive grammar will show us whether Fillmore's model is applicable.

Our deal pedagogical grammar should suggest a certain hierarchy of difficulty, but not so much in the sense of determining the gradation of teaching materials as rather in the sense of emphasis that particular structures should receive in teaching.

A complete grammar of this kind must comprise the phonological, syntactic and, if possible, lexical components, although it is difficult to conceive how a lexical contrastive study may be carried out. The only practical solution seems to be to limit it to only the most typical errors as established empirically by error analysis.

As far as a direction of such a contrastive grammar is concerned, it is not really crucial whether the analysis proceeds from the target to the native language or the other way round. It is also possible to arrange the analysis along certain universal grammatical categories and to show how they are realized in each of the two languages. Anyway, it is a practical problem and in each particular case it may be solved in a different way depending on a lot of circumstantial factors. Also, depending on who we address our work to, descriptions of certain structures in at least one of the languages will have varying degrees of delicacy. For instance, in a contrastive grammar of Polish and English written for the Polish learner there will be no need to give more attention to such structures as the imperfective and perfective aspects of the verb, as they have no formal correspondents in English.

Another essential remark concerns the necessity of often going beyond the limits of the sentence in our analysis, as certain syntactic and even phonological phenomena cannot be explained without reference to some broader context. We can consider here the use of the articles in English, or the use of *some* and *any* in a certain type of questions.

Summarizing, we can say that pedagogical contrastive grammar, the construction of which is the ultimate purpose of contrastive studies, will be an important aid in the processes of learning and teaching foreign languages, although by no means can it be regarded as a sort of pedagogical panacea. Its usefulness will certainly be limited but still great enough to justify a considerable expenditure of time and effort spent on its preparation. A grammar of this kind can be expected to be widely used by the following types of individuals involved in language teaching: the teacher, the learner, the materials writer and the translator.

(a) For the foreign-language teacher it will systematize and explain his pedagogical experience, and thus enable him to use it to a better advantage. It may be conceived as a kind of reference book for the teacher, of the same importance as a dictionary or a descriptive grammar of the target language.

It may prove particularly useful for the teacher who does not know the native language of his students. The contrastive grammar will also help the teacher to explain the most essential structural differences between the two languages to his students in a clear and systematic way. This, of course, will apply to those teachers who believe in pedagogical usefulness of this procedure or who can see its expediency in certain circumstances.

(b) The foreign-language learner will be able to use the contrastive grammar also, as one of the reference books for language learning, whenever he really needs it. I have here in mind a particular kind of learner, who bases his language learning on a cognitive approach and intellectual analysis. Also, learners following programmed materials may profit from this kind of grammar.

(c) The materials writer will find in the contrastive grammar a ready-made inventory of at least some of the special tasks and problems in language teaching, and, particularly, if this grammar is based on a psycholinguistic contrastive analysis, it may prove to be an extremely useful tool in his preparation of the materials. The same applies to a person responsible for the syllabus and organization of a language course. The grammar can also provide good material for the preparation of some types of language tests.

(d) The translator will also be able to use the contrastive grammar as a reference book that may often prompt the best solution of a particular problem in translation. Less experienced translators will probably profit from a systematic reading of the grammar as a part of the theoretical preparation for their work. The same applies to translator trainers and those organizing courses in translation. We can also notice that although translation is not recommendable as a language teaching technique, it is *par excellence* an exercise in contrastive analysis.

We may conclude with a remark that pessimism concerning the pedagogical application of contrastive studies is certainly unwarranted. Although some premature hopes and expectations of dramatic advancements in language teaching connected with the introduction of contrastive studies must be abandoned, these studies will play an important role as a contribution to better organization and guidance in foreign language teaching and learning.

References

Brière, E J (1966) 'An experimentally defined hierarchy of difficulties of learning phonological categories.' *Lg* 42, 768–796.
Brière, E J (1968) *A psycholinguistic study of phonological interference.* The Hague: Mouton.
Cleveland, H, Mangone, G J and Adams J C (1960) *The overseas Americans.* New York: McGraw-Hill.

Jakobovits, L A (1970) *Foreign language learning: a psycholinguistic analysis of the issues*. Rowley, Mass: Newbury House.

Nemser, W (1969) 'Approximative systems of foreign language learners.' *The Yugoslav Serbo-Croatian–English contrastive project*, ed by R Filipović, 3–12. Zagreb: U. Press.

Nemser, W and Slama-Cazacu T (1970) 'A contribution to contrastive linguistics (psycholinguistic approach: contact analysis). *Revue roumaine de linguistique* 15/2, 101–128.

Newmark, L (1970) 'How not to interfere with language learning' *Readings in applied transformational grammar*, ed by Mark Lester, 219–227. New York: Holt.

Norris, W E (1970) *Teaching English as a second language*. Washington, DC: Center for Applied Linguistics.

Oléron, G (1964) 'Le transfert.' *Traité de psychologie expérimentale*, ed by P Fraisse and J Praget, 115–178. Paris: PUF.

Rivers, W M (1970) 'Contrastive linguistics in textbook and classroom.' *English Teaching Forum* 8/4, 7–10.

Slama-Cazacu, T (1970) 'Psycholinguistics and contrastive studies.' (Mimeographed copy of the paper read at the Zagreb Conference on English Contrastive Projects, 7–9 Dec. 1970.)

Stockwell, R P, Bowen, J D and Martin, J W (1965) *The grammatical structures of English and Spanish*. Chicago: U. of Chicago Press.

Strevens, P (1970) *Two ways of looking at error analysis*. Washington, DC: Center for Applied Linguistics.

Weinreich, U (1968) *Languages in contact*. The Hague: Mouton.

11. Some More Remarks on the Pedagogical Use of Contrastive Studies

Waldemar Marton

Adam Mickiewicz University, Poznań

In one of my earlier papers I already recommended using some of the results of contrastive studies for explicit contrastive comparisons in the classroom, which would take the form of grammatical comments and explanations provided by the teacher before intensive drilling or other forms of language practice (Marton, 1973). In this paper I would like to further develop and specify these ideas and to show more explicitly how and in what ways contrastive analyses can be used in language pedagogy.

At the beginning I would like to make it clear that the analysis which follows will be developed within the framework of a broadly conceived cognitive approach and that it will concern only the teaching of syntactic structures. It will also be mostly concerned with teaching them to adults at a certain level of intellectual sophistication, such as high school and university students. This does not mean, of course, that I cannot see the usefulness of contrastive studies in teaching phonology and lexicon, it only means that neither my present interests nor the limits of this paper allow me to consider these other components of language. As the term *cognitive approach to foreign language teaching* is still not a very well-defined notion, I would like to say now what I mean by it, emphasizing those features of the cognitive approach which are particularly relevant to the problems discussed in this paper. In other words, I would like to present some relevant articles of my glottodidactic credo, which, to the best of my knowledge and judgement, are very much in agreement with the basic principles of the cognitive approach.

171

First of all, I must admit that I believe in language teaching, being thus in opposition to the now very popular 'naturalistic' trends in glottodidactics (whose representatives are often referred to as the 'new orthodoxy' group), which manifest their disbelief in the notion of language teaching and emphasize language learning. Of course, I realize and agree that language has to be ultimately learned by the language student, but I believe that effective teaching helps him and guides him in his learning so that his learning is much more efficient and economical than it would be if he relied only on his own heuristic procedures and learning strategies. I particularly believe in the value of language teaching in the conditions of foreign-language learning, in contradistinction to the conditions of second-language learning in which the student has ample opportunities for out-of-school contacts with the language. In my understanding teaching is not only organizing the input to the student's 'black box' and providing feedback to the output. It also, or even primarily, consists in steering the student's mental activities during his fulfilment of the learning task and can thus be seen as interfering with the processes within the 'black box'. Accordingly, I am very much for the use of such pedagogical devices as mediators and algorithms since to me they represent the very essence of teaching.

Secondly, I believe that the native language of the learner should be treated as an ally in the process of foreign-language teaching and that it should be consciously used instead of being ignored and avoided at all costs. I am convinced that, from a psychological point of view, it cannot be avoided and that, from a pedagogical point of view, it can facilitate learning if used wisely and deliberately. I completely agree with D P Ausubel, one of contemporary cognitive psychologists, who condensed all of his educational research and thinking in the following statement (Ausubel, 1968: vi):

> 'If I had to reduce all of educational psychology to just one principle, I would say this: The most important single factor influencing learning is what the learner already knows. Ascertain this and teach him accordingly.'

There is little doubt that what the language learner already knows is his mother tongue, through which, more or less consciously, he tries to perceive and assimilate the elements of the target language. Utilizing and controlling this tendency instead of ignoring or fighting it will to a long way towards facilitating learning and ensuring success.

Thirdly, I believe that in learning many syntactic structures of the target language the difficulty is primarily conceptual and not formal, ie—it is rather connected with learning a new grammatical concept or principle than a new form. Accordingly, the teacher's primary task is to make this concept or principle as clear to the student as possible, and his subsequent task is to help him in assimilating it and making it operative in his attempts at using the language.

Fourthly, I do not believe that language is a set of habits, at least *habits* in the behavioristic sense of the word, ie seen as mechanically established and mechanically-reproduced stimulus—response associations. I might agree that there are habits in language performance, but, as far as the use of syntactic structures is concerned, they are different in nature from behavioristically conceived, mechanical habits. They could be rather more appropriately labelled *generative habits*, to use R Leeson's (1975: 7) term, and, as such, they would not be very much different from the notions of a rule or a principle. Anyway, whatever the term, the point is that the conceptual and formal characteristics of a given structure have to be grasped and realized by the student in a flash of understanding before he starts practising this structure in exercises or other forms of language training. That is why, in my opinion, learning syntactic structures rather resembles concept and principle learning than mechanical conditioning processes used in animal training. This concerns also the low-level syntactic operations, such as, for example, the uses of inflectional endings.

Accordingly, I do not believe in habit formation in teaching grammar and I particularly do not believe that any syntactic habits can be formed in the phase of drilling or pattern practising, as our audio–lingual colleagues tended or still tend to think. The relevant point is that in drills and pattern practices it is the syntactic form itself which is the stimulus to which the student is trained to respond, while in any communication activity it is the overall semantic plan of the utterance which triggers the choice of particular syntactic structures. The conclusion is that actual syntactic habits, if we still want to use this term, can be formed only in communicative activities, be they real or simulated, in which the student is supposed to express his own meanings and not to just manipulate sentences made by someone else. This again does not mean that I see no use for grammar exercises, it means only that I see their functions very differently from audio–lingualists. I think that, first of all, they should serve the function of the clarification of a given syntactic concept or principle introduced by the teacher or the textbook, being thus, psychologically, the continuation or prolongation of the phase of perception. I see them also as serving the purpose of hypothesis testing, but in this case I do not have in mind hypotheses arrived at completely by the student himself but rather hypotheses formed by him with the help of the teacher, which, in spite even of the teacher's skill, can be and very often are erroneous.

Having presented some of the relevant articles of my glottodidactic faith I would like now to pass on to explaining what types of contrastive studies I do have in mind discussing here their pedagogical uses. Of course, I am very much aware of the distinction between theoretical and applied contrastive studies, introduced and supported by J Fisiak (1973: 8), and it is undoubtedly the latter which would form a theoretical basis for all kinds of pedagogical applications. Yet within the category of specific applied studies, still using J Fisiak's (1973: 8) terms, I would see a place for a pedagogical contrastive grammar, in a rather restricted sense of the word *pedagogical*. The point is that very often this word is used in the sense synonymous with the word *simplified* and although the term *pedagogical contrastive grammar* has been often used lately it is quite clear that the only pedagogical notion it has utilized has been the notion of simplification, which, in turn, has been most often meant as getting rid of the formidable technical apparatus with the help of which linguistic facts are presented in contemporary theoretical studies. Yet in my understanding of the term and in accordance with the principles sketched above, we can call pedagogical only such materials which are arranged according to a definite pedagogical theory and which utilize special pedagogical devices helping the student to assimilate the learning material in the most economical way. In other words, a pedagogical grammar should aim at something more than just presenting a necessary minimum that the student is supposed to know, it should also strive to shape the student's learning activities and guide him in his learning, thus guaranteeing him a certain measure of success. Since, to the best of my knowledge, no such pedagogical contrastive grammar exists, in this paper I will use as examples facts and statements taken from theoretical contrastive studies, mostly published in the periodicals *Studia Anglica Posnaniensia* and *Papers and Studies in Contrastive Linguistics*. At this point it has to be admitted that rather few of the contrastive analyses published so far in these periodicals and in other places lend themselves to any pedagogical uses. This is not so much caused by their high level of theoretical sophistication, which, after all, should never be an obstacle for the writer of a pedagogical grammar, but rather by two other facts. One of them is that the studies published so far have striven to establish correspondencies at the deep structure level and to compare corresponding transformational derivations, which is rather less important to the learner than the comparison of surface structure differences and similarities. The other reason is that these studies deal very often with structures which do not cause much conceptual difficulty and which do not require the strategy of meaningful learning. The point is that not every syntactic structure requires a contrastive presentation in teaching. Generally speaking, it is useful and profitable to contrastively present these structures which are conceptually difficult to grasp by the student of a given language background, or, in other word, such structures whose usage is rather specific for the given language and not immediately obvious to the learner. On the other hand, there are structures in the target language which are more economically acquired in a rote fashion since either the learning problem they represent is purely formal in nature (ie the student has only to learn a new form while the concept or principle is the same as in his own language) or their syntactic analysis, although possible, is not necessary since, psycholinguistically speaking, they are probably stored and recalled as ready-made stereotypes rather than rules or principles. As a good example of the latter category we might mention nominal compounds in English, which can be analyzed syntactically in terms of relationships holding between their constituents (cf Marton, 1970) but it is rather doubtful whether showing these relationships to the

Polish student and comparing them with the relationships in equivalent Polish compounds would really help in the learning and retention of these units.

Probably the kind of contrastive study which lends itself best to pedagogical applications is one dealing with a chosen semanto-syntactic category and showing how this category is syntactically realized in the two languages under comparison. As a good example of this type of study we might mention here the two articles by A Szwedek (1974), entitled 'Some Aspects of Definiteness and Indefiniteness of Nouns in Polish' and 'A Note on the Relation between the Article in English and Word Order in Polish', both dealing with the category of definiteness and indefiniteness and revealing how the use of the articles in English corresponds to the use of other syntactic devices such as word order, sentence stress and pronominal reference in Polish. Actually, Szwedek's articles are also very useful for language pedagogy for the reason that they discover certain facts and correspondencies by no means obvious to the Polish teacher of English and Polish materials writer. This does not mean, on the other hand, that when such correspondencies are fairly clear and can be easily discovered by the teacher acting as an amateur comparativist, contrastive analyses have nothing pedagogically worthwhile to offer. It is my belief that they can always help the teacher and the materials writer by systematizing their knowledge, showing some additional facts that they may be not aware of and providing good examples. This last function is by no means insignificant since good examples have a great pedagogical value which lies in this that they can be used as very powerful mediators facilitating the learning and retention of a more abstract principle.

And now, using some facts and examples from Szwedek's papers, I would like to demonstrate how contrastive information can be utilized in the teaching/learning process. For the sake of order and convenience this process will be seen here as consisting of the four natural stages which can be distinguished in it irrespective of what approach or method we are trying to follow and which can be named as: (a) the stage of presentation of a new material, (b) the stage of exercises, (c) the stage of communication, (d) the stage of reviewing and testing. Let us assume then that we want to teach some of the basic uses of the English articles which constitute a great conceptual difficulty to the Polish learner.

First the very concept of definiteness and indefiniteness of nouns in Polish could be introduced in the initial part of the presentation stage in the form of an advance organizer. The advance organizer is a pedagogical device, very much supported by D P Ausubel (1968: 148–149) and other cognitive psychologists, whose function is to present some relevant concepts and ideas in advance of the learning material itself so as to bridge the gap between what the learner already knows and what he needs to know before he can successfully learn the task at hand. These organizers have to be distinguished from previews of the learning material to follow because, in contradistinction to previews, they are presented at a higher level of abstraction, generality, and inclusiveness than the learning material itself. In our hypothetical case the advance organizer would be introduced before the presentation of the language material containing some examples of the basic uses of the definite and indefinite articles. As far as the format of this advance organizer is concerned, it certainly would not be commendable for the teacher to deliver a lecture on the category of definiteness and its realization in Polish syntax since a procedure like this might only confuse the learner and waste the previous classroom time. But the teacher might instead put on the board the two following sets of sentences, taken from Szwedek's article (1974a: 206, 208):

W pokoju siedziała dziewczyna.
Wszedł chłopiec.
Chłopiec wszedł.

Do domu, który obserwowałem, wszedł mężczyana.
O 3:00 mężczyzna wyszedł.
O 3:00 wyszedł mężczyzna.

Then the teacher through asking appropriate questions might make his students aware of the relationship between word order and definiteness of nouns connected with the phenomenon of anaphoric reference. Actually, his task would be simply to introduce and clarify the very concept of syntactic definiteness, which his students might know intuitively as part of their knowledge of Polish and which could yet not be available to them in their attempts to understand the principles guiding the use of the English articles. The teacher would finish his presentation by telling the students that in English the definiteness and indefiniteness of nouns are marked in a different way and that their next task would be to discover this way in the language material to be subsequently presented. Certaintly, in his presentation and discussion of these examples the teacher would not use all these metalinguistic terms and would try to make his presentation as simple and as brief as possible.

After the introduction of the advance organizer the essential part of the presentation stage follows. It is not the purpose of this paper to describe each of the four stages of the teaching process in detail so let it suffice to say that in our hypothetical case the cognitively oriented teacher would introduce a text or a dialog containing some illustrative examples of the usage of the articles and would then try to elicit the principle from his students by the technique of guided discovery, ie by asking them appropriately framed questions about these examples. Discovering the principle should not prove too difficult to the students since they would have been already prepared for this task by the introduction of some relevant ideas and facts in the advance organizer, and, of course, the teacher might consciously refer to these ideas and facts in discussing the examples. The guided discovery technique would, of course, eventually lead to the formulation and verbalization of the principle of usage, which could be done either by the teacher himself or by one of the brighter students. The principle would thus represent a fragment of the conscious knowledge about the language which would have to be subsequently converted into a functional rule or stereotype readily available to the student in his attempts at constructing utterances in the target language. This would have to take place since the rule in its totality would take too long to recall and would be too cumbersome to have any operational value in very rapid processes of speech production. This is also where many believers in the traditional grammar-translation techniques fail since they erroneously assume that the presentation of the rule and its understanding by the student will automatically result in the transfer of the rule to all the mental operations performed in the process of speech production. The truth is, however, that, as any experienced teacher will confirm, in very many students this transfer never seems to occur. Probably these students, when called upon to construct sentences in the target language in real or simulated communicative conditions, ie under considerable time pressure, find it too difficult to refer to the fragments of conscious knowledge about the language stored in their minds and naturally fall upon various simplification strategies in the fulfilment of their communicative task. The point is, then, that the student should be deliberately trained in this transfer and reduction of his conscious knowledge and, being here in complete agreement with L K Engels (1974), I think that this is where mediators have a particularly relevant function to fulfill. By a mediator I mean in this case some condensed and visually representable form of the rule which might mediate between the student's stored knowledge about the language and his use of this knowledge in a communication task. The purpose and the limits of this paper do not allow us to discuss all possible types of mediators in language learning but the point I want to make here is that very often these mediators, just like advance organizers, can be contrastive in nature and can refer a given target language element to its functional correspondent in the native language. Very often, as I have already said, typical and illustrative examples of the usage of a given structure can function very effectively as mediators. For instance, taking again advantage of Szwedek's (1974a: 207) data, we might construct the following mediator with reference to the use of the articles in English:

Widziałem w oknie kobietę.
↓
(nieokreślona → a)
Kobieta wyszła na ulicę.
↓
(określona → the)

After the presentation of new language material the teacher and his students pass on to the next stage which might be called the stage of exercises. Again, discussing all the types and the whole sequence of grammar exercises agreeable with the principles of the cognitive approach would take us beyond the purpose and the scope of this paper so I want just to repeat what I have already said before that I see the primary function of these exercises as gaining by the student a clear understanding of a given principle and its accompanying concepts and relating this principle to the other elements of the target language system that the student already has in his cognitive structure. Accordingly, as an essential type among these exercises I consider a problem-solving task in which the student has the opportunity of testing and correcting his own hypotheses about the rule or principle being learned. Giving the student this opportunity is necessary because even though his hypotheses are formed with the help of the teacher in the stage of presentation, this fact does not guarantee that the student grasped the full scope and all the implications of the rule being acquired. Among these hypothesis-testing and problem-solving exercises a translation exercise from the native into the target language should certainly play a prominent role since this type of exercise controls the student's natural tendency to rely in his learning on his intuitive knowledge of the native language. As translation exercises have lately fallen from favor with many language teaching methodologists I would like to emphasize that I do not consider them to be the only type of grammar exercise but, on the other hand, I would see at least one good translation exercise as a necessary element in the whole sequence of grammar-teaching techniques. And since a grammar translation exercise is *par excellence* a practical contrastive analysis there is no doubt that contrastive studies can provide very good models for the construction of such exercises. For instance, coming back to our case of teaching the English articles, we could find in Szwedek's (1974a: 207) paper many interesting sets of simple sentences in Polish which would be ideal for a translation exercise, like the following two pairs:

Na podwórzu bawił się piłką chłopiec.
Chłopiec dał piłkę kotu.

Na podwórzu bawił się chłopiec z kotem.
Chłopiec dał kotu piłkę.

In the next stage of the teaching process, the stage of communication, the student is supposed to have practice in expressing his own meanings (however trivial they might be) and in constructing his own utterances in the target language. According to the assumptions of the cognitive approach this is also the stage in which actual language habits or, to use a somewhat different terminology, schemata (Herriot 1970: 163) are formed in response to stimuli, which have the form of meanings originating in the student's mind. There is no doubt that communicative activities in this stage are very difficult for the student who, trying to encode his meanings into the signs of the target language, is faced with many difficult choices and decisions at a time. Yet in nearly all the teaching techniques suggested for this stage so far no real help has been offered to the struggling student except for the teacher's occasional prompting and correction of errors. Still it is the stage in which the student needs a lot of help which would facilitate transfer from the activities in which he was involved in the two preceding stages to the activities of spontaneous utterance construction. This help should be offered to him in the form of mediators of all kinds and even simple language production algorithms, which should be displayed in the classroom, right in front of the student, on specially prepared charts or on the board. The student should not only be allowed but even encouraged to consult these special cognitive aids when in doubt about the use of a given grammatical rule or principle in his attempts at spontaneous speech production. Since many of these mediators might have a contrastive format utilizing in this way the results of contrastive analyses, we can see now that these results could be pedagogically useful even in the third stage of the teaching process.

As far as the fourth stage, that of revision and testing, is concerned it is fairly obvious that contrastive studies can again provide good models for translation tests, very similar in format to the translation exercises used in the second stage, the main difference being that they would serve not a learning but a testing purpose.

Talking about translation exercises based on the models provided by contrastive analyses, it is also worthwhile to mention that some of these exercises could be particularly useful and appropriate for the advanced level of language teaching. Their usefulness is connected with the fact that advanced learners are often marked by a certain syntactic rigidity and fixedness in their performance in the target language. This rigidity can be described in this way that they functionally overload some of their syntactic schemata, constantly choosing certain structures to the exclusion of other syntactic possibilities, very often, but not always, guided in their preferences by the criterion of formal congruence holding between the native language and the target one. To teach these students some more flexibility in their handling of the target language syntactic structures the performance of syntactic and semantic paraphrases of target language sentences should be highly recommended, perhaps along the lines suggested by L A Jakobovits in his popular book *Foreign language learning* (1970: 21–22). The relevant point is that some contrastive studies very well reveal what are the possible syntactic correspondents in the target language of a given native language structure and thus provide very good models for the construction of appropriate translation exercises. For example, in M Grala's (1974) study of negated adverbial participles in Polish and their corresponding forms in English I found some Polish sentences accompanied by sets of their possible translational equivalents in English, which could be directly incorporated into an exercise of this kind. Here are two of these sentences (Grala, 1974: 282):

Janek był bardzo zmartwiony nie zdawszy egzaminu.

John was very upset
{
(a) not having passed the exam
(b) at not having passed the exam
(c) at failing the exam
(d) not to have passed the exam
(e) because he didn't pass the exam
(f) as he failed the exam
(g) to have failed the exam
}

Nie lubiąc ludzi nie znajdziesz przyjaciół.

Not liking people   (a)
Without liking people   (b)
Disliking people   (c)   } you won't find friends.
If you don't like people   (d)

To conclude this discussion I would like to say that it was supposed to demonstrate to the reader that if we get rid of the fear of using our student's minds in their task of foreign language learning and if we adopt at least some of the cognitive principles, we will be able to find many more pedagogical uses for the data provided by contrastive studies than it has been suggested so far.

References

Ausubel, D P (1968) *Educational psychology: a cognitive view.* New York: Holt, Rinehart & Winston.

Engels, L K (1974) 'Foreign-language learning processes.' *Communication and cognition* 7, 237–256.

Fisiak, J (1973) 'The Polish–English contrastive project.' *PSiCL* 1, 7–13.

Grala, M (1974) 'Negated adverbial participles in Polish and their corresponding forms in English.' *PSiCL* 2, 281–294.

Herriot, P (1970) *An introduction to the psychology of language.* London: Methuen.

Jakobovitis, L A (1970) *Foreign language learning: a psycholinguistic analysis of the issues.* Rowley, Mass: Newbury House.

Leeson, R (1975) *Fluency and language teaching.* London: Longman.

Marton, W (1970) 'English and Polish nominal compounds: a transformational contrastive study.' *SAP* 2, 59–72.

Marton, W (1973) 'Contrastive analysis in the classroom.' *PSiCL* 1, 15–22.

Szwedek, A (1974a) 'Some aspects of definiteness and indefiniteness of nouns in Polish.' *PSiCL* 2, 203–211.

Szwedek, A (1974b) 'A note on the relation between the article in English and word order in Polish.' *PSiCL* 2, 213–220.

12. On The Feasibility of Pedagogical Contrastive Sociolinguistics

Karol Janicki

Adam Mickiewicz University, Poznań

The following considerations originate from the recent upsurge of interest in pedagogical implications of sociolinguistic research. Although the number and quality of the articles on the subject to date are by no means impressive, the general lack of cohesion in the line of research undertaken can be detected.

The underlying claim of the present paper is that no systematic and effective teaching of sociolinguistic facts can be undertaken before a sound methodological basis is worked out.

Generally, the present article is an attempt at pointing out ways of systematic application of sociolinguistic data to the foreign-language learning–teaching process. In particular, our aim here is to define the framework within which sociolinguistic contrastive analyses for pedagogical purposes could evolve.

Such a framework would imply the existence of or need for the isolation of pedagogical sociolinguistics from sociolinguistics proper.

The term *pedagogical* can refer to both first and foreign-language phenomena (Hartmann and Stork, 1972: 167). We suggest, however, that in the present article the term *pedagogical* apply only to the learning and teaching of a foreign language.

The term *pedagogical sociolinguistics* has been proposed, obviously, as an analog to the already widely used pedagogical linguistics. However, extensive modifications should be made as to the range of concerns possibly dictated by the analogy. We suggest that objective of pedagogical sociolinguistics (at least at the present stage of research in the field) should be the circumscribing of the sociolinguistics areas, topics, issues and phenomena which will be foci of the foreign-language material compiler.

It follows that some sociolinguistic facts which may be of utmost

significance to sociolinguistics proper are not relevant to the preparation of foreign-language materials for teaching purposes.
We will now try to exemplify both pedagogically relevant and pedagogically irrelevant sociolinguistic facts. For example, the origin of Black English Vernacular (Trudgill, 1974) is by no means pedagogically relevant, although it remains a central problem of present-day American sociolinguistics. The methods of isolating contextual styles (Labov, 1972) will not be of interest to pedagogical sociolinguistics although the styles isolated and their linguistic correlates obviously will. Deep categories underlying the use of pronouns (Brown and Gilman, 1972) will have no bearing to foreign-language teaching but the surface pronoun system in a particular language and its application will be relevant. Likewise, rules of address, that can be explicitly formulated (Ervin-Tripp, 1973) and those pertinent to other forms of social interaction, will be valid.

Thus, pedagogical sociolinguistics will aim at selecting only those sociolinguistic facts that can potentially contribute to the native-like mastery of the foreign language. Moreover, this skill seems to be much facilitated when sociolinguistic data is presented to both the teacher and the student in a systematic and explicit way. This, in turn, will be plausible when *sociolinguistic grammars* are constructed.

The estrangement of pedagogical sociolinguistics from sociolinguistics proper, as defined above, may be taken to mean the possible emergence of a new discipline. For the time being, however, the term does not claim such a status; it has been tentatively used as a convenient tool for the handling of sociolinguistic data relevant to foreign-language instruction.

The relation of pedagogical sociolinguistics data to the entirety of sociolinguistic data might be graphically illustrated as follows:

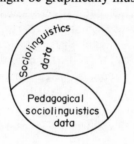

The relation of sociolinguistics to pedagogical sociolinguistics, however, will be entirely different since pedagogical sociolinguistics is not meant to be a subdiscipline of sociolinguistics but rather an independent domain which gets information from sociolinguistics and applies it in the foreign-language learning–teaching process. Graphically the relation might be presented as follows:

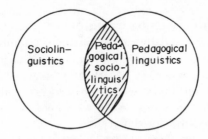

The shaded area, which circumscribes the limits of pedagogical sociolinguistics, refers to those socio-linguistic facts which are relevant to foreign-language teaching, and to those aspects of pedagogical linguistics which turn out to be relevant to the teaching of the mentioned sociolinguistic facts.

Having defined the term *pedagogical sociolinguistics*, we now turn to the discussion of *pedagogical contrastive sociolinguistics*. If it is assumed that any study of L2 involving concern about differences and similarities between L2 and L1 is of a contrastive nature, then pedagogical contrastive sociolinguistics seems to be a corollary of the existence of pedagogical sociolinguistics. This will be true unless we posit the operation of pedagogical sociolinguistics with no references to L1 sociolinguistic structure. In view of the present advances in language didactics such a procedure in turn would have to ignore, among other things, the interlanguage sociolinguistic interference which definitely exists but which has not yet been systematically explored.

In my opinion, which is based to a large extent on impressionistic judgments, a study of sociolinguistic interference (both inter- and intra-) would most probably reveal a number of interference categories possibly parallel to those isolated by Richards (1974).[1]

At this point we might tentatively say that pedogogical contrastive sociolinguistics is possible, but still a great many questions remain to be raised before the potential student of pedagogical contrastive sociolinguistics knows what his field actually is, and what are some of the tasks he is confronted with. If contrastive analysis is to be taken to mean systematic juxtaposition of equivalent and different structures, elaboration on the notions mentioned so far becomes necessary.

As has already been mentioned one of the goals of pedagogical sociolinguistics is the isolation of sociolinguistic data relevant to its (pedagogical sociolinguistics's) operation. Another target of pedagogical sociolinguistics will, however, be systematic application of this sociolinguistic data in the foreign language learning–teaching process. Such a procedure will be the easiest to pursue once sociolinguistic grammars have been constructed.

A sociolinguistic grammar might be arrived at by means of matching two grammar systems:

1. a linguistic grammar,
2. a grammar of social interaction.

A grammar of social interaction would be a finite set of rules on the basis of which an infinite number of social behaviours would be generated, eg the grammar of social interaction for language community X might include a rule stating that when two people see each other for the first time during the day they greet each other (it is a categorical rule for Polish and English, and possibly a universal one). A lower-level variable rule would, in turn, prescribe either a verbal realization of the greeting, a non-verbal one, or a combination of the two (in each of the cases a number of options being possible). Grimshaw (1973: 104) corroborates the validity of 2: 'I . . . want to underline for you the importance of at least acknowledging the existence of a complex set of rules in a grammar of social interaction and the further reality that while there may be a grammar of social interaction there are also grammars (plural) of social interaction for different groups'.

Recapitulating, in order for pedagogical contrastive sociolinguistics to exist the following line of reasoning has to be accepted:

1. Alongside a linguistic grammar, a grammar of social interaction has to be constructed for each language
2. These two grammars have to be combined to yield a socio-linguistic grammar of, say, language X
3. After individual sociolinguistic grammars for languages X and Y have been formulated, *contrastive sociolinguistics* singles out equivalent and different relationships
4. Pedagogical sociolinguistics comes in and utilizes grammatical[2] information for foreign-language teaching purposes
5. If pedagogical sociolinguistics uses data collected by contrastive sociolinguistics then it naturally becomes pedagogical contrastive sociolinguistics.

We now turn to the feasibility of steps 1 through 5. It seems that steps 1 and 2 involve a methodological alternative with regard to the process of combining linguistic grammars and those of social interaction. If we accept the view that legitimate sociolinguistic grammars can be constructed by means of matching linguistic grammars with those pertaining to the social structure, then in a number of languages (those for which relatively complete linguistic grammars have been written) our task is reduced to the construction of grammars of social interaction and then combining the two. Such an approach brings us to define the underlying categories and surface structure relationships of a potential grammar of social interaction of a language.

Even in a highly heterogeneous society whose overall pattern of language use is extensively diversified regularities can be arrived at. 'One may not need to know all the contexts and categories of a community to discern the essentials of its patterns in these regards, but one must know the dimensions on which contexts and categories contrast' (Hymes, 1974: 158). Countless situations 'in which language activity takes place can be grouped into situations types to which correspond the various uses of language' (Halliday *et al*, 1964: 95).

We follow Grimshaw in assuming that a grammar of social interaction endemic to an individual society would be derived from an underlying universal grammar of social interaction. 'I have become increasingly convinced that the varieties of behavior described by scholars who studied questioning, or teaching or learning in different societies may obscure—in their richness—the probable existence of a set of underlying principles and relations which hold for all such behavior—however different surface manifestations may be...I suspect, in short, that there are interactional universals for all societies and interactional rules for individual societies in a fairly precise analog to linguists' rules for languages and rules for language' (Grimshaw, 1973: 107).

The writer of a grammar of social interaction for a particular social group would thus have to take into account such relationships (which we assume to be universals) as subordination–superordination; possibly universal dimensions such as social distance; criteria for categorizing settings, topics, personnel; and content[3] of actual interaction, ie social behaviour commonly labelled as deference, compliance, effrontery, acquiescence, etc.

Following Simmel's (1950) model, a sociolinguistic grammar within the approach adumbrated above would involve a three-level analysis:

1. Identifying the forms which can be viewed as abstract, eg the accommodative relationship of subordination–superordination
2. Matching, in a particular language, the occurring content categories, eg compliance, deference, respect demand, etc, with the underlying abstract labels
3. Assigning the occurring linguistic forms to the observed social behavior, ie identified content categories.

Whatever the outcome of such a behaviour in a sociolinguistic description, the approach outlined above toward the development of a general method or theory in sociolinguistics is found by some scholars to be erroneous since it does not imply natural integration, from the very beginning, of sociological and linguistic facts.

The alternative view stresses that 'there must develop a partially independent body of method and theory—what might be termed—...an integrated theory of sociolinguistic description' (Hymes, 1974: 74) where no post-descriptive matching but outright integration would be attempted. The integrated theory of sociolinguistic description would account for the 'creative language use [which] is often not a matter of a novel sentence, or a novel context either, but a novel relation. Sentences and context may be familiar, the use of one in the other may be what is new' (Hymes, 1974: 156).

Provided sociolinguistic grammars have been constructed for any two languages (whatever the underlying methodology) contrastive sociolinguistics can commence to function. Having selected the sociolinguistic information relevant to foreign language teaching (cf p 187), pedagogical sociolinguistics, in turn, introduces the collected data into the learning–teaching process.

Before pedagogical contrastive sociolinguistics is clearly defined in terms of its immediate goals we have to refer to contrastive sociolinguistics which has not emerged yet, and which we need in the form of a systematic analysis of different sociolinguistic systems. As Higa (1971) points out, information on the use of relational utterances[4] is indispensable for successful foreign-language teaching. Since gross differences in the use of these utterances can be detected among languages, for foreign-language teaching the juxtaposition of the two systems pertaining to L1 and L2 is found to be of paramount importance. With regard to relational utterances Higa says: 'Contrastive sociolinguistic studies can determine how universal or culture-specific these factors of relational utterances are that are found in one language' (Higa 1971: 216).

The question that has to be asked at this point is whether the scope of contrastive sociolinguistics would go beyond the sociolinguistic facts that are of interest to pedagogical sociolinguistics. If we define contrastive sociolinguistics goal as discovery and explicit elicitation of differences and similarities between two sociolinguistic grammars, then the answer to the above question would be negative. If, however, contrastive sociolinguistics extends its concerns to exogrammatical (cf note 2) phenomena the answer would be positive. In other words, if contrastive sociolinguistics is concerned with the entirety of sociolinguistic data, then, a large part of contrastive sociolinguistics data will be irrelevant to pedagogical sociolinguistics and, by extension, to pedagogical contrastive sociolinguistics.

If the former concept of contrastive sociolinguistics is accepted then pedagogical contrastive sociolinguistics can come into being only after contrastive sociolinguistics juxtaposes two sociolinguistic systems (with the descriptive limits mentioned) and points to entities of equivalence or those exhibiting differences.

Thus we are getting to the final definition of pedagogical contrastive sociolinguistics in terms of its objectives. Pedagogical contrastive sociolinguistics is meant to be an approach within pedagogical sociolinguistics which would aim at effective utilization in the foreign-language teaching process of the systematically presented data included in the field of contrastive sociolinguistics (the scope of contrastive sociolinguistics concern not going beyond sociolinguistic grammars). The existence of contrastive sociolinguistics will be possible if the conditions pertaining to the ordering of data collection and rule formulation, listed above, are met.

Throughout this paper we have been referring to linguistic, socio-interactional, sociolinguistic and contrastive sociolinguistic grammars. Although the implications may have been those of a necessity of first completing the grammatical[5] description at a particular level of operation, and only later passing on to the next level, the author is fully aware of the present futility of such endeavour. How could we possibly think of complete sociolinguistic grammars if linguistic grammars are incomplete let alone grammars of social interaction, which do not exist at all?

Does it mean, then, that the field of central interest to us—pedagogical contrastive sociolinguistics cannot come into being until those complete source grammars have been constructed? Obviously not.

As is known, contrastive studies have been taken up although no complete grammatical information on the languages contrasted has been provided. Likewise pedagogical contrastive sociolinguistics can start operating on the fragmentary sociolinguistic data whose collection is being encouraged or which, in some isolated cases, has already been gathered.

A note must be made of the relationship of pedagogical contrastive sociolinguistics to *language didactics*, a label assigned to the general theory of language teaching. Unlike pedagogical linguistics, which does not concern itself with the exolinguistic aspects of human communication but only implements theoretical linguistic descriptions in the foreign-language teaching process, language didactics collects linguistic, psycholinguistic, sociolinguistic and pedagogical information, and incorporates all of these kinds of information in its working procedures.

In this way, it can be seen that pedagogical contrastive sociolinguistics along with pedagogical psycholinguistics (?), psychology of learning, and other disciplines relevant to foreign-language teaching are complementary to one another and thus subordinate to the more general and allinclusive language didactics.

Being aware of the hindrances and difficulties that pedagogical contrastive sociolinguistics faces we should not get discouraged, however. On the contrary, we should follow Bickerton (1973: 18) who, while being cognizant of the difficulties underlying the construction of polylectal grammars, says: 'One could, like some linguists..., spend forever discussing where and how to start, it seems more useful simply to get started.'

Notes

1. Among other categories Richards lists over-generalization, markers of transitional competence, errors due to strategies of communication and assimilation, etc.
2. Grammatical here means 'pertaining to sociolinguistic grammar'.
3. Simmel (1950) differentiates between the forms which interaction takes and the content of an interaction. Grimshaw (1973: 108) refers to Simmel's model: 'The forms can be discussed and understood in the abstract, without regard to the personalities or other characteristics of the particular incumbents in the particular roles involved. Simmel defined four such forms: competition, conflict, accommodation and assimilation.' Content, in turn, refers to the actual social behaviour.
4. Higa differentiates between *factual statements* and *relational utterances*. The former are those by means of which the speaker does not particularly attempt to relate himself to any other persons, eg *The sun rises in the east: The lion is a mammal*, etc. The latter are 'utterances which assume that there is a listener and the speaker is relating himself to the listener' (Higa, 1971: 211), eg *Good Morning: hi: so long*, etc.
5. Here *grammatical* is an overall term which may pertain to linguistic, sociointeractional or contrastive sociolinguistic grammar.

References

Bickerton, D (1972 'The structure of the polylectal grammars.' In Shuy, R W (*ed*) (1972), 17–42.

194   Karol Janicki

Brown, R and Gilman, A (1972) 'The pronouns of power and solidarity.' In Giglioli, P P (ed) (1972), 252–282.

Ervin-Tripp, S M (1973) Language acquisition and communicative choice. Stanford, Cal.: Stanford University Press.

Giglioli, P P (ed) (1972) Language and social context. Harmondsworth: Penguin Books.

Grimshaw, A D (1973) 'Rules, social interaction and language behavior.' TESOL Quarterly 7/1, 99–115.

Halliday, M A K, McIntosh, A and Strevens, P (1964) The linguistic sciences and language teaching. London: Longmans.

Hartmann, R R K and Stork, F C (1972) Dictionary of language and linguistics. London: Applied Science Publishers.

Higa, M (1971) Towards contrastive sociolinguistics.' Working papers 3/1, 211–218. Department of Linguistics, University of Hawaii.

Hymes, D (1974) Foundations in sociolinguistics. Philadelphia: University of Pennsylvania Press.

Labov, W (1972) Sociolinguistic patterns. Philadelphia: University of Pennsylvania Press.

Richards, J C (1974) 'Error analysis and second language strategies.' In Schumann, J H and Stenson, N (eds) (1974) 32–53.

Schumann, J H and Stenson, N (eds) (1974) New frontiers in second language learning. Rowley, Mass.: Newbury House Publishers.

Shuy, R W (ed) (1972) MSLL 25. Washinton, DC: Georgetown University Press.

Simmel, G (1950) The sociology of Georg Simmel. Translated, edited and with an introduction by Kurt, H Wolff. Glencoe: The Free Press.

Trudgill, P (1974) Sociolinguistics: an introduction. Harmondsworth: Penguin Books.

13. Contrastive Analysis as a Predictor of Errors, with Reference to Punjabi Learners of English[1]

Howard Jackson

City of Birmingham Polytechnic

1. Contrastive analysis

Contrastive linguistics is a branch of linguistics which seeks to compare (the sounds, grammars and vocabularies of) two languages with the aim of describing the similarities and differences between them. Such a description may be carried out for its own sake, or its purpose may be to contribute to the task of foreign-language teaching. Contrastive analysis is the technique associated with contrastive linguistics, and it may be defined as: 'a systematic comparison of selected linguistic features of two or more languages, the intent of which is ... to provide teachers and textbook writers with a body of information which can be of service in the preparation of instructional materials, the planning of courses, and the development of classroom techniques' (Hammer and Rice, 1965).

The aim of this paper is to explore the nature of the information that contrastive analysis can be reasonably expected to provide, and to suggest why this information should be useful to the teacher of English as a second language.

2. The claims of contrastive analysis

Contrastive linguistics developed in the 1950s in America out of the behaviourist inclined second-language learning theories and foreign-language programmes of the time. The notions of 'transfer' and 'interference' were borrowed from psychological learning theory and applied to second-language learning. If a structure to be learned in the target (foreign) language (L2) had a counterpart in the learner's mother tongue (L1), then 'positive' transfer would take place and learning be facilitated. If, on the other hand, an L2 structure did not have a counterpart in the L1, or if an L1 structure did not have a counterpart in the L2, or if the equivalent structures in L1 and L2 exhibited a measure of difference, then 'negative' transfer (alias interference) would take place and learning would be hampered. It was therefore concluded, in the words of C C Fries, that: 'The most efficient materials are those based upon a scientific description of the language to be learned carefully compared with a parallel description of the native language' (Fries, 1945: 9).

This position was stated even more strongly by Banathy, Trager and Waddle (1966):

> 'The change that has to take place in the language behaviour of a foreign language student can be equated with the differences between the structures of the student's native language and culture and that of the target language and culture.... Differences between two languages can be established by contrastive linguistic analysis.... What the student has to learn equals the sum of the differences established by contrastive analysis' (Banathy *et al*, 1966: 37).

This strong claim of contrastive analysis to provide all the information necessary for the foreign-language course planner will hardly hold up in practice: other considerations, such as immediate usefulness, simplicity, motivational strength, condition the choice and sequencing of items and structures in a foreign language course. A more modest form of this claim was expressed by Robert Lado in his book *Linguistics across cultures*, a seminal work that prompted a number of contrastive studies: 'The teacher who has made a comparison of the foreign language with the native language of the students will know better what the real learning problems are and can better provide for teaching them' (Lado, 1957). But even this stance is somewhat unrealistic: not many teachers have the time or the skill to undertake a detailed and systematic comparison of the L1 and L2 of their pupils; and many of the problems in the language-learning classroom would not in any case be solved by the kind of information provided by contrastive analysis.

Indeed, in practice it soon became clear that contrastive analysis could not deliver the goods that it had promised, and contrastive linguists were forced to make less far-reaching claims for their discipline (Jackson, 1976).

Nemser, for example, in 1971, states:

> 'I take contrastive linguistics to be a field concerned with drawing the implications in terms of learning facilitation and inhibition, of structural similarities and differences between the language or languages a learner has already acquired and the language he is seeking to acquire. On the basis of a comparison of the descriptions of the phonologies, grammars and lexicons of the languages in question ... contrastive linguistics offers hypotheses concerning identifications a learner will make between elements of his base and target systems, thus providing predictions and explanations concerning his learning behaviour of presumed high value in planning learning and teaching strategy' (Nemser, 1971).

Contrastive analysis is now limited to providing 'hypotheses', 'predictions' and 'explanations' about learning behaviour. Krzeszowski, three years later, was even less sanguine about the usefulness of contrastive analysis to language learning and teaching:

> 'The pedagogical value of contrastive analysis is becoming less and less obvious and the solutions therein more and more removed to a remote area near the horizon. ... The best that contrastive analysis can do is to predict areas of potential mistakes without making any claims as to whether or not and in what circumstances they are likely to occur in actual performance' (Krzeszowski, 1974: 281).

Here we are left with the prediction not of learning behaviour but merely of areas of potential mistakes.

It is this much weaker claim for contrastive analysis that I would like to make in this paper for the English as a second-language teaching situation. A contrastive analysis of English and the mother tongues of ethnic minorities is able to predict the potential mistakes of such learners of English. To this claim I would like to add the further and related one, cited by Nemser (q.v.): contrastive analysis is able to explain many of the actually occurring errors in the English of such learners, in particular those that arise from interference from the learners' mothers tongue. Prediction and explanation of errors have, then, become the modest goals of contrastive analysis and I hope to demonstrate how a comparison of the grammars of English and Punjabi can achieve these goals in some measure.

3. The English as a second-language classroom

Classical contrastive analysis was developed with the traditional foreign-language classroom situation in mind. In particular, it was assumed that the native language was English, which would probably also be the native language of the teacher, and that the students would be learning probably one of the usual European languages. The first contrastive studies done in America (following Lado, 1957) under the auspices of the Center for Applied Linguistics in Washington were on English/German, English/Spanish and English/Italian, with work on English/French and English/Russian unpublished. Contrastive projects currently running are mostly in European countries, contrasting their native languages with English-Polish, Finnish, Serbo-Croat, German.

Quite clearly the English as a second-language teaching situation differs markedly from the traditional foreign-language teaching 'one—in two ways. Firstly, the learners in the ESL classroom very probably do not have the same mother tongue, which means that they will not necessarily be making the same kinds of interference errors. Secondly, the teacher of English as a second language will not usually know the mother tongue of his students, and his own L1 will be the target language of his students and not their L1. In the usual foreign-language teaching situation, the learners will have a homogeneous L1, and the teacher will probably also share that L1, or will at least be familiar with both the L1 and L2 of his students. So, for example, in the teaching of German in an English school, the teacher and students will most likely share English as L1, and the teacher will, of course, additionally be competent in German, the target of his students. The English as a second-language teacher, on the other hand, will most likely have English as L1—the target language of his students—and he cannot be expected to be competent in Punjabi, Bengali, Hindu/Urdu, Gujarati, not to mention Farsi, Greek and West Indian.

4. Why contrastive analysis should be useful in the English as a second language teaching situation

Because of the situation outlined above, it is my contention that contrastive analysis, although it did not deliver the goods for the traditional foreign-language teaching situation for which it was designed, can be more useful to the teacher of English as a second language. For traditional foreign-language teaching it was said that a competent or experienced teacher would be able to predict and explain his students' errors without the help of contrastive analysis; and this was undoubtedly true in a significant number of cases. Familiarity with both languages, and the experience of having learned the foreign language himself anyway, would provide the competent foreign-language teacher with the basis for understanding interference errors in his students' target language performance.

Since the teacher of English as a second language does not usually have competence in both the mother tongue and target language of his students and does not have the experience of having learned English as a foreign language, he does not have the basic knowledge with which to understand the interference errors of his students, or even to detect which errors are caused by interference from the mother tongue and which are from other sources. It seems to me that contrastive analysis can provide this information to the ESL teacher. Contrastive analysis will predict areas of potential error and explain actually occurring errors which are caused by interference from the mother tongue of the learner. This information should help the teacher of English as a second language understand, and then perhaps more readily remedy at least some of the errors of his students caused in this way.

5. Examples from a contrastive analysis of Punjabi/English[2]

(i) One clear difference between the grammars of Punjabi and English is with words like 'in', 'on', 'to', 'at': in English these words are prepositions, they come before the noun or noun phrase to which they refer; in Punjabi these words are postpositions, they come after the noun or noun phrase to which they refer. So, 'in the garden' in

English is equivalently in Punjabi 'garden in' (there is no definite article in Punjabi). Contrastive analysis would predict that this clear difference would manifest itself in interference errors in the English of Punjabi learners; but in fact it does not.[3] There seems to be a principle operating that if the contrast is as gross as this one, learners do not generally make errors. Errors appear to occur most readily where there are some similarities and some contrasts between equivalent items or structures in the two languages.

There is, however, one context where the preposition/postposition contrast between English and Punjabi does cause errors, but there are other factors involved as well. The context is that of possessive expressions. In English, possessive constructions may be formed in two ways: either by an 's phrase before the noun, or by an 'of' phrase after it; eg 'the man's hat'—'the hat of the man'. In Punjabi there is only one possessive construction, coming before the noun, but similar in structure to the English 'of' phrase which comes after the noun, equivalently 'man of hat'. These contrasts appear to be the cause of errors like the following:

'There's a shoe of a pair'	for	'There's a pair of shoes'
'Some crisps of packets'	for	'Some packets of crisps'
'His hand of the fingers'	for	'The fingers of his hand'

These contrasts would predictably be a source of error, and the actually occurring errors may be explained as interference from the L1 caused by a contrast between the L1 and L2 language systems.

(ii) Some differences in ordering are not as gross as that between preposition and postposition and do cause interference errors. One of this kind occurs in questions. In forming polar questions (those expecting the answer 'yes' or 'no') from statements in English the first verbal auxiliary and the subject invert; eg 'I may come'—'May I come?'. If there is no auxiliary present in the verb phrase in the statement form, then the 'do' auxiliary is inserted in the question; eg 'He came'—'Did he come?'. In Punjabi the verb normally comes at the end of a clause, but in questions there is no inversion and no change of word order. Predictably this contrast gives rise to interference errors, like the following:

'You can run?'	for	'Can you run?'
'You know where they finding?'	for	'Do you know where to find them?'

The contrast in the position of the verb appears to be gross enough a contrast not to cause interference errors.

In information questions in English, the 'wh—' question word (who?, what?, why?, where?, etc) comes first in the clause, then the first verbal auxiliary (or 'do'), then the subject (unless this is the 'wh—' word itself), then the remainder of the verb phrase and any other clausal elements; eg 'Who is coming to the party?' ('wh—' word as subject), 'What did you have for breakfast?' ('wh—' word as object), 'Why has he gone home?' ('wh—' word as adjunct/adverbial). When the 'wh—' word is subject there is no inversion, but in all other cases there is inversion of subject and first auxiliary. In Punjabi there is again no inversion of subject and verb, and the 'wh—' question word comes immediately before the verb, usually the last item in the clause; eg equivalently, 'Party to who coming is?', 'You breakfast for what have?', 'He home why gone has?'. The contrast in position of the 'wh—' word appears to be a gross enough difference not to cause interference errors; but the lack of inversion causes errors here, as with polar questions, like the following:

'What this is?'	for	'What is this?'
'How I do this?'	for	'How do I do this?'
'How big he was?'	for	'How big was he?'

(iii) Our first two examples have been concerned mostly with differences in the order of items. We turn now to differences of form, and first of all to the tense system, a common cause of errors for Punjabi learners of English. English and Punjabi are the same in that they both have progressive and non-progressive tenses ('I am walking'—'I walk'). They differ, however, in that the *form* of the present progressive tense in English is the same as that of the simple present tense in Punjabi, except for the order (Eng. pres. prog.: Aux + Present participle; Pun. simp. pres.: Present participle + Aux). The present progressive in Punjabi is formed with: Verb root + progressive particle ('rya') + aux, thus having some similarities with the English present progressive form, eg presence of 'aux'. These contrasts are predictably a source of interference error and clearly explain the following kinds of error:

'He is eat the dinner'	for	'He is eating the dinner'
'He eat the dinner'	for	'He is eating the dinner'
'She ringing the bell'	for	'She is ringing the bell'
'At school I am playing with my friends'	for	'At school I play with my friends'.

In the simple past tense in Punjabi the form of the verb is usually just the past participle of the verb, with no auxiliary present; and errors of the following kind are found:

'She pushing her'	for	'She pushed her'
'I dog come out with me'	for	'My dog came out with me'.

Another contrast of form in the verb system is the occurrence in the English simple present tense of the '-s' inflexion in the 3rd person singular. Apart from the auxiliary the only verb forms that inflect for person and number in Punjabi are the future and the subjunctive forms. The '-s' inflexion in English represents a contrast with Punjabi, but it is also a maverick form in English; the interlanguage contrastive factor is therefore not the only cause of the following errors:

'He clean his leg'	for	'He cleans his leg'
'We cleans his face'	for	'We clean his face'
'Does a cat drinks water?'	for	'Does a cat drink water?'.

The last example, with the marker on both verb forms, reflecting over-application of the suffix, may be due directly to inadequate learning or teaching, but ultimately the cause of the error is the contrast between Punjabi and English at this point.

Moving away from the area of the verb, a further contrast in form exists between English and Punjabi in the systems of determiners. By determiners are meant words like the articles ('a', 'the'), the demonstratives ('this', 'that') and the possessives ('my', 'your', etc), which 'determine' the contextual status of a noun. The Punjabi system differs from the English system in that there are no articles in Punjabi. The demonstrative determiner, however, sometimes functions like a definite article. These contrasts are predictably a source of error, and indeed the following kinds of error occur:

'Boy is cutting the paper'   for   'A/The boy is cutting the paper'
'This man is go the house'   for   'The man is going to the house';

and the insertion of articles in inadmissible positions:

'I bought a biscuits'   for   'I bought (some) biscuits'
'Where's the Linda?'   for   'Where's Linda?'
'with a glue'   for   'with glue'
'She wear the black shoes'   for   'She wears black shoes'.

(iv) Finally, I would like to bring two examples from another aspect of grammar: the realisation of grammatical categories. The first of these examples is a further instance of a gross difference, which for this reason does not give rise to errors. It concerns the grammatical category of *case*, associated with the noun. In English there is a simple two-way case distinction between 'common' case and 'genitive' case or 'possessive' case ('boy' and 'boy's'). In Punjabi there are five case forms, of which three are restricted in use; and they do not include a genitive/possessive case, since possession is indicated by means of the 'of' phrase equivalent in Punjabi. As we have seen, Punjabi learners do have difficulty with the possessive noun phrase in English because of this contrast. Otherwise there is virtually a reduction of five cases to one, and no errors occur which suggest that a Punjabi learner tries to form equivalent cases in the English noun to those in his native language.

The second example concerns the category of gender in the pronoun. Punjabi nouns are divided into two gender classes—masculine and feminine—like French, indicated by the ending of the noun: this contrast causes no problems in learning English, since it again represents a reduction in categories (from 2 to 1). In the pronouns, however, there is a problem: the only place in the grammatical system where English exhibits gender distinctions is in the 3rd person singular pronouns ('he', 'she', 'it'), a maverick relic, rather like the '-s' ending in the 3rd person singular present tense of verbs. What is more, Punjabi does not have 3rd person pronouns as such, but uses the demonstrative pronouns for this purpose. This contrast predictably gives rise to a number of errors in the English of Punjabi learners, and explains errors such as the following:

'Whenever she goes to school she takes his work with him'	for	'Whenever she goes to school she takes her work with her'
'She don't brought'	for	'He didn't bring'
'He's got the same noses'	for	'They've got the same noses'
'It's not black'	for	'They're not black'.

These examples demonstrate that a contrastive analysis can both predict areas of potential error, even if not pinpoint precise errors, and that it can provide the explanation of a great number of errors that arise from the interference of the mother tongue. I hope that I have gone some way to commending contrastive analysis as a useful contributor of information to the English as a second-language teaching task.

Notes

1. A first version of this paper was presented at a conference on 'Language Pluralism in Schools', held at the University of Birmingham on 24 March 1979, organised by the Midland Association for Linguistic Studies and the Faculty of Education, University of Birmingham.
2. These examples are based on research being done in the Department of English & Foreign Languages, City of Birmingham Polytechnic, comparing English with the languages spoken by the major ethnic minorities in Birmingham. So far a comparison of the grammars of Punjabi and English has been reported on (Jackson, 1979).
3. The error corpus quoted from in this paper was compiled from lists provided by ESL teachers in the Sandwell English to Immigrants Service, West Midlands.

References

Banathy, B H, Trager, E C and Waddle, C D (1966) 'Use of contrastive data in foreign language course development.' In Valdman (1966), 35–56.
DiPietro, R J (1971) *Language structures in contrast* Rowley, Mass.: Newbury House.

Filipović, R (ed) (1971) *Zagreb Conference on English Contrastive Projects 7–9 December 1970*. Zagreb: Institute of Linguistics.

Fries, C C (1945) *Teaching and Learning English as a foreign language*. Ann Arbor: Wahr.

Hammer, J and Rice, F A (1965) *A bibliography of contrastive linguistics*. Washington, DC: Center for Applied Linguistics.

Jackson, H (1976) 'Contrastive linguistics—what is it?' *ITL 32*, 1–32.

Jackson, H (1979) 'Errors of Punjabi learners of English, a comparison of the grammars of Punjabi and English.' CORE 3/3.

Krzeszowski, T P (1974) Review of DiPietro (1971) *PSiCL* 3, 281–290.

Lado, R (1957) *Linguistics across cultures*. Ann Arbor: University of Michigan Press.

Nemser, W (1971) 'Recent Center activities in contrastive linguistics.' In Filipović (1971), 11–30.

Valdman, A (ed) (1966) *Trends in language teaching*. New York: McGraw–Hill.

14. Contrastive Analysis, Error Analysis and Interlanguage: Three Phases of One Goal

S. N. Sridhar

State University of New York

0. Introduction

The mistakes or 'errors' that students make in the process of learning a second or foreign language (target language) have always been a cause of much concern to the teachers and textbook writers alike.[1] This concern is reflected not only in the way writers of pedagogical grammars draw attention to the potential 'pitfalls' in the target language, but also in the many lists of 'common errors' prepared by experienced teachers.[2] A systematic approach to the problem of errors, in an effort to account for their linguistic and psychological origin, regularity, predictability, variability, etc, is, however, relatively recent. The 'one goal' mentioned in the title of this paper refers to the attempt to facilitate the process of target language learning (and teaching) by studying the phenomenon of 'errors' within a scientific framework that is consistent with both linguistic theory and learning theory. In so far as the three areas of research under review have this as one of their primary goals, if not the main goal, they may be said to constitute three phases of one goal.

0.1. The 'outreach' of the areas of research

This is not to imply, of course, that the areas of research mentioned in the title have this pedagogical goal as their only concern. On the contrary, each of the three fields of study has been claimed to have important contributions to make in a variety of related areas. Contrastive analysis is claimed to be central to all linguistic research—in developing a general theory of language based on the discovery of the 'universals' of language, in the study of diachronic change and of dialectal variation, in longitudinal studies of language acquisition, as well as in interlingual translation[3] (see Ferguson, 1968). Error analysis, it is claimed, is significant for the insights it provides into the strategies employed in second-language acquisition, and in turn into the process of language learning in general (see Corder, 1967). The study of Interlanguage, it is claimed, has implications for theories of language contact, language change and language acquisition, besides its usefulness in describing special language types such as immigrant speech, non-standard dialects, non-native varieties of language and the language of aphasics and of poetry, among others (see Nemser, 1971a; Richards, 1972; Corder, 1971a). Despite these many and varied claims, it is still correct, however, to say that the primary goal of all the three areas of research has been to facilitate target language learning by providing insights into the nature of the learner's performance.

In addition to the diversity of claims regarding their applications, contrastive analysis, error analysis and Interlanguage also differ from one another in a number of respects—in their theoretical assumptions, methodologies, the nature and scope of data considered relevant in each area, the kind of insights they provide into the nature of target language learning, and in the implications of the studies carried out for practical classroom teaching and materials preparation.

It is the purpose of this paper to present a 'state of the art' in each of these areas of research from the point of view of the 'one goal' explained above. In particular, with respect to each field of study, we shall examine the current trends in theory, methodology, claims and empirical validations thereof and its contribution to target language teaching. The following discussion is organized in four parts—the first, second and third parts deal with contrastive analysis, error analysis and Interlanguage respectively and the last part is the conclusion. There will be a good deal of overlap among the sections, but this is unavoidable given the fact that the three fields have developed at times as rivals, and as complementary to one another at other times.

1.0. Contrastive analysis

Although several prominent linguists and pioneers in the field of target language pedagogy, including Henry Sweet, Harold Palmer and Otto Jespersen, were well aware of the 'pull of the mother tongue' in learning a target language, it was Charles C. Fries who firmly established contrastive linguistic analysis as an integral component of the methodology of target language teaching.[4] Declaring that

> The most effective materials (for foreign language teaching) are based upon a scientific description of the language to be learned carefully compared with a parallel description of the native language of the learner (1945, p 9).

Fries may be said to have issued the charter for modern contrastive analysis. In doing so, he also made the first move in what has turned out to be one of the most spirited controversies in the field of foreign language teaching, namely on the role and relevance of contrastive analysis, but more on this later (see Sections 1.7 and 2.2). The challenge was taken up by Lado, whose work *Linguistics across cultures* (1957) soon became a classic field manual for practical contrastive studies. The Chomskyan revolution in linguistics gave a fresh impetus to contrastive analysis, not only making it possible for the comparisons to be more explicit and precise, but also giving it what seemed to be a more solid theoretical foundation by claiming the existence of 'language universals' (but cf Bouton, 1975). The volumes of *The contrastive structure series* (eg Stockwell and Bowen, 1965; Stockwell, Bowen and Martin, 1965) represent this phase of contrastive analysis. The papers from the three conferences on contrastive analysis held at Georgetown, Cambridge, and Stuttgart (Alatis, 1968; Nickel, 1971a; Nickel, 1971b, respectively) present scholars as, by and large, optimistic about the possibilities of contrastive analysis. But by early 1970s, contrastive analysis was already open to attack on both external grounds (of empirical validity) and internal (theoretical foundations), leading Selinker to wonder that contrastive analysis was still thriving 'at a period when a serious crisis of confidence exists as to what it is' (Selinker, 1971, p 1) and Wardhaugh to forecast a 'period of quiescence' for it (Wardhaugh, 1970). Contrastive analysis today, however, is not entirely on the defensive—not only do 'messages of hope' keep appearing from time to time (eg Schachter, 1974; Wode, 1978), but even the proponents of alternate approaches (error analysis and Interlanguage) implicitly or explicitly incorporate contrastive analysis in their methodology (see Section 3.5). If anything, the controversy seems to have clarified the possibilities and limitations of contrastive analysis and its place, along with other components, in the task of accounting for the nature of the learner's performance.

1.1. The rationale for contrastive analysis

The rationale for undertaking contrastive studies comes mainly from three sources: (a) practical experience of foreign language teachers; (b) studies of language contact in bilingual situations; and (c) theory of learning.

Every experienced foreign language teacher knows that a substantial number of persistent mistakes made by his students can be traced to the 'pull of the mother tongue'. Thus, when a Hindi speaker learning English says, 'The plants were all right till we kept them in the study' in the sense of 'as long as' or an Arabic speaker persists in retaining a pronominal reflex of the relativized noun in his relative clauses as in 'The boy that he came' (cf Catford, 1968; Schachter, 1974), or to give a different type of example, the Indian learners of English systematically replace the alveolar consonant with their retroflex counterparts, there is no doubt that the learner is 'carrying over' patterns of the mother tongue into his target language performance. Moreover, such a 'carry over' seems to result in the largest number of deviant sentences in areas where the structures of the native language and the target language differ the most.

Students of language contact have also noted the phenomenon of 'interference', which Weinreich defines as 'those instances of deviation from the norms of either language which occur in the speech of bilinguals as a result of their familiarity with more than one language' (1953, p 1). Weinreich (1953) was the first (and perhaps still the best) extensive study of the mechanisms of bilingual interference.

The third source that has been considered to support the contrastive analysis hypothesis (see Section 1.2) is learning theory—in particular, the theory of *transfer*. In its simplest form transfer refers to the hypothesis that the learning of a task is either facilitated ('positive' transfer) or impeded ('negative' transfer) by the previous learning of another task, depending on, among other things, the degree of similarity or difference obtaining between the two tasks. The implications of transfer theory for target language learning are obvious. (For an excellent study of the application of transfer theory to second-language learning, see Jakobovits 1969; see also Carroll 1968.)

1.2. Contrastive analysis hypothesis

The 'strong' version of the contrastive analysis hypothesis is clearly stated by Lee (1968, p 186). Contrastive analysis is based on the assumption, he says,

1. That the prime cause, or even the sole cause, of difficulty and error in foreign-language learning is interference coming from the learners' native language;
2. that the difficulties are chiefly, or wholly, due to the differences between the two languages;
3. that the greater these differences are, the more acute the learning difficulties will be;
4. that the results of a comparison between the two languages are needed to predict the difficulties and errors which will occur in learning the foreign language;
5. that what there is to teach can best be found by comparing the two languages and then subtracting what is common to them, so that 'what the student has to learn equals the sum of the differences established by the contrastive analysis.'

It must be mentioned that not all theoreticians and practitioners of contrastive analysis would go along with this version of the contrastive analysis hypothesis. In particular, scholars differ on how strongly they wish to claim for interlingual interference the pride of place among error types, and the rather 'simpliste' correlation in Lee's version, between differences in structure and learning difficulty.[5] Nevertheless, some version of this hypothesis, with the qualifications noted above (or similar ones) is assumed by most practitioners of contrastive analysis. (For a detailed discussion of the 'predictive' versus 'explanatory' version of the contrastive analysis hypothesis, see Sections 1.7 and 2.2)

1.3. Contrastive analysis: its pedagogical claims

On the basis of these, or similar assumptions, various claims have been made as to the potential role of contrastive analysis in target language teaching. Hall (1968) asserts that the era of the uniform, standard textbook for all learners of a target language irrespective of their language backgrounds is over; the structure of the textbook—selection of teaching items, degree of emphasis, kinds of practice drills, nature of exposition, etc—should be geared to the native language of the learner: Nickel and Wagner (1968) also make similar claims about the crucial role of contrastive analysis in both 'didactic' (limitation [selection], grading, and exposition) as well as 'methodic' (actual classroom presentation) programming (see Lado, 1957 and Halliday et al, 1964 on this point). It is also claimed (by Lado, 1957) that the results of contrastive analysis provide ideal criteria for selecting testing items (for an opposite view, see Upshur, 1962). It is also generally agreed that basing teaching materials on the results of contrastive studies necessarily entails a more 'mentalistic' technique of teaching—explicit presentations of points of contrast and similarity with the native language, involving an analytical, cognitive activity (Rivers, 1968; Jakobovits, 1969; Stockwell, 1968).

1.4. Contrastive analysis and linguistic models

Since comparison depends on description, there exists an inevitable implicational relationship between contrastive analysis and linguistic theory. Accordingly, the assumptions of contrastive analysis, the delicacy of its comparisons and forms of contrastive statements have changed from time to time, reflecting the changes in linguistic theory. The earlier contrastive studies were conducted in the structural framework, although structural linguistics, with its insistence on describing each language in its own terms, theoretically precluded any comparison across languages. However, characteristic of a practice that has been endemic in contrastive analysis, the theoretical and methodological contradictions did not deter practitioners of contrastive analysis. Taxonomic contrastive analysis displayed the similarities and differences between languages in terms of similarities and differences in (i) the form and (ii) the distribution of comparable units (comparability being based on nothing more spectacular than 'gut feelings').

With the advent of generative grammar, taxonomic contrastive analysis, like taxonomic descriptive linguistics in general, has been criticized for its preoccupation with the surface structure of language (cf Di Pietro, 1968 and 1971). Three aspects of the transformational grammar model have profoundly influenced contrastive analysis: (1) the universal base hypothesis; (2) the deep and surface structure distinction; and (3) the rigorous and explicit description of linguistic phenomena. The universal base hypothesis, it is claimed, provides a sounder theoretical foundation for contrastive analysis as contrasted with the structuralists' relativity hypothesis, for the assumption that all languages are alike at an abstract, underlying level provides, theoretically at least, a basis for comparability.[6] Methodologically, the description of this underlying level of representation in terms of a universal (non-language specific) set of basic grammatical primes, semantic features and phonetic (distinctive) features makes it easier to state similarities and differences in a uniform manner. The explicit incorporation of two levels of linguistic organization makes it possible for the contrastive linguist to capture and represent the intuitions of bilinguals about the translation equivalence of utterances in two languages, although they are disparate on the surface. Finally, the adaptation of mathematical models for the description of natural language phenomena has enabled descriptions to be rigorous and explicit. This in turn has enabled comparisons to be rigorous and explicit as contrasted with, for example, statements such as

> The past definite, or preterite, *je portai* corresponds to the English *I carried* ...

modified by a 'fiction',

> The past indefinite is frequently used for the past definite in colloquial style (cf Halliday *et al*, 1964, p 118).

This is not to say that the use of the transformational grammar model has solved the problem of contrastive analysis; on the contrary, it has made explicit the intricate problems facing contrastive analysis which had not previously been appreciated. Nevertheless, it will not be disputed that the application of the transformational grammar model has made it possible for comparisons and contrasts to be insightful and sophisticated to a degree unimaginable two decades ago.

1.5. Contrastive analysis: the methodology

The prerequisite for any contrastive study is the availability of accurate and explicit description of the languages under comparison. It is also essential that the descriptions be theoretically compatible. Given such descriptions, how does one go about comparing two languages?

1.5.1. Selection. It is generally agreed that attempting to compare two languages in entirety is both impractical and wasteful. An alternative is suggested by the British linguists, who advocate a Firthian 'polysystemic' approach. This approach is based on the assumption that language is a 'system of systems'. Hence comparisons are made in terms of particular systems and subsystems (eg the personal deictic system, the auxiliary verb system, etc) cf Halliday *et al*, 1964; Catford, 1968). While this approach may work in contrasting 'closed systems' such as the determiner system, or even for phonology as a whole, which can be reduced, according to one view, to an 'item by item analysis of segment types', it does not seem to be suited for syntactic comparison, which must handle 'a boundless class of possible sentences' (cf Langacker, 1968).

A second criterion for selection has often been advocated by scholars who consider the role of contrastive analysis to be primarily 'explanatory' and not 'predictive' (see Catford, 1968; Lee, 1968). According to these scholars, contrastive analysis should limit itself to 'partial' comparisons, analyzing those parts of the grammar which are known (through error analysis) to present the greatest difficulty to learners. But such an approach, as Hamp rightly points out, is of limited value—we need contrastive analysis to provide a 'theory adequate to explain cases not in our corpus' (1968, p 146).

A reasonable approach to this problem is taken by Langacker (1968), who suggests that syntactic comparison should cover

> approximately the same ground that the language teacher is called on to deal with explicitly in the classroom. Within this area, common productive processes (such as infinitive embedding, for example) should be compared for the two languages with respect to the rules generating them.

This is essentially the approach adopted by Stockwell *et al* (1965). While Stockwell admits that their approach was 'somewhat tempered by [error-analysis]' (used as a delimitation device in selection), he insists that 'the most useful basis for contrastive analysis is entirely theoretical' (1968, p 25).

1.5.2. Comparability: the problem of equivalence. The discussion in the previous section dealt with the general problem of selection. A much more difficult and crucial problem is that of 'comparability', ie of establishing just what is to be juxtaposed for comparison. Despite the extensive study of various aspects of contrastive analysis, this problem which lies at the heart of contrastive analysis has yet to be satisfactorily resolved. The question can be approached from three points of view, viz those of (i) structural (or formal) equivalence; (ii) 'translation' equivalence; (iii) both structural and translation equivalence. While the most widely used criterion in the literature has been that of *translation equivalence*, the term has been used rather loosely. Harris seemed to work on the assumption that for a given sentence in language A there would be only one 'roughly unique' translation in language B, and proposed to construct a 'transfer' grammar on the basis of the 'minimal grammatical differences' (1954, p 259). Levenston (1965), on the other hand, points out the possibility of multiple translation equivalents (cf also Halliday *et al*, 1964, p 121) and hence advocates constructing 'translation paradigms'—ie tabulation of the various structural configurations by which a given item may be translated, with specification of the contextual restrictions governing the use of each equivalent. Catford, on the other hand, believes that 'the only basis for equating phonemes or for equating grammatical units in two languages is extra-linguistic—is substantial rather than formal' (1968, p 144). For him, the test of translation equivalence is the interchangeability of the items in a given situation (1965, p 49).

Is it possible to formalize the relationship that should hold between constructions that are considered translation equivalents by a 'competent bilingual'? There have been a few attempts to confront this crucial problem. Dingwall (1964) proposed that 'languages are more likely to be similar in their "kernel" than in their total structure, and that which is obligatory in the most valued grammar is more basic than that which is optional', but with the demise of the notion of 'kernel' sentences, his hypothesis has become somewhat outdated. Perhaps the single most influential work on this question is Krzeszowski (1971). This paper, although it does not solve the problem of equivalence, shows how much contrastive analysis has gained in rigor and sophistication from the application of current generative theory. In this paper, Krzeszowski proposed that 'equivalent sentences have identical deep structures even if on the surface they are markedly different' (1971, p 38), 'deep structures' being defined in the sense of Lakoff (1968), in terms of basic grammatical relations, selectional restrictions and co-occurrence relations. While this is probably the closest we have ever come to rigorously defining the notion of 'equivalence', even this formulation is still far from satisfactory, as is apparent from the works discussed below.

Bouton (1975) points out that there are large classes of constructions which are translation equivalents but cannot be derived from a common deep structure (in the sense of Krzeszowski—instances where deep structure parts contain crucial information with regard to notions of stativity, transitivity, tense/aspect, polarity of presupposition, etc—thus calling for either a redefinition of 'deep structure' to include 'contextual' structure or the rejection of Krzeszowski's hypothesis as it stands.

Y Kachru (1976) has shown the limitation of a purely structural notion of equivalence and the relevance of pragmatics and 'conversational implicature' for defining 'equivalence'. Fillmore (1965) had earlier pointed out instances of translation equivalence 'which are constructed along non-analogous (structural) principles' and 'cases where sentences in one language cannot be translated into another language at all' (1965, p 122).

A different approach to defining equivalence is suggested in Sridhar (1979). In his cross-linguistic experimental study of sentence production, Sridhar found that common perceptual stimuli often produced structurally different responses in different languages which, nevertheless, were functionally similar. For example, in describing a scene in which an inanimate object (eg a ball) acts upon an animate, human object (eg a doll), the inherent salience of the latter causes the movement of the object NP to the sentence-initial position, resulting in passives and topicalized sentences in English, but active sentences with object fronting in other languages like Hungarian, Japanese, Kannada, Turkish, etc. This technique, therefore, demonstrates the possibility of establishing functional equivalence across structures in empirical terms.

While discussion, formalization and refinement of the notion of equivalence proceeds on the theoretical plane, the problems involved in this endeavor have not significantly impeded the flow of practical contrastive studies and their application to classroom and text materials. I will now briefly consider the state of the art in practical contrastive analysis.

1.6. The scope of contrastive studies

By 'scope' here I mean the levels of linguistic structure and language use covered by contrastive studies. Even a cursory glance at the extensive bibliographies by Hammer and Rice (1965) and Gage (1961), as well as the volumes of *IRAL, Language Learning* and other journals, reveals that the major emphasis has been on contrasting phonological systems. Also, it is consistent with the structuralist dictum regarding the primacy of speech. However, as Stockwell rightly reminds us, it is time to face up to the fact that 'pronunciation is simply not that important ... Grammar and meaning are at the heart of the matter' (1968, p 22). Despite the 'kiss of life' that syntax has received with the advent of generative grammar, the number of sophisticated studies of contrastive syntax still remains rather small. (Part of the problem may have to do with the rapid change in syntactic theory in the last thirty years that has left the 'applied' linguist constantly trying to catch up with the new developments.) the best full-length studies of contrastive syntax still remain in the volumes produced under *The contrastive structure series* of the Center for Applied Linguistics, Washington, DC. The area of vocabulary has hardly been touched at all. One of the notable exceptions is Oksaar

(1972), In that work, Oksaar reports on research using the semantic differential technique (Osgood, Hofstatter) in order to measure intra- and interlingual differences (German–Swedish) in the area of connotative meaning. Taking certain operational terms to demonstrate the approach, she comes to the following conclusion: the 'competing' terms differ from each other in the two languages; and interferences are likely on the non-denotative meaning level of the second language, the source of which lies in the influence of the mother tongue. The extensive work done in bilingual lexicography has not been, as Gleason correctly points out, 'deeply theory-informed work' (1968, p 40). The huge area of usage still remains practically unchartered, and in the absence of a viable theory, the best that can be done in this area is, in the words of Stockwell, 'listing with insight'. Lado (1957) strongly advocated the need to include comparison of cultures as an integral part of contrastive linguistics, yet his example does not seem to have been pursued seriously. Thus the picture of contrastive studies today is rather lopsided—leaning heavily on the side of phonology, moderately inclined to syntax, but (to mix metaphors) leaving entire flanks of lexicography, semantics and usage almost completely exposed.

1.7. Critics of contrastive analysis

For convenience of discussion, we may consider the major criticisms of contrastive analysis under two heads: (i) criticism of the predictions made by contrastive analysis and (ii) criticism of the theoretical basis of contrastive analysis.

Critics of contrastive analysis have argued that since native language interference is only one of the sources of error, indulging in contrastive analysis with a view to predicting difficulties is not worth the time spent on it; moreover, they argue, many of the difficulties predicted by contrastive analysis do not show up in the actual learner performance at all; on the other hand, many errors that do turn up are not predicted by contrastive analysis. In the light of this, they suggest, the only version of contrastive analysis that has any validity at all is the *a posteriori* version, ie the role of contrastive analysis should be explanatory, restricted to the recurrent problem areas as revealed by error analysis, rather than the *a priori* or predictive version (see Whitman and Jackson, 1972; Gradman, 1971; Lee, 1968; Ritchie, 1971, among others).

These, and some other criticisms of contrastive analysis, have been, in my opinion, ably answered in James (1971). Suffice it here to say that the proponents of the strong version of contrastive analysis are the first to concede that contrastive analysis does not account for *all* errors; they never claimed that it did (see the caveats in Section 1.2). Secondly, the non-occurrence of error does not necessarily invalidate the prediction—on the other hand, it may confirm it in that it provides evidence that the student is avoiding the use of problematic structures (cf Corder, 1973; Schachter, 1964; Celce-Murcia, 1978). Contrastive analysis cannot merely be a subcomponent of error analysis because, for one thing, what we need is not only a taxonomic classification of a corpus of date but a corpus-free theory of errors and, for another, 'predictive' contrastive analysis brings to light areas of difficulty not even noticed by error analysis (cf Schachter, 1974). Moreover, the failure of the predictions of contrastive analysis in particular instances does not necessarily invalidate the theory itself—a distinction often lost sight of by the extremist critics of contrastive analysis. All that it shows is that we need a more precise characterization of what type of, and under what conditions, prior linguistic knowledge is made use of (see Wode, 1978 for an attempt to define this in structural terms). After all, there have been scores of instances in the published literature of the last decade where the predictions of contrastive analysis have been borne out by empirical results (see, for example, Duškova, 1969; Schachter, 1974; Bieritz, 1974 among others). George (1972) estimates that approximately one-third of all errors made by target language learners can be traced to native language interference. Therefore, as Stockwell (1968) says, as long as one of the variables that contributes to success or failure in language learning is the conflict between linguistic systems, contrastive analysis has a place in target language methodology. The critics of contrastive analysis have not conclusively proved this is not so. If anything, recent developments in the theory and methodology of error analysis and Interlanguage have explicitly incorporated the assumptions and methodology of contrastive analysis in their models (see Section 2.3.4). Saying that contrastive analysis should be only one component among others of target language methodology is not a criticism of contrastive analysis *per se*—after all, it was meant to be exactly that. Those who have attempted to 'put contrastive analysis in its place' may have revealed their own insecurity.

The second type of criticism seeks to show that given its theoretical and methodological assumptions, contrastive analysis is *in principle* incapable of accounting for learner behavior. For instance, Newmark and Reibel (1968) contend that interference is an otiose idea and that ignorance is the real cause of errors. Dulay and Burt (1972), among others, accuse contrastive analysis of being based on the behaviorist conditioning principle, which has now fallen on evil days. Dickerson (1974) says that contrastive analysis, by denying the 'variability' (ie presence of a wide assortment of pronunciations) and the 'systematicity' characteristic of the learner's output, is necessarily forced to predict 'categorical' (ie non-variable) performance, which does not exist.

The argument of Newmark and Reibel (1968) has been answered by James (1971) and I shall not go into it here. As for the second criticism, despite the authors' dismissal of Corder's argument, I think Corder (1967) is essentially correct in claiming that contrastive analysis is not incompatible with the generativists' view of language learning as a hypothesis testing process. Only with this view the psychological basis of 'interference' would shift to something more like that of transfer of training, in that the learner may be said to select his experience with the learning of his native language as one of the initial hypotheses (or 'processing strategies') to be tested in the course of learning a target language. As for the third criticism (Dickerson, 1974), it must be granted that this is one of the most serious criticisms leveled against contrastive analysis and calls for a deliberate response. At this point, I shall content myself with a few observations. There is nothing in the contrastive analysis hypothesis that denies the learner's language systematicity: in fact, the very premise of predictability is the systematicity of the learner's performance. The presence of elements other than those due to interlingual interference is, though correct, not a criticism of contrastive analysis *per se*. On the question of 'variability', it is true that none of the current models of contrastive analysis incorporates this feature. After all, variability still remains a challenge to descriptive linguistics as well, and contrastive analysis can only be as good as the description on which it is based. Certainly variability must be accounted for in synchronic description as well as contrastive analysis. Selinker's impressionistic observations on the emergence of 'fossilized' elements in the learner's language under certain circumstances is the first step toward recognition and exploration of this important aspect (cf Selinker, 1972). Krashen's (1976, 1978) 'monitor' model target language performance is another. I submit that by treating unsuppressed or unmonitored access to native language patterns as one of the 'variables' responsible for the 'variability' of target language performance, we can reconcile contrastive analysis with the variability model. Models of contrastive analysis in the past have shown considerable resilience, and claims such as that variability analysis is the 'Waterloo of contrastive analysis' seem to be a bit premature at this point.

2.0. Error analysis

2.1. Traditional error analysis

Of the three areas of study under review, error analysis has probably the longest tradition. Yet, until recently a typical error analysis went little beyond impressionistic collections of 'common' errors and their taxonomic classification into categories (mistakes of agreement, omission of articles, etc). Little attempt was made either to define 'error' in a formally rigorous and pedagogically insightful way or to systematically account for the occurrence of errors either in linguistic or psychological terms. Hence it is substantially correct to say that traditional error analysis was an *ad hoc* attempt to deal with the practical needs of the classroom teacher.

2.1.1. The goals of traditional error analysis. The goals of traditional error analysis were purely pragmatic—error analysis was conceived and performed for its 'feedback' value in designing pedagogical materials and strategies. It was believed that error analysis, by identifying the areas of difficulty for the learner, could help in (i) determining the sequence of presentation of target items in textbook and classroom, with the difficult items following the easier ones; (ii) deciding the relative degree of emphasis, explanation and practice required in putting across various items in the target language; (iii) devising remedial lessons and exercises; and finally, (iv) selecting items for testing the learner's proficiency. The 'applied' emphasis in this approach to error is obvious.

2.1.2. The methodology. The methodology of error analysis, in so far as traditional error analysis can be said to have followed a uniform method at all, consisted of the following steps:

1. Collection of data (either from a 'free' composition by students on a given theme or from examination answers);
2. identification of errors (labelling, with varying degrees of precision depending on the linguistic sophistication brought to bear on the task, with respect to the exact nature of the deviation, eg dangling preposition, anomalous sequence of tenses, etc);
3. classification into error types (eg errors of agreement, articles, verb forms, etc;
4. statement of relative frequency of error types;
5. identification of the areas of difficulty in the target language;
6. therapy (remedial drills, lessons, etc).

While the above methodology is roughly representative of the majority of error analyses in the traditional framework, the more sophisticated investigations (for example, Rossipal, 1971; Duškova, 1969) went further, to include one or both of the following:

1. Analysis of the source of errors (eg mother tongue interference, over-generalization, inconsistencies in the spelling system of the target language, etc);
2. determination of the degree of disturbance caused by the error (or the seriousness of the error in terms of communication, norm, etc).

Notice that the inclusion of the two tasks just mentioned brings with it the possibility of making error analysis broadbased and of evolving a theory of errors. This possibility, however, has only recently begun to be explored.

2.2. Resurgence of interest in error analysis

It was with the advent of contrastive analysis and its claim to predict and explain (some major types of) errors that serious interest began to be taken in error analysis. Although in the beginning contrastive analysis, with its relatively sophisticated linguistic apparatus and the strong claim to predict a majority of errors in target language learning, seemed to condemn error analysis to obsolescence, as the claims of contrastive analysis came to be tested against empirical data, scholars realized that there were many kinds of errors besides those due to interlingual interference that could neither be predicted nor explained by contrastive analysis. This led to renewed interest in the possibilities of error analysis. The claim for using error analysis as a primary pedagogical tool was based on three arguments: (1) error analysis does not suffer from the inherent limitations of contrastive analysis—restriction to errors caused by interlingual transfer: error analysis brings to light many other types of errors frequently made by learners, for example, *intralanguage* errors arising from the particular teaching and learning strategy employed (cf Richards, 1971a). (2) error analysis, unlike contrastive analysis, provides data on actual, attested problems and not hypothetical problems and therefore forms a more efficient and economical basis for designing pedagogical strategies (Lee, 1968). Error analysis is not confronted with the complex theoretical problems encountered by contrastive analysis (eg the problem of equivalence) (Wardhaugh, 1970).

Based on arguments such as these, some scholars (eg Wilkins, 1968) have argued that there is no necessity for a prior comparison of grammars and that an error-based analysis is 'equally satisfactory, more fruitful, and less time consuming' (p 102). The experimental evidence, the little that there is, however, does not support such an extreme position. The investigations in Duškova (1969), Banathy and Madarasz (1969), Richards (1971b), Schachter (1974), and Celce-Murcia (1978), among others, reveal that just as there are errors that are not handled by contrastive analysis, there are those that do not surface in error analysis, and that error analysis has its role as a testing ground for the predictions of contrastive analysis as well as to supplement its results.

2.3. The reorientation of error analysis

At the same time that the extended domain of error analysis *vis-à-vis* contrastive analysis came to be appreciated, a development took place, largely as a result of the insights of British linguists and those influenced by them (Corder, 1967, 1971a, 1971b, 1973, 1974; Strevens, 1970; Selinker, 1969, 1972; Richards, 1971a, 1971b, 1973) which has not only revolutionized the whole concept of error analysis, but also opened up an exciting area of research commonly referred to as Interlanguage. Although in the current literature the distinction between error analysis and Interlanguage is not always clear, we will, for the purpose of this paper, study the developments in two parts—those directly relevant to the theory and practice of error analysis in this part and those having to do with Interlanguage in the next.

2.3.1. On the notion of 'error.' Pit Corder, in his influential paper (1967), suggested a new way of looking at the errors made by the learner of a target language. He justified the proposed revision in viewpoint on the basis of the 'substantial similarities between the strategies employed by the infant learning his native language and those of the second language learner'. The notion of 'error', he argued, is a function of the traditional practice to take a teacher-centered viewpoint of the learner's performance and to judge the latter in terms of the norms of the target language. From the perspective of the language learner, the observed deviations are no more 'errors' than the first approximations of a child learning his mother tongue are errors. Like the child struggling to acquire his language, the second-language learner is also trying out successive hypotheses about the nature of the target language, and from this viewpoint, the learner's 'errors' (or hypotheses) are not only inevitable but are a necessary part of the language-learning process.

2.2.3. Errors versus mistakes. At this point, Corder introduces an important distinction between 'errors' and 'mistakes'. Mistakes are deviations due to *performance* factors such as memory limitations (eg mistakes in the sequence of tenses and agreement in long sentences), spelling pronunciations, fatigue, emotional strain, etc. They are typically random and are readily corrected by the learner when his attention is drawn to them. Errors, on the other hand, are systematic, consistent deviances characteristic of the learner's linguistic system at a given stage of learning. 'The key point', he asserts, is that the learner is using a definite system of language at every point in his development, although it is not...that of the second language.... The learner's errors are evidence of this system and are themselves systematic (1967, p 166).

Corder proposed the term 'transitional competence' to refer to the intermediate systems constructed by the learner in the process of his language learning.

2.3.3. The goals of error analysis. Given this redefinition of the notion of error, it follows that the goals of error analysis as conceived previously also need to be redefined. In a subsequent paper (1971b), Corder makes a distinction between the theoretical and applied goals of error analysis. Error analysis has too often, he argues, concerned itself exclusively with the 'applied' goal of correcting and eradicating the learner's errors at the expense of the more important and logically prior task of evolving an explanatory theory of learner's performance. The study of the systematic errors made by the learners of a target language yields valuable insights into the nature of language-learning strategies and hypotheses employed by learners and the nature of the intermediate 'functional communicative systems' or languages constructed by them. Thus the theoretical aspect of error analysis is as worthy of study in and of itself as is that of child language acquisition and can, in turn, provide insights into the process of language acquisition in general.

2.3.4. The data and method of error analysis. We have already noted Corder's distinction between 'mistakes' and 'errors'. Corder proceeds to point out that not all errors are overtly observable, ie the traditional reliance on obvious observable deviations in the learner's productive use of the target language is not a reliable procedure for data-collection purposes. The 'covertly erroneous' utterances, ie utterances that are superficially well formed and acceptable, but produced by a set of rules different from those of the target language (eg 'I want to know the English' in the sense of 'I want to learn English') should also be considered part of the data for error analysis. Learner's performance may also be right 'by chance', ie due to holophrastic learning or systematic avoidance of problem structures. All this goes to show that the learner's errors—overt or covert—'are not properly to be regarded as right or wrong *in themselves* but only as evidence of a right or wrong system' (Corder, 1973, p 274). Hence, the object of error analysis is to describe the whole of the learner's linguistic system and to compare it with that of the target language. That is why error analysis is 'a brand of comparative linguistic study' (Corder, 1973, p 274).

As Corder correctly observes, the crucial element in describing the learner's system is the correct interpretation of the learner's utterance. This is to be done, he says by reconstructing the correct utterance of the target language, matching the 'erroneous' utterance with its equivalent in the learner's native language. If this can be done by asking the learner to express his intentions in the mother tongue (the translation guaranteeing its appropriateness), then it is an *authoritative* reconstruction. If the learner is not available for consultation, and the investigator has to rely on his knowledge of the learner's system, his intentions, etc then it can only be called *plausible* reconstruction (Corder, 1973, p 274).

On the basis of these data, the investigator can reconstruct the learner's linguistic system. This is to be complemented with a psychological explanation in terms of the learner's strategies and the process of learning (see Section 2.3).

2.4. Is the notion of error obsolescent?

The proposed change in the attitude toward the learner's deviant utterances raises several important questions from the pedagogical point of view. Since the assumptions underlying the current approach to error analysis and Interlanguage are identical, I shall postpone discussion of these questions until after we have examined the concept of Interlanguage in more detail. In this section, I shall merely point out some of the issues that need to be clarified in the new framework of error analysis.

For one thing, we need criteria to distinguish between *productive*, systematic deviations and non-productive deviations in the learner's performance in order to make learning more efficient. Secondly, we need criteria to determine the seriousness of 'errors' in terms of the degree of disturbance to effective communication (intelligibility, etc) caused by them. Thirdly, we need to reexamine the notion of errors in the context of second-language teaching, especially in those settings where the primary object of learning a second language is not so much to communicate with the native speakers of that language, but for 'internal' purposes, and where full-fledged, functionally adequate non-native varieties of a target language are in wide use (for example, English in India; see B Kachru, 1976). It is only when we have clarified these issues that error analysis will have a pedagogically useful role to play. We shall take up these questions again in Section 3.6.

3.0. Interlanguage

The successive linguistic systems that a learner constructs on his way to the mastery of a target language have been variously referred to as 'idiosyncratic dialects' (Corder, 1971a), 'approximative systems' (Nemser, 1971a) and 'interlanguages' (Selinker, 1969). The term 'Interlanguage' is becoming established in the current literature on the subject, possibly because it is neutral as to the directionality of attitude—the other two terms imply a target language-centered perspective.

The term Interlanguage seems to be appropriate also for the following reasons: (1) it captures the indeterminate status of the learner's system between his native language and the target language; (2) it represents the 'atypical rapidity' with which the learner's language changes, or its instability; (3) focussing on the term 'language', it explicitly recognizes the rule-governed, systematic nature of the learner's performance and its adequacy as a functional communicative system (from the learner's point of view, at least).

The single most important influence on the study of Interlanguage phenomena has been the findings of the (post-structuralist) studies of child language acquisition (see Cook, 1969, 1973). In a sense, the progression from traditional error analysis to the concept of Interlanguage may be said to parallel the shift from the 'telegraphic speech' model of child language to the recent study of the stages of child language acquisition in *sui generis* terms. The earlier model treated the child's speech as a truncated, 'telegraphic' version of adult language and proceeded to derive the child's utterances by means of deletion rules operating on the adult system, just as error analysis looked upon the second-language learner's performance as 'inadequate approximations of the target language norm'. Recent studies in child language acquisition (cf Brown, 1973) have recognized the absurdity of describing the child as possessing all the rules of the adult language together with a suspiciously large number of deletion rules. The current approach treats child language learning as a progression of self-contained, internally structured systems, getting increasingly similar to the adult language system. This was essentially the approach advocated as early as 1941 by Jakobson.[7] The parallelism between this change of approach in developmental psycholinguistics and the change from traditional error analysis to the concept of Interlanguage is obvious.

3.1. Interlanguage: assumptions

Defining an 'approximative system' (L_a) as a 'deviant linguistic system actually employed by the learner attempting to utilize the target language', Nemser (1971a) states the assumptions underlying the concept of L_a's:

> ... Our assumption is three-fold: (1) Learner's speech at a given time is the patterned product of a linguistic system, L_a, distinct from learner's speech and learner's target [the source and the target language] and internally structured. (2) L_a's at successive stages of learning form an evolving series $L_a i ... n$, the earliest occurring when a learner first attempts to use LT, the most advanced at the closest approach to learner's target ... (3) In a given contact situation, the L_a's of learners at the same stage of proficiency roughly coincide, with major variations ascribable to differences in learning experience (p 116).

Similar views are put forth by Corder (1967, 1971a), Selinker (1969, 1972) and Richards (1971b, 1973).

3.2. Toward an explanatory theory of Interlanguage

Selinker (1972) has proposed a theoretical framework to account for Interlanguage phenomena in second-language learning. According to Selinker, the most crucial fact that any description of Interlanguage must account for is the phenomenon of fossilization.

Fossilizable linguistic phenomena are linguistic items, rules, and subsystems which speakers of a particular native language will tend to keep in their Interlanguage relative to a particular target language, no matter what the age of the learner or amount of explanation or instruction he receives in the target language (p 215).

In order to account for this phenomenon, Selinker posits the existence of a genetically determined *latent psychological structure* (different from Lenneberg's 'latent linguistic structure') 'which is activated whenever an adult attempts to produce meanings, which he may have, in a second language he is learning' (p 229). This latent psychological structure contains five central processes (language transfer, transfer of training, strategies of second-language learning, strategies of second-language communication and overgeneralization of target language linguistic material) and a few minor ones (eg hypercorrection, spelling pronunciation, cognate pronunciation, holophrase learning, etc). Each process, he suggests, 'forces fossilizable material upon surface Interlanguage utterances, controlling to a very large extent the surface structures of these sentences' (p 217). It follows from this that 'each of the analyst's predictions as to the shape of Interlanguage utterances should be associated with one or more of these ... processes' (p 215).

Before proceeding to consider the suggested methodology for describing Interlanguages in terms of the processes listed above, it may be fruitful to clarify some of the terms used to refer to the processes. 'Language transfer' is, of course, self-explanatory. So is 'over-generalization' (eg 'What did he intended to say?'). 'Transfer of training' is different from either of these, and refers to cases such as the one where Serbo-Croatians find it hard to use the he/she distinction in English correctly, due to the presentation of drills in textbooks and classroom exclusively with *he* and never with *she*. An example of a 'second-language learning strategy' would be the tendency to reduce the target language to a simpler system (eg omission of function words, plural markers, etc). 'Second-language communication strategy' would be the tendency to stop learning once the learner feels he has attained a 'functional competence' in the target language, or that certain elements in the target language are not crucial for effective communication.

3.3. Methodology for studying Interlanguage systems

Both Selinker (1972) and Corder (1971b, 1974) agree that since Interlanguages are internally patterned autonomous systems, the data for Interlanguage should be based on sources other than those used in conventional error analysis. Selinker argues that

> the only observable data from meaningful performance in controlled situations (as opposed to classroom drills and experiments with nonsense material) we can establish as relevant for interlingual identification are (1) utterances in the learner's native language produced by the learner; (2) Interlanguage utterances produced by the learner; and (3) target languages utterances by the native speakers of that target language (p 214).

As opposed to Selinker who feels that 'the analyst in the interlingual domain cannot rely on intuitive grammatical judgments since he will gain information about another system ... ie, the target language' (pp 213, 219), Corder (1974) does not consider this a drawback, because the judgments of the learner will give crucial information on what he *thinks* is the norm of the target language, thus (unconsciously) revealing his own Interlanguage system.

3.4. Interlanguage: the empirical evidence

Nemser (1971a) provides some arguments for the structural independence of Interlanguage from the native language and target language systems. Based on his study of the acquisition of English phonology by Hungarian learners (Nemser, 1971b), he points out that the learner's Interlanguage (i) exhibits frequent and systematic occurrence of elements not attributable to either the learner's native or target language; (ii) constitutes a system exhibiting true internal coherence when studied in *sui generis* terms. Supporting his second assumption (with regard to the evolutionary stages, Nemser notes that the amount and type of deviation in the successive stages of language learning varies systematically, the earlier stages being characterized by syncretism (under-differentiation), while the later stages are marked by processes of reinterpretation, hypercorrection, etc. In order to account for the systematicity of deviant forms (or their 'fossilization' at a given stage), Nemser posits the play of two forces:

demands of *communication* force the establishment of phonological, grammatical and lexical categories, and the demands of *economy* force the imposition of the balance and order of the linguistic system. Richards (1971a, 1971b), extrapolating from the results of error analysis in various second-language learning situations, shows that many of the 'deviant' forms produced by learners can be accounted for in terms of one or more of the processes posited by Selinker.

The acid test for the Interlanguage hypothesis would be, of course, longitudinal studies of second-language learning. This task is made extremely complicated by what has earlier been referred to as the instability of the learner's Interlanguage. In this difficult area of research, one of the most rigorous studies to have appeared to date is Dickerson (1974).

In her study of the acquisition of selected consonant sounds of English by a group of Japanese learners, Dickerson demonstrates that the learner's output at every stage is both *systematic* and *variable*, the variability being a function of the internal linguistic environment of the sounds as well as the external style stratification (eg in-class versus out-of-class contexts). Dickerson's use of the Labovian variability model to the study of target language acquisition is significant for at least two reasons: (i) methodologically, it is ideally suited for the study of manifestly *unstable* language phenomena such as learners' intermediate systems; and (ii) theoretically, it provides a more plausible explanatory account of the so-called backsliding to Interlanguage norms noted by Selinker, Krashen, and many others in the performance of language learners (cf Section 1.7).

It is obvious that the studies reported above seem to provide at best partial evidence for the Interlanguage hypothesis. What the study of Interlanguage needs is empirical evidence validating each of the psychological constructs posited by Selinker. This task is impeded at present by the lack of a rigorous discovery procedure that can unambiguously identify whether a given utterance in the learner's Interlanguage is produced by the operation of one process as against another. As long as we lack such procedures, the greater explanatory power claimed for Interlanguage will remain no more explanatory than that of the much maligned lists of errors organized into error types.

3.5. Interlanguage in relation to contrastive analysis and error analysis

At this point, we may pause to consider in what respects, if any, the theory and methodology of Interlanguage differ from those of the two other approaches to learner's performance discussed in this paper, and to try to assess whether this difference actually amounts to an improvement.

The most obvious difference, of course, is in the attitude toward learner's performance, especially toward the 'errors'. While contrastive analysis *per se* does not take any position on this issue, traditional error analysis considers errors to be harmful and seeks to eradicate them; in the framework of Interlanguage, the deviations from the target language norms are treated as exponents of the learner's system.

Secondly—and perhaps this is the most important difference—while contrastive analysis is concerned exclusively with that aspect of the learner's performance which can be correlated with the characteristics of his native language, Interlanguage avoids this limitation. Native language interference is only one of the explanatory tools in the repertoire of the Interlanguage investigator. Thus Interlanguage is explanatorily more powerful inasmuch as it includes the explanatory power of contrastive analysis and extends beyond it.

Methodologically, Interlanguage may be said to incorporate the assumptions of both contrastive analysis and error analysis. While contrastive analysis contrasts the learner's native language and the target language, and conventional error analysis involves contrast between the learner's performance and the target language, Interlanguage takes all three systems into account, explicitly incorporating the contrastive analysis of the learner's Interlanguage with both his native language and the target language. The difference is that, in Interlanguage, the contrastive analysis is an initial filtering device, making way for the testing of hypotheses about the other determinants of the learner's language.

3.6. Pedagogical implications

It is perhaps too early to expect concrete suggestions for practical classroom teaching and preparation of materials based on the assumptions of the new approach to error analysis and the study of Interlanguage. Yet one may wish to at least speculate on the possible pedagogical implications of the recent studies, if only to generate controversy.

A major outcome of the application of Interlanguage studies to target language pedagogy would be a radical change in the teacher's attitude toward the learner's performance (cf Corder, 1967; Cook, 1969; Richards, 1971a). In particular, the teacher should give up the unreasonable expectation of target language performance from the learner from the very start. Instead, as Dickerson (1974) suggests, he is asked to 'expect variability', to measure the learner's attempts not in terms of the target language versus non-target language opposition, but in terms of the 'proportion of target language on non-target language variants' in the learner's performance in a given stylistic/sociolinguistic situation. From this it follows that the so-called backsliding to the Interlanguage norm does not indicate regression but a natural sensitivity to style difference. This in turn suggests that the traditional monolithic format of proficiency tests should give way to a more flexible, multi-factor format sampling learner performance in various styles and structural environments.

A similar change in viewpoint is also warranted in deciding on the model of instruction (and consequently the norms of correctness) in those second language (or dialect) learning contexts where indigenous non-native varieties of a target language or 'non-standard' native varieties of the target language are in wide use. English in India and West Africa, and Black English in the US are cases in point. While the systematicity, contextual determination and functional adequacy of these varieties have been recognized for some time now (see B Kachru, 1966; Labov, 1969, among others), the pedagogical problems posed by them are only recently being appreciated. Richards (1972) suggests that these varieties are properly to be regarded as Interlanguages which have developed as a result of the particular social contexts of their learning and use. In these contexts, he suggests, we need to distinguish not only between 'errors' versus 'non-errors' but also between 'errors' and 'deviations', in the sense of Kachru (1966). According to Kachru, 'deviations' are explainable in terms of the sociocultural context in which English functions in India, while 'errors' are breaches of the linguistic code of English. Richards (1972) points out the relevance of this distinction in second/foreign language teaching: 'in the foreign language setting', he observes, 'all differences between the learner's use of English and overseas English are *mistakes* (= errors) or signs of incomplete learning' (p 182); there is no scope for 'deviations' here, whereas in a second-language setting *deviations* (in the sense just defined) are 'reflections of interlingual creativity' (p 181). Given this distinction, it follows that questions of instructional model, etc, are to be decided keeping in mind the pragmatics of language use in such contexts (cf B Kachru, 1976). If the target language is to be used primarily for communicating with other members of the interlingual community and only very marginally for communicating with the native speakers of the target language, one wonders if the enormous time, effort and resources expended on polishing the *t*'s, *d*'s, *θ*'s and *ð*'s of the learners is justified. Thus the notion of 'error' in such learning contexts needs a redefinition.

This does not mean that teachers are asked to abandon comparison of the learner's language with the norms of the target language altogether and replace the notion of error with that of Interlanguage. On the contrary, as Zyatiss (1974) remarks, a pedagogically oriented description of the learner's language is 'always *contrastive* and eventually *evaluative*' (p 234). This viewpoint is shared by Richards (1971b), who agrees that we still need the notion of 'errors', and to 'correct' them

> simply because speech is linked to attitudes and social structure. Deviancy from grammatical or phonological norms of a speech community elicits evaluational reactions that may classify a person unfavorably (p. 21).

To sum up some of the problems raised in this section and in Section 2.4, if the proposed reorientation in the perspective toward learner's errors is to be pedagogically useful, we need to clarify the following: (i) the criteria to distinguish between errors which are productive hypotheses and errors resulting from false generalizations; (ii) the methodology to clearly identify the sources of errors in terms of the processes outlined in Section 3.2; (iii) a hierarchy of types of errors in terms of their disturbance to effective communication and attitudinal reactions; and finally, (iv) the notion of 'error' versus acceptable 'deviations' in second-language learning contexts.

4.0. Conclusion

In the course of this paper, I have attempted to show that contrastive analysis, error analysis and Interlanguage may be looked upon as three evolutionary phases in the attempt to understand and explain the nature of the target language learner's performance. This 'evolution' may be said to involve an extension of perspective in many ways—in the attitude toward the learner's 'errors', in the explanatory hypotheses regarding the source(s) of the 'errors', in the data considered relevant for study and in the suggested methodology. In other words, the approach toward the learner's performance has become more broadbased in trying to come up with an explanatory account of why the target language learner speaks and writes the way he does. Perhaps the most significant outcome of the research into target language acquisition over the last decade or so is the recognition of the similarities with first-language acquisition, both in strategies (eg, overgeneralization) and developmental sequences (eg in the order of acquisition of grammatical morphemes, cf Brown, 1973). Thus target language acquisition is viewed as a process of 'creative construction' (Dulay and Burt, 1976). However, this recognition of creativity is somehow felt to be inconsistent with the notion of interference. Thus one sees a tendency in the current literature to downplay the role of first-language interference, and an overeagerness to explain away what seem to be patently interference errors in terms of some other strategy felt to be more respectable or consistent with the view of the target language, learner as an active experimenter with language.

Yet, as I have tried to show earlier, creativity and transfer are not at all incompatible with each other, and to suggest that transfer theory necessarily presupposes a 'conditioning' model of learning betrays a naïve understanding of both transfer and creativity. After all, child language acquisition research is full of instances of transfer—for, what else is 'overgeneralization', the single most important strategy in language learning, if not the transfer of hypotheses formed on the basis of previous experience to new situations? The target language learner's errors arising from first-language interference are no more instances of conditioning than are the child's over-regularizations. If the latter can be touted as instances of creative construction, as indeed they have been, there seems to be no reason why the same explanation could not be given of the former.

What this implies, therefore, is not that the contrastive analysis approach should be thrown overboard, but that more rigorous research is needed to identify the precise conditions under which the trade language learner utilizes the hypotheses developed on the basis of his experience with the first language. Consequently, while one readily grants that an explanatory account of target language learner's performance must include other components besides inter-lingual interference, contrastive analysis still remains the most rigorously worked-out component of the theory. The next few years will probably see a flurry of proposals for the study of the other major processes claimed to influence the target language learner's performance.

Notes

1. I am grateful to Professor Braj Kachru and Yamuna Kachru for their suggestions on an earlier version of this paper.
2. See, for example, the following: George Whitworth (1907). *Indian English: An examination of the errors made by Indians in writing English.* Letchworth: Herts; T L M Pearse-Smith (1934) *English errors in Indian schools.* London: Oxford University Press; F Q French (1949) *Common errors in English.* London: Oxford University Press.
3. The possibility of evolving a scientific theory of translation that could, in turn, be used in machine translation has been one of the additional motivations for pursuing contrastive analysis (see Catford, 1965).
4. Cf Sweet (1899): 'There is another class of difficulties which may be regarded as partly external, partly internal—those which depend on the relations of the foreign language to the learner's native language, especially as regards similarity in vocabulary and structure' (pp 53–54 in the 1964 edition). Sweet warned against the formation of wrong 'cross-associations' across seemingly similar items in 'closely allied languages'. Jespersen recognized native language interference, but advocated comparative analysis only as an 'interesting' adjunct to the main task of teaching the target language. 'Comparisons between the languages which the pupils know, for the purpose of showing their differences of economy in the use of linguistic means

of expression ... may often become very interesting, especially for advanced students.... The teacher may call attention to the inconsistency of the languages; what is distinctly expressed in one case is in another case not designated by any outward sign (haus:häuser ... sheep:sheep)' (Jespersen, 1904, p 135). H E Palmer deals at some length with the 'illegitimate' substitutions made by English learners in speaking French—in phonology, lexis and grammar. He also recognizes cases of positive transfer. However, he sternly warns against 'the temptation to replace habit-forming by analysis and synthesis of problem items' (Palmer, 1964, p 58).

5. This view seems to derive from Lado (1957, p 2): 'Those elements that are similar to his native language will be simpler for him, and those elements that are different will be difficult.'

6. Boulton (1976) points out that the universal base hypothesis and the notion of equivalence in the sense of Krzeszowski are not strictly compatible.

7. See Jakobson (1941). In the words of Ferguson (1968); '... Jakobson made clear the notion that a child's language is always a coherent system [although with more marginal features and fluctuation than adult language] and that the development of a child's language may profitably be regarded as a succession of stages, just as the history of a language may be.'

References

Alatis, James E (ed) (1968) 'Contrastive linguistics and its pedagogical implications'. Monograph series on languages and linguistics, no. 21. Washington, DC: Georgetown University.

Banathy, B H and Madarasz, P H (1969) 'Contrastive analysis and error analysis.' Journal of English as a second language 4, 77–92.

Bieritz, W D (1974) 'Phonologische Interferenzen—Französiche Aussprachefehler deutscher Studenten.' IRAL 12, 193–230.

Brown, Roger (1973) A first language: The early stages. Cambridge, Mass.: Harvard University Press.

Bouton, Lawrence F (1976) 'The problem of equivalence in contrastive analysis.' IRAL 14, 143–163.

Carroll, John B (1968) 'Contrastive linguistics and interference theory.' In Alatis (1968) 113–122.

Catford, J C (1965) A linguistic theory of translation. London: Oxford University Press.

Catford, J C (1968) 'Contrastive analysis and language teaching'. In Alatis (1968).

Celce-Murcia, Marianne (1978) 'The simultaneous acquisition of English and French in a two-year-old child.' In Hatch (1978) 38–53.

Cook, Vivian J (1969) 'The analogy between first and second language learning.' IRAL 7, 207–216.

238   S N Sridhar

Cook, Vivian J (1973) 'The comparison of language development in native children and foreign adults.' *IRAL* 11, 13–28.

Corder, Stephen Pit (1967) 'The significance of learner's errors.' *IRAL* 5, 161–170.

Corder, Stephen Pit (1971a) 'Idiosyncratic dialects and error analysis'. *IRAL* 9, 147–159.

Corder, Stephen Pit (1971b) 'Describing the language learner's language'. *CILT* reports and papers 6, 57–64.

Corder, Stephen Pit (1973) *Introducing applied linguistics.* Harmondsworth: Penguin.

Corder, Stephen Pit (1974) 'The elicitation of interlanguage.' *IRAL* (Special issue on the occasion of B Malmberg's 60th birthday, edited by G Nickel), 51–63.

Dickerson, Lonna J (1974) *Internal and external patterning of phonological variability in the speech of Japanese learners of English: Toward a theory of second language acquisition.* PhD dissertation. Urbana-Champaign: University of Illinois.

Dingwall, William O (1964) 'Transformational generative grammar and contrastive analysis.' *Language learning* 14, 147–160.

Di Pietro, Robert (1968) 'Contrastive analysis and notions of deep and surface grammar.' In Alatis (1968) 65–80.

Di Pietro, Robert (1971) *Language structures in contrast.* Rowley, Mass.: Newbury House.

Dulay, Heidi C and Burt, Marina K (1972) 'Goofing: An indicator of children's second language learning strategies.' *Language learning* 22, 235–252.

Dulay, Heidi C and Burt, Marina K (1976) 'Creative construction in second language teaching and learning.' In Brown, H Dr (ed) (1976) *Papers in second language acquisition.* Ann Arbor: University of Michigan.

Duškova, L (1969) 'On the sources of errors in foreign language learning.' *IRAL* 7, 11–30.

Ferguson, Charles A (1968) 'Contrastive analysis and language development'. In Alatis (1968), 101–112.

Fillmore, Charles J (1965) 'On the notion of "equivalent sentence structure".' The Ohio State University project on linguistic analysis. Report 11.

Fries, Charles C (1945) *Teaching and learning English as a foreign language.* Ann Arbor: University of Michigan Press.

Gage, William W (1961) *Contrastive studies in linguistics. A bibliographical checklist.* Washington, DC: Center for Applied Linguistics.

George, H V (1972) *Common errors in language learning.* Rowley, Mass.: Newbury House.

Gleason, H A, Jr (1968) 'Contrastive analysis and discourse structure.' In Alatis (1968), 39–63.

Gradman, J (1971) 'The limitations of contrastive analysis predictions.' *Working papers in linguistics, University of Hawaii* 3, 73–77.

Hall, Robert A Jr (1968) 'Contrastive grammar and textbook structure.' In Alatis (1968), 175–183.

Halliday, Michael A K, McIntosh, A and Strevens, P (1964) *The linguistic sciences and language teaching.* London: Longmans.

Hammer, John J (in consultation with Rice, F A) (1965) *A bibliography of contrastive linguistics.* Washington, DC: Center for Applied linguistics.

Hamp, Eric P (1968) 'What a contrastive grammar is not, if it is.' In Alatis (1968), 137–147.

Harris, Z S (1954) 'Transfer grammar.' *International journal of American linguistics* 20, 259–270.

Hatch, Evelyn, M (1978) *Second language acquisition.* Rowley, Mass.: Newbury House.

Jackson, Kenneth L (1971) 'The verification and comparison of contrastive analyses.' *Working papers in linguistics, University of Hawaii* 3, no. 4, 201–210.

Jakobovits, Leon A (1969) 'Second language learning and transfer theory.' *Language learning* 19, 55–86.

Jackobson, Roman (1941) *Kindersprache, aphasie und allgemeine lautgesetze.* Uppsala. [English version: 1968. *Child language, aphasia and linguistic theory.* The Hague: Mouton.]

James, Carl. 'The exculpation of contrastive linguistics.' In Nickel (1971a), 53–68.

Jespersen, Otto. 1904. *How to teach a foreign language.* New York: Macmillan.

Kachru, Braj B (1966) 'Indian English: A study in contextualization.' [C C Bazell, *et al* (eds) (1966) *In memory of J R Firth.* London: Longmans.

Kachru, Braj B (1976) 'Models of English for the Third World: White man's linguistic burden or language pragmatics? *TESOL quarterly* 10, 221–239.

Kachru, Yamuna (1976) 'Defining equivalence in contrastive analysis; causative constructions in South Asian Languages.' *The bulletin of the Central Institute of English and Foreign Languages* 12, 1–13.

Krashen, Stephen (1976) 'Monitor theory: A model of adult second language performance'. Paper presented at the USC–UCLA second language acquisition forum.

Krashen, Stephen (1978) 'Individual variation in the use of the monitor.' (1978) W C Ritchie, (ed) *Second language acquisition research: Issues and implications.* New York: Academic Press.

Krzeszowski, Tomasz P (1971) 'Equivalence, congruence and deep structure.' In Nickel (1971a), 37–48.

Labov, William (1969) 'The logic of non-standard English.' *Monograph series on languages and linguistics* no. 22. Washington, DC: Georgetown University.

Lado, Robert (1957) *Linguistics across cultures.* Ann Arbor: University of Michigan Press.

Lakoff, George (1968) 'Instrumental adverbs and the concept of deep structure.' *Foundations of language* 4, 4–27.

Langacker, Ronald W (1968) 'Review of Stockwell *et al*, 1965 and Stockwell and Bowen, 1965.' *Foundations of language* 4, 211–218.

Lee, W R (1968) 'Thoughts of contrastive linguistics in the context of foreign language teaching. In Alatis (1968), 185–194.

Levenson, E A (1965 'The "translation paradigm": A technique for contrastive syntax.' *IRAL* 3, 223–228.

Nemser, William (1971a) 'Approximative systems of foreign language learners.' *IRAL* 9, 115–124.

Nemser, William (1971b) *An experimental study of phonological interference in the English of Hungarians.* (Revision of his 1961 dissertation.) Bloomington: Indiana University Press.

Newmark L and Reibel, D (1968) 'Necessity and sufficiency in language learning.' *IRAL* 6, 145–164.

Nickel, Gerhard (*ed*) (1971a) *Papers in contrastive linguistics* Cambridge: Cambridge University Press.

Nickel, Gerhard (*ed*) (1971b) *Papers from the International Symposium on Applied Contrastive Linguistics.* Bielfield: Cornelsen-Vellagen and Klasing.

Nickel, Gerhard and Wagner, K H (1968) 'Contrastive linguistics and language teaching.' *IRAL* 6, 233–255.

Oksaar, E. 'On contrastive semantics: Experiments with the polarity-profile method.' In Nickel (1971b), 201–211.

Palmer, Harold E (1964) *The principles of language study.* London: Oxford University Press.

Richards, Jack C (1971a) 'A non-contrastive approach to error analysis.' *English language teaching* 25, 204–219.

Richards, Jack C (1971b) 'Error analysis and second language strategies.' *Language sciences* 17, 12–22.

Richards, Jack C (1972) 'Social factors, interlanguage, and language learning.' *Language learning* 17, 159–188.

Ritchie, W C (1967) 'Some implications of generative grammar for the construction of courses in English as a foreign language.' *Language learning* 17, 45–131.

Rivers, Wilga M (1968) 'Contrastive linguistics in textbook and classroom.' In Alatis (1968), 151–154.

Rossipal, H (1971) Om felanalys och om en felanalys av svenskars tysk. Sprakforskning i relation till sprekundervisning. Copenhagen: Nordik Sommeruniversitets Generalsekretariat, *Fiolstraede* 26 (1972) 109–127.

Schachter, Jacquelyn (1974) 'An error in error analysis.' *Language learning* 24, 205–214.

Selinker, Larry F (1969) 'Language transfer.' *General linguistics* 9, 67–92.

Selinker, Larry F (1971) 'A brief reappraisal of contrastive linguistics.' *Working papers in linguistics, University of Hawaii*, 1–10.

Selinker, Larry F (1972) 'Interlanguage.' *IRAL* 10, 209–231.

Sridhar, S N (1980) *Perceptual and cognitive determinants of syntactic structures:*

A cross-linguistic study in sentence production. PhD dissertation. Urbana-Champaign: University of Illinois.

Stockwell, Robert P (1968) 'Contrastive linguistics and lapsed time.' In Alatis (1968), 11–26.

Stockwell, Robert P and Bowen, J D (1965) *The sounds of English and Spanish.* Chicago: The University of Chicago Press.

Stockwell, Robert P and Martin, J W (1965) *The grammatical structure of English and Spanish.* Chicago: The University of Chicago Press.

Strevens, Peter S (1970) 'Two ways of looking at error analysis.' *ERIC: ED* 037 714.

Sweet, Henry (1889) *The practical study of languages.* London: J M Dent. (Reprinted London: Oxford University Press, 1964.)

Upshur, John A (1962) 'Language proficiency testing and the contrastive analysis dilemma.' *Language learning* 12, 123–127.

Wardhaugh, Ronald (1970) 'The contrastive analysis hypothesis.' *TESOL quarterly* 4, 123–130.

Weinreich, Uriel (1953) *Languages in contact: Findings and problems.* New York: Linguistic Circle of New York.

Whitman, R A (1970) 'Contrastive analysis: Problems and procedures.' *Language learning* 20, 191–197.

Whitman, R A and Jackson, K L (1972) 'The unpredictability of contrastive analysis.' *Language learning* 22, 29–41.

Wilkins, D A (1968) 'Review of trends in language teaching.' *IRAL* 6, 99–107.

Wode, Henning (1978) 'Developmental sequences in naturalistic L2 acquisition.' In Hatch (1978), 101–117.

Zydatiss, Wolfgang (1974) 'A "kiss of life" for the notion of error.' *IRAL* 12, 231–238.

15. A Bibliography of Applied Contrastive Studies

Kari Sajavaara and Jaakko Lehtonen

University of Jyväskylä

This bibliography of applied contrastive studies consists of a selection of titles from *A Select Bibliography of Contrastive Analysis* edited by Kari Sajavaara and Jaakko Lehtonen (Jyväskylä Contrastive Studies 1, Jyväskylä: Department of English, University of Jyväskylä, 1975), which covers the years 1965-1975, and of those from the years 1976-1980.

The bibliography does not aim at exhaustiveness. The material for the bibliography was originally collected for the Finnish–English Contrastive Project, which means that it reflects, to some extent at least, the orientation of the personal interests of the compilers and the composition of the data sources available at Jyväskylä. Thus, the non-inclusion of a title must not be interpreted as being due to the non-relevance of this title for contrastive studies. In many cases we have not simply had access to the title.

The threefold division of the original bibliography into general studies; morphology, syntax and semantics; and phonetics and phonology was not retained in the present bibliography, nor does it include the topic index of the original work.

Our thanks are due to Pirjo Lätti, Helen Niskanen and Henna Vesterinen. Without their assistance this version of the bibliography would never have been possible.

Abbreviated titles

Amer. Speech. *American Speech*. New York, NY.
Audiovis. Lang. J. *Audio-visual Language Journal*. Birmingham.

243

Found. Lang. *Foundations of Language*. Dordrecht.
HCLP. *The Hungarian–English Contrastive Project*. The Linguistics Institute of the Hungarian Academy of Sciences. Budapest.
Inc. Linguist. *The Incorporated Linguist*. The Institute of Linguists. London.
J.ESL. *Journal of English as a Second Language*. Philadelphia, Pa.
J.IPA. *Journal of International Phonetic Association*. London.
J.Ling. *Journal of Linguistics*. London.
J.Phon. *Journal of Phonetics*. London.
LL. *Language Learning*. Ann Arbor, Michigan.
MLJ. *The Modern Language Journal*. St. Louis, Missouri.
MST Engl. Quart. *The MST English Quarterly*. Manila.
PAKS Arbeitsberichte. *Projekt für angewandte kontrastive Sprachwissenschaft*. Stuttgart.
The PCCLLU Papers. The Pacific Conference on Contrastive Linguistics and Language Universals. University of Honolulu, Hawaii.
PILUS. *Papers from the Institute of Linguistics, University of Stockholm*. Stockholm.
PSiCL. *Papers and Studies in Contrastive Linguistics*. Poznań.
Quart. J. Sp. *The Quarterly Journal of Speech*. New York, NY.
RELC Journal. *The Regional English Language Centre Journal*. Singapore.
RUUL. *Reports from Uppsala University, Department of Linguistics*. Uppsala.
SAP. *Studia Anglica Posnaniensia*. Poznań.
SECS Report. *Swedish–English Contrastive Studies*. Lund.
SRAZ. *Studia Romanica et Anglica Zagrebiensia*. Zagreb.
STL-QPSR. *Speech Transmission Laboratory. Quarterly Progress Report*. Department of Speech Communication. Royal Institute of Technology, Stockholm.
TEFL. *A Bulletin for the Teaching of English as a Foreign Language*. American University of Beirut, Beirut.
TESOL Quart. *TESOL Quarterly*. Washington, DC.
YSCECP Ped. Mat. *The Yugoslav Serbo-Croatian–English Contrastive Project: Pedagogical Materials*. Zagreb.
YSCECP Studies. *The Yugoslav Serbo-Croatian–English Contrastive Project: Studies*. Zagreb.
YSCECP Studies 4. *Zagreb Conference on English Contrastive Projects Dec. 1970*. Zagreb.
YSCECP Reports. *The Yugoslav Serbo-Croatian–English Contrastive Project: Reports*. Zagreb.
Z. Dialektol. Ling. *Zeitschrift für Dialektologie und Linguistik*. Wiesbaden.
Z. Phon. *Zeitschrift für Phonetik, Sprachwissenschaft und Kommunikationsforschung*. Berlin.
Z. Slaw. *Zeitschrift für Slawistik*. Berlin.

The Bibliography

Abraham, W, Some semantic properties of some conjunctions, *Some impli-cations of linguistic theory for applied linguistics, ed* S P Corder and E Roulet, Brussels, 1975, 7–31.

Adams, C, English speech rhythm and the foreign learner, *Proceedings of the 7th International Congress of Phonetic Sciences, Montreal 1971*, The Hague and Paris, 1972, 824–832.

Adjemian, C, On the nature of interlanguage systems, *LL* 26 (1976), 297–321.

Afolayan, A, Contrastive linguistics and the teaching of English as a second or foreign language, *ELT* 25 (1971), 220–229.

Aid, F M, Semantic universals in instructional materials, *TESOL Quart.* 8 (1974), 53–64.

Alatis, J E (*ed*) *Bilingualism and language contact: Anthropological, linguistic psychological and sociological aspects.* Report on the 21st Annual Round Table Meeting on Linguistics and Language Studies. Monograph Series on Language and Linguistics 23. Washington DC, 1970.

Alatis, J E (*ed*) *Contrastive linguistics and its pedagogical implication.* Report on the 19th Annual Round Table Meeting on Linguistics and Language Studies. Monograph Series on Language and Linguistics 21. Washington DC, 1968.

Aleithe, R, *Zur Problematic der Konfrontation. Forschungskollektiv Fach-sprachen und Sprachunterricht: Arbeitsmaterial.* Martin-Luther-Univ., Sektion Sprach- und Literaturwissenschaft 34. Halle-Wittenberg, 1974.

Allen, J B and Pit Corder, S (*eds*) Techniques in applied linguistics. *The Edin-burgh course in applied linguistics* Vol 3. Oxford, 1974.

Allen, R L, The use of rapid drills in the teaching of English to speakers of other languages, *TESOL Quart.* 6 (1972), 13–32.

Anderson, K O, Some aspects of English language interference in learning German intonation, *Proceedings of the 7th International Congress of Phonetic Sciences, Montreal 1971*, The Hague and Paris, 1972, 837–841.

Andrassy, V, Errors in the morphology and syntax of the parts of speech in the English of learners from the Serbo-Croatian-speaking area, *VSCECP Ped. mat.* 1 (1971), 7–31.

Angelis, P J, Listening comprehension and error analysis, *Proceedings of the 3rd AILA congress, Copenhagen 1972*, Vol 1, *ed* G Nickel, Heidelberg, 1974, 1–11.

Anthony, E M, A 'traditional' linguistic basis for language teaching, *TESOL Quart.* 4 (1970), 3–16.

Arabski, J, Contrastive studies and interlanguage, *PSiCL* Vol 10, *ed* J Fisiak, Poznań, 1979, 135–143.

Arabski, J, A linguistic analysis of English composition errors made by Polish students, *SAP* 1 (1968), 71–79.

Arabski, J, Selected bibliography on error analysis and related areas, *Errata. Papers in error analysis, ed* J Svartvik, Stockholm, 1973, 161–170.

Awedyk, W, Towards a pedagogical contrastive phonology, *PSiCL* Vol 10, *ed* J Fisiak, Poznań, 1979, 125–134.

Aziz, Y Y, Some problems of English consonant sounds for the Iraqui learner, *ELT* 28 (1974), 166–168.

Aziz, Y Y, Some problems of the English diphthongs for the Iraqui learner, *ELT* 29 (1974), 68–70.

Backmann, N, Intonation errors in second language pronunciation of eight Spanish-speaking adults learning English, *ISB Utrecht* 4 (1979), 239–265.

Baird, A, Contrastive studies and the language teacher, *ELT* 21 (1967), 130–135.

Bald, W D, Englische und deutsche Intonation in Forschung und Unterricht, Paper read at the 4th Polish–English Contrastive Conference, Ustronie, 1973.

Banathy, B H and Madarasz, P H, Contrastive analysis and error analysis, *J. ESL* 4 (1969), 77–92.

Banathy, B H, Trager, E C and Waddle, C D, The use of contrastive data in foreign language course development, *Trends in modern language teaching*, *ed* A Valdman, New York, 1966, 35–56.

Banczerowski, J, The transposition of Polish stops by Chinese speakers, *Glottodidactica* 2 (1967), 47–51.

Barrera-Vidal, A and Kühlwein, W *et al* (*eds*) *Kritische Bibliographie zur angewandten Linguistik.* Dortmund, 1976.

Barrera-Vidal, A and Kühlwein, W, *Angewandte Linguistik für den Fremdsprachlichen Unterricht. Eine Einführung.* Dortmund, 1975.

Bartley, D E, *Soviet approaches to bilingual education.* Philadelphia, 1971.

Barrutia, R, Creating schemata for teaching Spanish phonetics, *IRAL* 9 (1971), 347–351.

Barry, W J, Language background and the perception of foreign accent, *J. Phon.* 2 (1974), 65–89.

Barry, W J, Remedial pronunciation practice for German-speaking students of English, *ELT* 26 (1971), 43–47.

Barry, W J and Gutknecht, C, *A university course in English phonetics and a comparative study in English and German phonology*, LB-Papier 3. Brunswick, 1970 and LB-Papier 15. Brunswick, 1971.

Bausch, K-R, Ausgewählte Literatur zur kontrastiven Linguistik und zur Interferenzproblematik, *Babel* 17 (1971), 45–53.

Bausch, K-R and Raabe H, Der Filter 'Kontrastivität' in einer Lehrer-grammatik, Eine Skizze der Probleme und Perspektiven, *Beiträge und Materialien zur Ausbildung von Fremdsprachenlehrern*, Dokumentation zur Projektarbeit des Zentralen Fremdsprachenistituts der Ruhr-Universität Bochum, Workshop 74, Band II, 415–439.

Bausch, K-R and Gauger, H-M (*eds*) *Interlinguistica: Sprachvergleich und Übersetzung: Festschrift zum 60. Geburtstag von Mario Wandruszka.* Tübingen, 1971.

Bausch, K-R, Kontrastive Linguistik, *Perspektiven der Linguistik*, *ed* W A Koch, Stuttgart, 1973, 159–182.

Bausch, K-R, Kontrastive Linguistik und Übersetzen, *Linguistica Antverpiensia* 6 (1972), 7–15.

Bausch, K-R, La linguistica contrastive e il tradurre, *La traduzione, Saggi e studi,* Trieste, 1973, 141–154.

Bausch, K-R, Klegraf, J and Wilss, W, *The science of translation: An analytical bibliography (1962–1969).* Tübingen.

Bausch, K-R, Übersetzungswissenschaft und angewandte Sprachwissenschaft: Versuch einer Standortbestimmung, *Lebende Sprachen* 15 (1970), 161–163.

Bausch, K-R and Kasper, G, Der Zweitsprachenerwerb: Möglichkeiten und Grenzen der 'grossen' Hypothesen, *Linguistische Berichte* 64/79.

Becica, B, First language background as it affects ESL teaching, *TESOL Quart.* 3 (1969), 349–353.

Bennett, W A, An applied linguistic view of errors of syntax, *Audiovis. Lang. J.* 11 (1973), 123–125.

Bennett, M, Comparative linguistics (as applied to learning and teaching English as a foreign language: Some basic theory), *Australian Journal of Adult Education* 11 (1971), 108–113.

Bennett, W A, The significance of article/verb colligation for English learners of French, *Modern Languages* 61 (1975), 117–122.

Berndt, R, A semantically based approach to language description and its potential impact on the teaching of foreign languages, *PSCL* Vol 2, *ed* J Fisiak, Poznań, 1974, 33–64.

Bernstein, W, Sprachvergleich und Bezugnahme auf die Muttersprache im Fremdsprachenunterricht, *Zielsprache Deutsch* 3 (1975), 17–25.

Bertkau, J S, An analysis of English learner speech, *LL* 24 (1974), 279–288.

Bhatia, A T, An error analysis of students' compositions, *IRAL* 12 (1974), 337–350.

Bickerton, D, Cross-level interference: The influence of L1 syllable structure on L2 morphological error, *Applications of Linguistics,* ed G E Perren and J L M Trim, Cambridge, 1971, 133–140.

Bieritz, W D, Phonologische Interferenzen: Französische Aussprachefehler deutscher Studenten, *IRAL* 12 (1974), 193–200.

Bierwisch, M, Fehlerlinguistik, *Linguistic Inquiry* 1 (1970), 397–414.

Bilinić, J, Errors in the morphology and syntax of the verb in the speech of learners of English in the Serbo-Croatian area, *YSCECP Ped. mat.* 1 (1971), 32–59.

Bîra, E, A pedagogical grammar of modal sentences with 'may'/'might' and 'can'/'could' and their nearest Romanian equivalents, *RECAP, Contrastive studies in the syntax and semantics of English and Romanian,* Bucharest, 1974, 195–226.

Bîra, E, Some theoretical and methodological observations on establishing semantic grammatical equivalences of modal verb phrases in English and Romanian, *RECAP, Studies, ed* D Chitoran and I Ionescu, Bucharest, 1972, 201–211.

Boeddingshaus, W, Lehrstrategie im Unterricht nah verwandter Sprachen, *Proceedings of the 3rd AILA congress, Copenhagen 1972*, Vol 1, ed G Nickel, Heidelberg, 1974, 21–32.

Bolinger, D L, The influence of linguistics: plus and minus, *TESOL Quart.* 6 (1972), 107–120.

Bouton, C-P, *L'acquisition d'une langue étrangère*. Paris, 1975.

Bowen, J D, Contextualizing pronunciation practice in the ESOL classroom, *TESOL Quart.* 6 (1972), 83–94.

Bowen, J D, Contrastive analysis and the language classroom, *On teaching English to speakers of other languages, Series 3*, ed B W Robinett, Washington, DC 1967, 80–87.

Bowerman, M, *Early syntactic developments: a cross-linguistic study with special reference to Finnish*. Cambridge Studies in Linguistics 11. London, 1973.

Bratt Paulston, C, Las escuelas bilingues en Perú: Some comments on second language learning, *IRAL* 10 (1972), 351–356.

Breitkreuz, H, 'False friends' und ihre unterrichtliche Behandlung, *Die Neueren Sprachen* 22 (1973), 70–74.

Brière, E J, Improving English speakers' pronunciation of French, *LL* 13 (1963), 33–40.

Brière, E J, An investigation of phonological interference, *Language* 42 (1966), 768–796.

Brière, E J, Phonological testing reconsidered, *LL* 17 (1967), 163–170.

Brière, E J, *A psycholinguistic study of phonological interference*. The Hague, 1968.

Brockhaus, K, Automatische Übersetzung, *Untersuchung am Beispiel der Sprachen Englisch und Deutsch*, Brunswick, 1971.

Brown, H D, Categories of spelling difficulties in speakers of English as a first and a second language, *Journal of Verbal Learning and Verbal Behavior* 9 (1970), 232–236.

van Buren, P, Contrastive analysis, Techniques in applied linguistics. *The Edinburgh course in applied linguistics* Vol 3, ed J P B Allen and S Pit Corder, London, 1974, 279–312.

Burgschmidt, E and Götz, D, *Kontrastive Linguistik—Deutsch/Englisch*. Munich, 1974.

Burgschmidt, E and Götz, D, Kontrastive Phonologie Deutsch–Englisch und Mundartinterferenz, *Linguistik und Didaktik* 3 (1972), 209–225.

Burke, S J, Language acquisition, language learning and language teaching, *IRAL* 12 (1974), 53–77.

Burt, M K, Dulay, H C and Hernandez, Ch, *Bilingual syntax measure*. New York, 1973.

Buteau, M F, Students' errors and the learning of French as a second language: A pilot study, *IRAL* 8 (1970), 133–145.

Cairns, H S, Cairns, C E and Williams, F, Some theoretical considerations of articulation substitution phenomena, *Language and Speech* 17 (1974), 160–173.

Calbris, G, Test sur la perception des voyelles orales françaises par des Français et des étrangers, *Phonetica* 30 (1974), 101–122.

Cammack, F M and van Buren, H, Paralanguage across cultures: some comparisons between Japanese and English, *ELEC Bulletin* 22 (1967), 7–10, 47.

Campbell, R N, On defining the objectives of a short-term training program: Grammar, *TESOL Quart.* 1 (1967), 44–49.

Canale, M *et al*, Aspects de l'usage de la préposition 'pour' en francais ontarien: interférence et/ou surgénéralisation? *Working papers on bilingualism* 12 (1977), 61–78.

Cancino, H, Rosansky, E and Schumann, J, Testing hypothesis about second language acquisition: the copula and negative in three subjects, *Working papers on bilingualism* 3 (1974), Toronto, 80–96.

Capell, A, The limits of second language learning, *Monda Lingvo-problemo* 1 (1969), 19–26.

Carlbom, U, Word order errors, *SECS Report* 2 (1973).

Carls, U, Interferenzerscheinungen zwischen dem Deutschen und Englischen im Bereich des attributiven Relativsatzes, *Wissenschaftliche Zeitschrift der Humboldt Universität zu Berlin, Gesellschaft- und Sprachwissenschaftliche Reihe* 22 (1973), 199–201.

Carr, E B, Teaching the *th* sounds of English, *TESOL Quart.* 1 (1967), 7–14.

Carroll, J B, Contrastive linguistics and interference theory, *Contrastive linguistics and its pedagogical implications*, ed J Alatis, Washington, DC, 1968, 113–122.

Carroll, J B, Linguistic relativity, contrastive analysis and language learning, *IRAL* 1 (1963), 1–20.

Carstensen, B, Contrastive syntax and semantics of English and German, *Active methods and modern kids in the teaching of foreign languages*, ed R Filipović, London, 1972, 206–216.

Carstensen, B, Griesel, H and Meyer, H-G, Zur Intensität des englischen Einflusses auf die deutsche Pressesprache, *Muttersprache* 82 (1972), 238–243.

Carter, R J, An approach to a theory of phonetic difficulties in second language learning, *Semiannual Technical Report* 2, Cambridge, Mass, 1967, 56–92.

Cassano, P, The influence of Guarani on the phonology of the Spanish of Paraguay, *Studia Linguistica* 26 (1972), 106–112.

Cassano, P, The influence of American English on the phonology of American Spanish, *Orbis* 1 (1973), 201–214.

Castelo, L M, Verb usage in educated Filipino English, *IRAL* 10 (1972), 153–165.

Catford, J C, Contrastive analysis and language teaching, *Contrastive linguistics and its pedagogical implications*, ed J Atlatis, Washington, DC, 1968.

Catford, J C, *A linguistic theory of translation*. London, 1965.

Catford, J C, Translation and language teaching, *Linguistic theories and their application*, Council for cultural co-operation AIDELA, Strasbourg, 1967, 125–146.

Chamot, A U, Phonological problems in learning English as a third language, *IRAL* 11 (1973), 243–249.

Chesterman, A, Error analysis and the learner's linguistic repertoire, *Jyväskylä Contrastive Studies* 4 (1977), 45–58.

Chiţoran, D, Contrastive analysis: questions other than linguistic theory and research methodology, *RECAP, Reports and studies*, Bucharest, 1971, 71–80.

Chiţoran, D, The contrastive hypothesis in second language acquisition, *RECAP Further developments in contrastive studies*, Bucharest, 1974, 49–64.

Chiţoran, D, A model for second language acquisition, *YSCECP Studies* 4 (1971), 173–180.

Chiţoran, D, *The Romanian English contrastive analysis project. Studies: Monograph studies*. Bucharest, 1972.

Cintas, P F and Valdman, A, Les apports de l'analyse contrastive et de l'analyse des erreurs à l'elucidation des mécanismes d'apprentissage du français langue seconde, *FIPF Bulletin* 10–11 (1975), 79–84.

Clas, A, Le système du pronom indéterminé on. Problemes de traduction, *Lebende Sprachen* 15 (1970), 13–16.

Clarke, M A, Arabic distractors for English vocabulary tests, *ELT* 27 (1972), 77–79.

Clyne, M G, *Transference and triggering*. The Hague, 1967.

Clyne, M C, Transference patterns among English–German bilinguals—a comparative study, *ITL* (14), 5–18.

Cohen, A and Robbins, M, Towards assessing interlanguage performance: the relationship between selected errors, learners' characteristics and learners' explanations, *LL* 26 (1976), 45–67.

Collins, B and Rodd, J, English pronunciation problems of francophonic West-Africans, *ELT* 27 (1972), 79–88.

Contrastive studies in phonetics and phonology. The Romanian–English contrastive analysis project. Bucharest, 1973.

Cook, V J, The analogy between first and second language learning, *IRAL* 7 (1969), 207–216.

Cook, V J, The comparison of language development in native children and foreign adults, *IRAL* 11 (1973), 13–28.

Cook, M J and Sharp, M A, Problems of Navajo speakers in learning English, *LL* 16 (1966), 21–29.

Cooper, R L, Olshtain, E, Tucker, G R and Waterbury, M, The acquisition of complex English structures by adult native speakers of Arabic and Hebrew, *LL* 29 (1979), 255–276.

Corder, S P, The elicitation of interlanguage, *Errata: Papers in error analysis*, ed J Svartvik, Stockholm, 1973, 36–47.

Corder, S P, Idiosyncratic dialects and error analysis, *IRAL* 10 (1971), 147–160.

Corder, S P, *Introducing applied linguistics*. Harmondsworth, 1973.

Corder, S P, Problems and solutions in applied linguistics, *Proceedings of the*

3rd AILA Congress, Copenhagen, 1972, Vol 3: Applied Linguistics, Problems and solutions, ed J Qvistgaard *et al,* Heidelberg, 1974, 3–23.

Corder, S P, Die Rolle der Interpretation bei der Untersuchung von Schüler-fehlern, *Fehlerkunde,* ed G Nickel, Berlin, 1972, 38–50.

Corder, S P and Roulet, E (eds) *Linguistic insights in applied linguistics.* Brussels, 1974.

Corder, S P and Roulet, E (eds) *Some implications of linguistic theory for applied linguistics.* Brussels, 1975.

Corder, S P and Roulet, E (eds) *Theoretical models in applied linguistics.* Brussels and Paris, 1973.

Corder, S P, The significance of learner's errors, *IRAL* 4 (1967), 161–170.

Corder, S P, Zur Beschreibung der Sprache des Sprachlerners, *Reader zur kontrastiven Linguistik,* ed G Nickel, Frankfurt, 1972, 175–184.

Court, C, Word-linking and unstressed words in English: A problem for speakers of Thai, *ELT* 26 (1972), 284–288.

Cowan, R, Reading, perceptual strategies and contrastive analysis, *LL* 26 (1976), 95–109.

Craig, D R, Teaching English to Jamaican Creole speakers: A multi-dialect situation, *LL* 16 (1966), 49–61.

Crome, E, Zur Konfrontation von semantischen Beziehungen bei der Aneignung fremdsprachiger Lexik, *Linguistische Arbeitsberichte* 8 (1973), 232–240.

Cronnell, B A, Spelling-sound relations in ESL instruction, *LL* 22 (1972), 17–27.

Cummins, J, The cross-lingual dimensions of language proficiency: implications for bilingual education and the optimal age issue, *TESOL Quart.* 14, (1980), 175–188.

Cygan, J, English question structures and the Polish learner, *Glottodidactica* 2 (1967), 85–93.

Czochralski, J, Zur sprachlichen Interferenz, *Linguistics* 67 (1971), 5–26.

Dabrowska, J, Le bilinguisme et l'enseignement d'une langue étrangère, *Glottodidactica* 8 (1975), 45–52.

Dahlstedt, K-H, Mother tongue and the second language: A Swedish view-point, *IRAL* 10 (1972), 333–350.

Dahlstedt, K-H, *Svårigheter i svenskans uttal.* Lund, 1971.

Darbelnet, J, Le français face à l'anglais comme langue de communication, *Le Français dans le Monde* 89 (1972), 6–9.

Dardjowidjojo, S, Contrastive analysis: Pros & cons, *Proceedings of the 3rd AILA congress, Copenhagen 1972,* Vol 1, ed G Nickel, Heidelberg, 1974, 45–58.

Davies, A, Language tests and language errors, *RELC English language testing report of the RELC fifth regional seminar, Bangkok, 1970,* ed R Cherrier, Singapore, 1971, 95–103.

Debyser, F, La linguistique contrastive et les interférences, *Langue française* 8 (1970), 31–61.

Dehghanpisheh, E. Language development in Parsi and English: implications for the second language learner. *IRAL* 16 (1978), 45–61.

Dimitrijević, N R. Problems and implication of contrastive analysis of vocabulary and culture. *PSiCL* Vol 7, *ed* J Fisiak, 1977, 133–144.

Dimitrijević, N R. Testing and contrastive analysis. *PSiCL* Vol 7, *ed* J Fisiak, 1977, 121–131.

Dimitrijević, N R and Djordjević, D. The reliability of the subjective assessment of the pupils pronunciation of English as a foreign language. *IRAL* 9 (1971), 245–265.

Diósy-Stephanides, E. Contrastive aspects of British and American English with implications for Hungarian learners of English. *HCLP* 4 (1973), 27–43.

DiPietro, R J. Contrastive analysis: Demise or new life. *Proceedings of the 3rd AILA congress, Copenhagen 1972*, Vol 1, *ed* G Nickel, Heidelberg, 1974, 69–80.

DiPietro, R J. Learning problems involving Italians [s], [z] and English /s/, /z/. *Proceedings of the 9th International Congress of Linguists, Cambridge, Mass., Aug. 27–31, 1962*, The Hague, 1964, 224–227.

DiPietro, R J. Student competence and performance in ESL. *TESOL Quart.* 4 (1970), 49–61.

Dordević, R. Pedagogical materials as a supplement to contrastive analysis projects. *Glottodidactica* 8 (1975), 81–89.

Dresdner, M P. Difficulties of Chilean students in pronouncing English consonant sounds. *The English Language Journal: Revista de la Lengua Inglesa* 1 (1970), 325–340.

Dresdner, M P. Difficulties of Chilean students in pronouncing English vowel sounds. *The English Language Journal: Revista de la Lengua Inglesa* 2 (1971), 5–14.

Drubig, B. Zur Analyse syntaktischer Fehlleistungen. *Fehlerkunde*, *ed* G Nickel, Berlin, 1972, 78–91.

Dubrow, M P. *A generative-transformational contrastive analysis of English and Hebrew for selected grammatical structures that are difficult for the Hebrew-speaking learner of English*. Diss. New York University, 1973.

Dulay, H C and Burt, M K. Errors and strategies in child second language acquisition, *TESOL Quart.* 8 (1974), 129–136.

Dulay, H and Burt, M. Should we teach children syntax? *LL* 23 (1973), 235–252.

Dusková, L. On source of errors in foreign language learning, *IRAL* 7 (1969), 11–36.

Ebneter, T. *Angewandte Linguistik 2. Eine Einführung. Sprachunterricht.* München, 1976.

Edström, E. Tense, aspect and modality: Problems in English for Swedish students, *Errata: Papers in error analysis*, *ed* J Svartvik, Stockholm, 1973, 124–133.

Efstathiadis, S and King, P, Some lexical and structural errors made by Greek learners of English, *ELT* 26 (1972), 159–167.

Eichberg, E, Über das Vergleichen im Fremdsprachenunterricht, *Die Neueren Sprachen* 19 (1970), 61–65.

Emons, R, Linguistik und Fremdsprachenunterricht: Vorüberlegungen zu einer pädagogischen Grammatik, *Praxis* 22 (1975), 341–346.

Engel, U, Unvorgreifliche Gedanken zur kontrastiven Grammatik, *Kongressbericht der 4. Jahrestagung der Gesellschaft für angewandte Linguistik GAL e.V.*, *IRAL-Sonderband*, ed G Nickel and A Raasch, Stuttgart, 1974, 128–136.

Englund, B and Waldin, J, Sekundärspråksinterferens i primärspråket, B Hammarberg (ed), *Kontrastiv Lingvistik och sekundärspråkforskning*, Stockholm, 1979, 19–30.

Enkvist, N E, The choice of transcription in foreign language teaching, *Proceedings of the 4th International Congress of Phonetic Sciences, Helsinki 1961*, The Hague, 1962, 586–589.

Enkvist, N E, The English and Finnish vowel system: A comparison, *Suomen englanninkielen opettajien yhdistyksen julkaisu VIA III*, Turku, 1963, 44–49.

Enkvist, N E, Kontrastive Textlinguistik und Übersetzung, *Grazer Linguistische Studien* 5 (1977), 47–73.

Enkvist, N E, Should we count errors or measure success? *Errata: Papers in error analysis*, ed J Svartvik, Stockholm, 1973, 16–23.

Erdmann, P H, Patterns of stress-transfer in English and German, *IRAL* 11 (1973), 229–241.

Erdmann, P, Die Strukturierung von Synonymen: zur Übersetzung von deutschen Rand ins Englisch, *Neophilologus* 58 (1974), 305–320.

Ervin-Tripp, S M, Is second language learning like the first? *TESOL Quart.* 8 (1974), 111–127.

Ervin-Tripp, S M, Methodological factors: contrastive, *A field manual for cross-cultural study of the acquisition of communicative competence*, ed D J Slobin, Berkeley, Calif., 1967, 61–70.

Erämetsä, E and Klemmt, R, *Grundlegung zu einer pädagogischen Phonetik des Deutschen auf kontrastiver Basis (Finnisch)*. Jyväskylän yliopiston saksan kielen laitoksen julkaisuja 2 (1974).

Erämetsä, E, Kontrastiivista pedagogista fonetiikkaa, *Fonetiikan paperit, Tampere 1974*, Tampereen yliopiston puheopin laitoksen monisteita 1 (1975), 53–55.

Esser, J, Contrastive analysis at the crossroads of linguistics and foreign language teaching, *IRAL* 18 (1980), 181–192.

Faiss, K, Übersetzung und Sprachwissenschaft—eine Orientierung, *IRAL* 10 (1972), 1–20.

Falkovich, M M, Vozmozhnye napravenya sopostavitelnykh leksicheskikh issledovanii, *Inostrannye yazyki v shkole* 1 (1973), 14–21.

Fant, G. Lindblom, B and de Serpa-Leitao, A, Consonant confusions in English and Swedish: A pilot study, *STL-QPSR* 4 (1966), 31–34.

Farsi, A, A, Some pronunciation problems of Swahili-speaking students, *ELT* 20 (1966), 136–140.

Felix, S, Wh-pronouns in first and second language acquisition, *Linguistische Berichte* 44 (1976), 52–64.

Ferguson, C A, Contrastive analysis and language development, *Contrastive linguistics and its pedagogical implications*, ed J Alatis, Washington DC, 1968, 101–112.

Fernando, C, English in Ceylon: a case study of a bilingual community, *Language in Society* 6 (1977), 341–360.

Filipović, R, A compromise system, a link between linguistic borrowing and the foreign language learning, *YSCECP Studies* 5 (1972), 19–29.

Filipović, R, Contrastive analysis and error analysis in pedagogical materials, *YSCECP Ped. mat.* 1 (1971), 1–6.

Filipović, R, Modern linguistics and foreign language teaching: International conference in Budapest 1–5 April 1971, *Contact* 18–19 (1972), 8–16.

Filipović, R, Testing the results of contrastive analysis, *Proceedings of the 3rd AILA congress, Copenhagen 1972*, Vol 1, ed G Nickel, Heidelberg, 1974, 97–109.

Filipović, R, The use of contrastive and error analysis to practicing teachers, *Deutsche Sprache im Kontrast*, ed U Engel, Tübingen, 1977, 5–22.

Filipović, R (ed) *Zagreb conference on English contrastive projects 7–9 Dec. 1970: Papers and discussion.* Zagreb, 1971 (= *YSCEP Studies* 4).

Fischer, M, Contrastive cultural features in foreign language teaching, *Slavonic and East European Journal* 11 (1967),

Fishman, J, The implications of bilingualism for language teaching and language learning, *Trends in modern language teaching*, ed A Valdman, New York, 1966, 121–131.

Fisiak, J (ed) (1973–1981) *Papers and Studies in Contrastive Linguistics*, Vols I–XIII. Poznań.

Fisiak, J, The Polish–English contrastive project, *PSiCL* Vol 1, ed J Fisiak, Poznań, 1973, 7–13.

Fisiak, J (ed) (1980) *Theoretical issues in contrastive linguistics.* Amsterdam: Benjamins.

Fisiak, J (1980) Some notes concerning contrastive linguistics, *AILA Bulletin* 21:1, 1–17.

Fougeron, I, Quelques remarques sur les fautes des français dans la prononciation des mots russes, *IRAL* 9 (1971), 13–29.

Fraser, B and Klatt, M M, A partial inventory of phonetic difficulties encountered in second language learning, *Semiannual technical report* 2, Cambridge, Mass, 1967, 26–55.

French, F G, *Common errors in English—Their cause, prevention and cure.* London, 1970.

Fried, V. Comparative linguistic analysis in language teaching, *Modern language teaching: Papers from the 9th FIPLV congress*, ed H Jalling, London, 1968, 38–46.

Friedman, H L and Johnson, R L. Some actual and potential use of rate-controlled speech in second language learning, *The psychology of second language learning*, ed P Pimsleur and T Quinn, Cambridge, 1971, 157–163.

Friedrich, W. Kontrastive Stilistik und Übersetzungstechnik dargestellt an Beispielen aus dem Englischen, Russischen und Deutschen, *Russisch: Zeitschrift für eine Weltsprache* 5 (1971), 7–13; 33–38.

Friederich, W. With + Partizip: ein Grammatik- und Übersetzungsproblem, *Idioma* 4 (1967), 156–160, 249–253.

Gage, W W. What's so hard about that? *Papers in contrastive linguistics*, ed G Nickel, Cambridge, 1971, 49–51.

Gässler, R. *Vom Satz zum Wort, ein englisch–deutsch–französisch–italienisch Übersetzungsvergleich. Transformation und Polymorphie.* Göppingen, 1973.

Gatto, M C. Une étude contrastive du français et de l'espagnol et ses implications pour l'enseignement du français langue étrangère, *Proceedings of the 3rd AILA congress, Copenhagen 1972*, Vol 1, ed G Nickel, Heidelberg, 1974, 120.

van Geest, J and Mulder, J. Is the past simple? An analysis of past-tense errors of second and third year MAVO pupils in the Netherlands, *ISB-Utrecht* 3 (1978), 292–318.

George, H V. *Common errors in language learning: Insights from English.* Rowley, Mass, 1972.

Gerbert, M. Konfrontation, Register und Leistungstests in der Fremdsprachen-ausbildung, *Wissenschaftliche Zeitschrift der Universität Berlin (Ost), Gesellschafts- und Sprachwissenschaftliche Reihe* 18 (1969), 437–442.

Gerbert, M. Syntaktisch-lexikalische Interferenz im Englischunterricht, *Wissenschaftliche Zeitschrift der Humboldt Universität zu Berlin, Gesellschaft- und Sprachwissenschaftliche Reihe* 22 (1973), 195–197.

Ghadessy, M. Error analysis: a criterion for the development of materials in foreign language education, *ELT* 31 (1977), 244–248.

Gillis, M and Weber, R M. The emergence of sentence modalities in the English of Japanese-speaking children, *LL* 26 (1976), 77–94.

Ginesy, M and Hirst, D. The influence of regional accents (southern French) on the learning of English as a foreign language, *Etudes de Linguistique Appliquée* 7 (1972), 28–37.

Gleason, H A, Jr. Contrastive analysis in discourse structure, *Contrastive linguistics and its pedagogical implications*, ed J Alatis, Washington DC, 1968, 36–64.

Glinz, H. *Die Sprachen in der Schule. Skizze einer vergleichenden Satzlehre für Latein, Deutsch, Französisch und Englisch.* Düsseldorf, 1965.

Goldstein, B Z and Tamura, K. *Japan and America: A comparative study in language and culture.* Vermont, 1975.

Golopentia-Eretescu, S, Towards a contrastive analysis of conversational strategy, *RECAP, further developments in contrastive studies*, Bucharest, 1974, 79–132.

Gonzáles-Mena LoCoco, V, A cross-sectional study on L₃ acquisition, *Working papers on bilingualism* 9 (1976), Toronto, 44–75.

Gnutzman, C, Zur Analyse lexikalischer Fehler, *PAKS* 5 (1970), 142–153.

Gorosch, M, Assessment intervariability in testing oral performance of adult students, *Errata: Papers in error analysis*, ed J Svartvik, Stockholm, 1973, 145–152.

Gradman, H L, The limitations of contrastive analysis predictions, *The PCCLLU papers*, ed K L Jackson and R L Whitman, Honolulu, 1971, 11–16.

Graham, H L, What methodologists ignore in 'contrastive' teaching, *The PCCLLU papers*, ed K L Jackson and R L Whitman, Honolulu, 1971, 73–77.

Granfors, T and Palmberg, R, Errors made by Finns and Swedish-speaking Finns learning English at a commercial-college level, *Errors made by Finns and Swedish-speaking Finns learning English*, AFTIL5, ed H Ringbom and R Palmberg, Åbo, 14–53.

Grauberg, W, An error analysis in German of first-year university students, *Applications of Linguistics*, ed G E Perren and J L M Trim, Cambridge, 1971, 257–263.

Grosjean, F and Deschamps, A, Analyse contrastive des variables temporelles de l'anglais et du français: Vitesse de parole et variables composantes, phénomènes d'hésitation, *Phonetica* 31 (1975), 144–184.

Grucza, F, Fehlerlinguistik, Lapsologie und kontrastive Forschungen, *Kwartalnik Neofilologiczny* 23 (1976), 237–247.

Grucza, F, Fremdsprachenunterricht und Übersetzung, *Glottodidactica* 5 (1970), 37–50.

Grucza, F, Zum Begriff des Interphons, *Glottodidactica* 2 (1967), 41–46.

Gründler, H, Investigation of auditory and articulatory competence in English-and German-speaking adults, *IRAL* 10 (1972), 123–143.

Gussmann, E, A note on phonological explanations of phonetic failings, *Lubelskie Materialy Neofilologiczne*, Lublin. *Polskie Towarzystwo Neofilologiczne* 1972, 85–96.

Gutknecht, C, *Kontrastive Linguistik. Englisch als Zielsprache*. Stuttgart, 1977.

Gutknecht, C and Panther, K-U, The role of contrastive grammars in foreign language learning, *The Incorporated Linguist* 10 (1971), 105–111.

Gutknecht, C and Panther, K-U, *The role of contrastive grammars in foreign language teaching*. LB-Papier 14. Brunswick, 1971.

Gutschow, H, Zur Analyse von Schülerfehlern, *Englisch* 3 (1967), 77–80.

Gårding, E, *Kontrastiv prosodi*. Lund, 1974.

Hadeli, O M, *A descriptive contrastive analysis of English and Arabic verbs: a study designed to improve the teaching of English to advanced Arab students*. Diss. New York University, 1971.

Hakes, D T, Psychological aspects of bilingualism, *MLJ* 49 (1965), 220–227.

Hakuta, K, A case study of a Japanese child learning English as a second language, *LL* 26 (1976), 321–353.

Hall, R M R and Hall, B L, Computer-aided instruction and contrastive analysis: a look to the future, *J. ESL* 2 (1967), 83–91.

Hall, R A, Contrastive grammar and textbook structure, *Contrastive linguistics and its pedagogical implications*, ed J E Alatis, Washington DC, 1968, 175–184.

Halliday, M A K, McIntosh, A and Strevens, P, *The linguistic sciences and language teaching*. London, 1965.

Hamayan, E, Markman, B R, Pelletier, S and Tucker, G R, Differences in performance in elicited imitation between French monolingual and English-speaking bilingual children, *IRAL* 16 (1978), 330–339.

Hammarberg, B, The insufficiency of error analysis, *Errata: Papers in error analysis*, ed J Svartvik, Stockholm, 1973, 29–35.

Hammarberg, B, Interference in American English-speakers' pronunciation of Swedish, *Studia Linguistica* 21 (1967), 15–36.

Hammarberg, B and Viberg, Å, *Anaforiska processer i svenskan i invandrarperspektiv—några utgångspunkter*. SSM Report 3, Stockholm, 1976.

Hammarberg, B and Viberg, Å, *Platshållartvånget, ett syntaktisk problem i svenskan för invandrare*. SSM Report 2, Stockholm, 1975.

Hammarberg, B and Viberg, Å, *Reported speech in Swedish and ten immigrant languages*. SSM Report 5, Stockholm, 1975.

Hammer, J H and Rice, F A, *A bibliography of contrastive linguistics*. Washington DC, 1965.

Hammerly, H, The correction of pronunciation errors, *MLJ* 57 (1973), 106–110.

Hammerly, H, Teaching pronunciation and generative phonology, *Foreign Language Annals* 6 (1973), 487–489.

Hamp, E P, What contrastive grammar is not if it is, *Contrastive linguistics and its pedagogical implications*, ed J E Alatis, Washington DC, 1968, 137–147.

Hanania, E A S and Gradman, H L, Acquisition of English structures: a case study of an adult native speaker of Arabic in an English-speaking environment, *LL* 27 (1977), 75–92.

Harris, D, *Testing English as a second language*. New York and London, 1969.

Hartmann, R R K (ed) *Contrastive analysis*. Papers in German–English contrastive applied linguistics, Occasional Papers in Linguistics and Language Learning, New University of Ulster, 1977.

Hauptman, P C, A comparison of first and second language reading strategies among English-speaking university students, *ISB Utrecht* 4 (1979), 173–201.

Häusler, F, Linguistik und Methodik im modernen Russisch-Unterricht, *Z. Slav.* 13 (1968), 730–731.

Hausmann, F J, *Linguistik und Fremdsprachenunterricht 1964–75*. Tübingen, 1975.

Heikkinen, H, Vowel reduction in the English of Finnish learners, *Jyväskylä Cross-Language Studies* 7 (1979), 15–52.

Helbig, G, Zu einigen Problemen der konfrontativen Grammatik und der Interferenz in ihrer Bedeutung für den Fremdsprachenunterricht, *Wissenschaftliche Zeitschrift der Humboldt Universität zu Berlin, Gesellschaft- und Sprachwissenschaftliche Reihe* 22 (1973), 171–177.

Helbig, G, Zur Rolle des kontrastiven Sprachvergleichs für den Fremdsprachenunterricht (Möglichkeiten, Voraussetzungen, Grenzen), *Deutsch als Fremdsprache* 13 (1976), 9–16.

Hell, G, Kontrastivität und sprachinnere Strukturen, *Modern Linguistics and Language Teaching, International Conference Budapest, 1–5 April 1971,* ed P Inkey and G Szépe, The Hague, 1975, 323–326.

Hellinger, M, Möglichkeiten und Grenzen der Fehleranalyse, *Ling. Berichte* 36 (1975), 73–83.

Hellinger, M, *Übungen zu einer kontrastiven Grammatik des Deutschen und Englischen.* Tübingen, 1976.

Henkel, H and Mehrer, H, Kontrastive Grammatik und Unterrichtspraxis, *Südwestdeutsche Schulblätter* 71 (1972), 151–157.

Henning, W A, Discrimination training and self-evaluation in the teaching of pronunciation, *IRAL* 4 (1966), 7–17.

Herranen, T, Errors made by Finnish university students in the use of the English article system, *Jyväskulä Contrastive Studies* 6 (1978) 74–95.

Heuser, J, Bewertung und Behebung von Fehlern, *English* 3 (1968), 68–74.

Higa, M, Toward contrastive sociolinguistics, *The PCCLLU papers,* ed K L Jackson and R L Whitman, Honolulu, 1971, 211–218.

Hill, J H, Foreign accents, language acquisition and cerebral dominance revisited, *LL* 20 (1970), 237–248.

Hirvonen, P, *Finnish and English communicative intonation.* Turun yliopiston fonetiikan laitoksen julkaisuja 8, 1970.

Hirvonen, P, *On the problems met by Finnish students in learning the rising interrogative intonation of English.* Turun yliopiston fonetiikan laitoksen julkaisuja 2, 1967.

Hocking, B D W, Implications of some clause-level problems of interference in advanced remedial teaching of English in Kenya, *The Journal of the Language Association of Eastern Africa* 1 (1970) 1, 56–63.

Hocking, B D W, Types of interference, *Focus on the learner,* ed J Oller and J Richards, Mass, 1973, 87–95.

Hodek, N, On teaching English intonation to Serbo-Croat learners, *ELT* 22 (1967), 67–72.

Hodge, C T, A contrastive note, *Anthropological Linguistics* 2 (1968), 32–34.

Hok, R, Cognitive and S-R learning theories reconciled through bisociation and contrastive studies, *IRAL* 10 (1972), 263–269.

Hok, R, Contrast: An effective teaching device, *ELT* 17 (1973), 118–122.

Huang, T-S, *A contrastive analysis of the syntactic errors in English made by Chinese students and its implications for the teaching of English syntax to Chinese.* Diss. Southern Illinois University, 1974.

Hughes, A, Aspects of a Spanish adult's acquisition of English, *ISB-Utrecht* 4 (1979), 49–65.

Hyldgaard-Jensen, K, Kontrolle der Aussprache des Deutschen, *Errata: Papers in error analysis*, ed J Svartvik, Stockholm, 1973, 134–138.

Hylgaard-Jensen, K and Zettersten, A (eds) *Kontrastiv Lingvistik i Danmark*. København, 1977.

Iarovici, E, Some pedagogical implications of lexical contrastive analysis, *2nd international conference of English contrastive projects, Bucharest 20–23 November, 1975*, ed D Chitoran, Bucharest, 1976, 287–293.

Ivir, V, Remarks on contrastive analysis and translation, *YSCECP Studies* 2 (1970), 14–26.

Jackson, K L, The verification and comparison of contrastive analyses, *The PCCLLU papers*, ed K L Jackson and R L Whitman, Honolulu, 1971, 201–210.

Jackson, K L and Whitman, R L (eds) *The PCCLLU papers (The Pacific conference on contrastive linguistics and language universals)*. Working papers in linguistics, University of Hawaii 3 (1971), 4.

Jäger, G, Konfrontation und Translation, *Wissenschaftliche Zeitschrift der Humboldt Universität zu Berlin, Gesellschaft- und Sprachwissenschaftliche Reihe* 22 (1973), 157–163.

Jäger, S, Kontrastive Grammatik: Ein Weg zur Rationalisierung des Deutschunterrichts, *Bericht über die Jahressitzung des Institus für deutsche Sprache*, Colloquia Germanica 3 (1969), 332–342.

Jaggi, S and Gandhi, D P, Perceputal interference and hierarchy of difficulties (seen in Hindi speech for English ears), *Indian Linguistics* 32 (1971), 1–17.

Jain, M P, Error analysis: source, cause and significance, Error analysis: perspectives on second language acquisition, *Applied linguistics and language study*, ed J Richards, London, 1974, 189–215.

Jakobovits, L A, *Foreign language learning: A psycholinguistic analysis of the issues*. Rowley, Mass, 1970.

Jakobovits, L A, Second language learning and transfer theory: A theoretical assessment, *LL* 19 (1969), 55–86.

James, C, Contrastive analysis versus error analysis, *IRAL-Sonderband: Kongressbericht der 3. Jahrestagung der GAL*, ed G Nickel and A Raasch, Heidelberg, 1972, 214–249.

James, C, Deeper contrastive study, *IRAL* 7 (1969), 83–96.

James, C, The diagnosis and analysis of error—some insights from linguistics, *Audiovis. Lang. J.* 10 (1972), 75–79.

James, C, The exculpation of contrastive linguistics, *Papers in contrastive linguistics*, ed G Nickel, Cambridge, 1971, 53–68.

James, C, The ignorance hypothesis in interlanguage studies, *ISB-Utrecht* 2 (1977), 152–165.

James, C, Linguistic measures for error gravity, *Audio-vis. Lang. J.* (1974), 3–9.

James, C, Zur Rechtfertigung der kontrastiven Linguistik, *Reader zur kontrastiven Linguistik*, *ed* G Nickel, Frankfurt, 1972, 21–38.

Janicki, K, Contrastive sociolinguistics—some methodological considerations, *PSiCL* Vol 10, *ed* J Fisiak, 1979, 33–40.

Janicki, K, On the feasibility of pedagogical contrastive socio-linguistics, *PSiCL* Vol 6, *ed* J Fisiak, Poznań, 1977, 17–24.

Jarosz, J, Versuch einer Fehleranalyse im Bereich der Verbalphrase, *Glottodidactica* 8 (1975), 71–80.

Jensen, M K, Physiologie et enseignement de la prononciation, *IRAL* 8 (1970), 221–225.

Jernudd, B H and Lindau, M, Approximations to Swedish phonetics by Australian English learners I, *IRAL* 11 (1973), 139–154.

Jernudd, B H and Lindau, M, Approximations to Swedish phonetics by Australian English learners II, *IRAL* 11 (1973), 211–227.

Jernudd, B, The linguist, the language teacher, and contrastive analysis, *Kivung* 5 (1972), 20–31.

Johansson, F A, Multiple contact analysis, *Errata: Papers in error analysis*, *ed* J Svartvik, Stockholm, 1973, 48–54.

Johansson, S, A case for studying Swedish–American, *Errata: Papers in error analysis*, *ed* J Svartvik, Stockholm, 1973, 55–59.

Johansson, F A, *Immigrant Swedish phonology: A study of multiple contact analysis.* Travaux de l'Institut de linguistique de Lund 9 (1973).

Johansson, S, *Kort lärobok i engelsk fonetik.* Lund, 1973.

Johansson, S, *Papers in Contrastive Linguistics and Language Testing.* Lund Studies in English 50, 1975.

Johansson, S, *Swedish and English phonemes: A perceptual study.* SECS Report 5, Lund, 1973.

Johansson, S, The uses of error analysis and contrastive analysis (I), *ELT* 29 (1975), 246–253.

Johansson, S, The uses of error analysis and contrastive analysis (II), *ELT* 29 (1975), 330–336.

Johnson, R L and Friedman, H L, Some temporal factors in the listening behavior of second language students, *The psychology of second language learning*, *ed* P Pimsleur and T Quinn, Cambridge, 1971, 165–169.

Jonasson, J and McAllister, R H, Foreign accent and timing: An instrumental phonetic study, *PILUS* 14 (1972), 11–40.

Jones, H, Error analysis in language teaching, *English for Immigrants* 4 (1971), 33–38.

Juhasz, J, Interferenzlinguistik, *Lexikon der germanistischen Linguistik*, *ed* H Althaus *et al*, Tübingen, 1973, 457–462.

Juhasz, J, *Probleme der Interferenz.* Munich, 1970.

Juhasz, J, Transfer und Interferenz, *Deutsch als Fremdsprache* (1969), 195–198.

Kacowsky, W, Ergenbnisse einer empirischen Untersuchung zur Fehlerhäufigkeit im Englischunterricht von der 5. Schulstufe bis zum Universitätseintritt, *Moderne Sprachen* 19 (1975), 1–20.

Kallioinen, V, Ääntämisen opetus fonemiikan ja fonetiikan kannalta, *Tempus* 1969, 2, 6–14.

Kalm, M, *Zur Anrede im Deutschen, im Finnischen und in Übersetzungen.* Germanistisches Institutu, Helsinki, 1972.

Kalogjera, D, A survey of grammatical characteristics of the English modal verbs with regard to interference problems, *YSCECP Reports* 1 (1969), 39–41.

Kaluza, H, Teaching the English articles to speakers of Slavic, *LL* 13 (1963), 113–124.

Kam, H W, An investigation of errors in English composition of some preuniversity students in Singapore, with suggestions for the teaching of written English, *RELC Journal* 4 (1973), 48–65.

Kandiah, T, The teaching of English in Ceylon: Some problems in contrastive statement, *LL* 15 (1965), 147–166.

Kaplan, R B, Contrastive grammar: Teaching composition to the Chinese student, *J. ESL* 3 (1968) 2, 1–13.

Kaplan, R B, Contrastive rhetoric and the teaching of composition, *TESOL* 1/4 (1967), 10–16.

Kaymer, G, Von der Notwendigkeit der Fehlerdiskriminierung im Englischunterricht, *Die Neueren Sprachen* 22 (1973), 573–580.

Kellerman, E, Elicitation, lateralisation and error analysis, *ISB-Utrecht* 1 (1976), 79–114.

Kellerman, E, The problem with difficulty, *ISB-Utrecht* 4 (1979), 27–48.

Kellerman, E, Towards a characterisation of the strategy of transfer in second language learning, *ISB-Utrecht* 1 (1977), 58–145.

Kelz, H P, Articulatory basis and second language teaching, *Phonetica* 24 (1971), 193–211.

Kessler, C, Syntactic contrasts in child bilingualism, *LL* 22 (1972), 221–234.

Khampang, P, Thai difficulties in using English prepositions, *LL* 24 (1974), 215–222.

Kielhöfer, B, Sprachkontrast und Lernschwierigkeit, *Französisch lehren und lernen,* ed W Börner, B Kielhöfer and K Vogel, Kronberg, 1976, 59–81.

Kirkwood, H W, Aspects of word order and its communicative function in English and German, *J. Ling.* 5 (1969), 85–107.

Kirsch, H, Fremdsprachenunterricht und kontrastive Phonematik, *Glottodidactica* 2 (1967), 21–31.

Kitzing, K, Contrastive acoustic analysis of vowel phonemes, pronounced by some North German and South Swedish high school pupils, *LUND Working Papers* 4 (1971), 48–57.

Kitzing, K, *Kontrastiv akustisk och perceptuell analys av vokalfonem has nordtyska och sydsvenska gymnasister.* Lund, 1972.

Koefoed, H A, *Structure and Usage as Applied to Word-order,* Oslo/Bergen, 1967.

262   Kari Sajavaara and Jaakko Lehtonen

Kohler, K J, Anwendungsorientierte Phonetik: Sinn und Unsinn der kontrastiven Phonologie für den Fremdsprachenunterricht, *Ling. Berichte* 26 (1973), 70–78.

Kohn, K, *Konfrontative Grammatik und Interferenzforschung*, Wissenschaftliche Zeitschrift der Humboldt Universität zu Berlin 12, 3, 1973.

Kohn, K, Kontrastive Syntax und Fehlerbeschreibung. *Skripten Linguistik und Kommunikationswissenschaft* 10. Kronberg, 1974.

Kohn, K, Kontrastive Syntax und Fehlerbeschreibung, *Skripten Linguistik und Kommunikationswissenschaft* 10, Regensburg, 1974.

Kohn, K, Lernersprache aus linguistischer Sicht, *Linguistische Berichte* 46 (1976), 47–60.

Koo, J H, Language universals and the acquisition of an unfamiliar sound, *IRAL* 10 (1972), 145–152.

Kopczyński, A, Degree of voicing in initial stops in educated Polish and American English, *SAP* 3 (1971), 75–79.

Kranjcević, S, Errors in the syntax of the sentence in the speech of learners of English in the Serbo-Croatian-speaking area, *YSCECP Ped. mat.* 1 (1971), 60–80.

Kreidler, C W, Teaching English spelling and pronunciation, *TESOL Quart.* 6 (1972), 3–12.

Kruatrachue, F, *Thai and English: A comparative study of phonology for pedagogical applications.* Bloomington, 1968.

Kruppa, U, Kontrastive Analyse von Interferenzerscheinungen im deutschen-englischen Bereich, *Neusprachliche Mitteilungen* 28 (1975), 92–99.

Krzeszowski, T P, Contrastive linguistics and its pedagogical applications, *Reports from the Department of English, University of Jyväskylä* 5 (1977), ed K Sajavaara, 17–20.

Krzeszowski, T P, English tense expressing verb phrases in the process of teaching Polish students, *Glottodidactica* 1 (1966), 115–124.

Krzeszowski, T P, Interlanguage and contrastive generative grammar, *ISB-Utrecht* 1 (1976), 58–79.

Krzeszowski, T P, The so-called deep structures and the foreign language learner, *Linguistic insights in applied linguistics,* ed S P Corder and E Roulet, Brussels, 1974, 77–87.

Krzeszowski, T P, *Teaching English to Polish learners,* Warszawa: PWN, 1970.

Kufner, H L, Deskriptive Grammatik—kontrastive Grammatik—pädagogische Grammatik, *Fragen der strukturellen Syntax und der kontrastiven Grammatik.* Sprache der Gegenwart: Schriften des Instituts für deutsche Sprache 17, Düsseldorf, 1971, 201–209.

Kufner, H L, Kontrastive Grammatik und dan...? *Angewandte Sprachwissenschaft und Deutschunterricht,* ed G Nickel, Munich, 1973, 17–31.

Kugler, W, Strukturmerksätze: ein Beitrag zur Fehlerkorrektur undprophylaxe auf kontrastiver Grundlage, *Neusprachliche Mitteilungen* 28 (1975), 132–140.

Kühlwein, W, Fehleranalyse im Bereich des englischen Vokalismus, *Fehlerkunde*, ed G Nickel, Berlin, 1972, 51–66.

Kühlwein, W, Intra- und interstrukturale Fehlleistungen auf der phonemischegraphemischen Ebene, *PAKS Arbeitsberichte* 5, 39–84.

Kühlwein, W, An outline of the project 'Forum applied linguistics' of the international Hasselt conference, *2nd international conference of English contrastive projects, Bucharest, 20–23 November, 1975*, ed D Chitoran, Bucharest, 1976, 67–75.

Kühlwein, W, Phonetik und Phonemik im englischen Anfangsunterricht, *Schule und Hochschule 1969*, ed I Braak, Kiel, 1970.

Kühlwein, W, The state of applied contrastive linguistics as reflected by the 19th Annual Round Table Meeting, *SAP* 4 (1972), 81–92.

Künne, W, Erstellung eine fremdsprachlichen Aussprachetests: Probleme und Methoden, *Die Sprachen* 72 (1973), 372–380.

König, E, Fehleranalyse und Fehlertherapie im lexikalischen Bereich, *Fehlerkunde*, ed G Nickel, Berlin, 1972, 73–77.

König, E, Syntax und Semantik der modalen Hilfsverben im Englischen: Ein Beitrag zu dem Thema 'Linguistik und Fremdsprachenunterricht', *PAKS Arbeitsberichte* 3/4 (1969), 1–26.

Kussmaul, P, Good-bye, my love, good-bye! Zur Übersetzung Kontextdeterminierter Ausdrücke, *Linguistische Berichte* 31 (1974), 47–53.

Kuusinen, J and Salin, E, Children's learning of unfamiliar phonological sequences, *Perceptual and Motor Skills* 33 (1971), 559–562.

Köster, J-P, Beurteilung synthetischer vokalartiger Signale durch deutsche Schüler unterschiedlicher Altersstufen und ihre Konsequenzen für den Sprachunterricht, *Hamburger Phonetische Beiträge 9: Miszellen, I*, Hamburg, 1973, 47–84.

Lado, R, Contrastive linguistics in a mentalistic theory of language learning, *Contrastive linguistics and its pedagogical implications*, ed J Alatis, Washington DC, 1968, 125–135.

Lado, R, *Language testing: The construction and use of foreign language tests*. London, 1967.

Lado, R, *Linguistics across cultures: Applied linguistics for language teachers*. Ann Arbor, 1957.

Lado, R, Meine Perspektive der kontrastiven Linguistik 1945–1972, *Reader zur kontrastiven Linguistik*, ed G Nickel, Frankfurt, 1972, 15–20.

Lamminmäki, R, The discrimination and identification of English vowels, consonant, junctures and sentence stress by Finnish comprehensive school pupils, *Jyväskylä Cross-Language Studies* 7 (1979), 165–73.

Lane, H, Foreign and speech distortion, *JASA* 35 (1963), 451–453.

Larnmouth, D W, Differential interference in American Finnish cases, *Language* 50 (1974), 356–366.

Laroche-Bouvy, D, Une pédagogie de perfectionnement linguistique pour les enseignants: l'étude contrastive, *Studi italiani di linguistica teorica et applicata* 5 (1976), 191–212.

Lawendowski, B, Some postulates concerning the role of translation in contrastive studies, *PSiCL* Vol 5, *ed* J Fisiak, Poznań, 1976, 19–27.

Lee, W R, The contribution of contrastive linguistics to the preparation of language teaching materials, *Proceedings of the 3rd AILA congress, Copenhagen 1972*, Vol 1, *ed* G Nickel, Heidelberg, 1974, 137–142.

Lee, W R, How can contrastive linguistic studies help foreign language teaching?, *YSCECP Studies* 5 (1972), 57–66.

Lee, W R, Language, experience, and the language learner, *ELT* 27 (1973), 234–245.

Lee, W R, Thoughts on contrastive linguistics in the context of language teaching, *Contrastive linguistics and its pedagogical implications, ed* J E Alatis, Washington DC, 1968.

Lee, W R, Types of interference and contrasting—the kinds of research needed, *PAKS: Papers from the international symposium on applied contrastive linguistics, Stuttgart, Oct. 11–13, 1971, ed* G Nickel, Bielefeld, 1972, 13–26.

Lee, W R, Überlegungen zur kontrastiven Linguistik im Bereich des Sprachunterrichts, *Reader zur kontrastiven Linguistik, ed* G Nickel, Frankfurt, 1972, 156–166.

Legenhausen, L, *Fehleranalyse und Fehlerbewertung. Untersuchungen an englischen Reifeprüfurgsnacherzählungen*. Berlin, 1975.

Lehiste, I, Grammatical variability and the difference between native and non-native speakers, *Papers in contrastive linguistics, ed* G Nickel, Cambridge, 1971, 69–74.

Lehtonen, J, *Kielenopetuksen fonologiaa*, Kasvatustieteen tutkimuslaotoksen julkaisuja 168. Jyväskylä, 1972.

Lehtonen, J, Sajavaara, K and May, A, *Spoken English*. Jyväskylä, 1977.

Leisi, E, Theoretische Grundlagen der Fehlerbewertung, *Fehlerkunde, ed* G Nickel, Berlin, 1972, 25–37.

Leiwo, M, Äännesubstituutioista: Erityisesti mustalaiskielen klusiilien mukautmisesta suomen fonologiseen järjestelmään, *Transformaatioita*, Turun yliopiston fonetiikan laitoksen juikaisuja 7, 1970, 41–51.

Léon, P, Teaching pronunciation, *Trends in language teaching, ed* A Valdman, New York, 1966, 57–80.

Levenston, E A, A classification of language differences, *IRAL* 4 (1966), 198–206.

Levenston, E A, Over-indulgence and under-representation: Aspects of mothertongue interference, *Papers in contrastive linguistics, ed* G Nickel, Cambridge, 1971, 115–121.

Levin, L, *Comparative studies in foreign language teaching*. Stockholm, 1972.

Lindblom, B and Sundberg, J, A quantitative theory of cardinal vowels and the teaching of pronunciation, *STL-QPSR* 2–3 (1969).

Linde, R, The analysis of grammatical errors in advanced spoken English. *JACET Bulletin* (Japan) 3 (1972), 87–118.

Lindgren, L, Ranskan vokaalien oppimiseen liittyviä vaikeuksia, *Tempus* 1972, 6, 16–19.

Lindner, G and Melika, G I, Mechanismus der Sprachinterferenz und Prinzipien seiner Wirkungsweise, *Z. Phon.* 25 (1972), 289–305.

Linnarud, M, Lexis in free production: An analysis of the lexical tc*r*ture of Swedish students' written work, *SECS Report* 6 (1975), Lung, 1975.

Linnarud, M, Some aspects of style in the source and the target language, *PSiCL* Vol 7, *ed* J Fisiak, 1977, 85–94.

Littlewood, W T, A comparison of first language acquisition and second language learning, *Praxis der neusprachlichen Unterrichts* 20 (1973), 343–348.

Lotz, J, Abramson, A S, Gerstman, L J, Ingemann, F and Nemser, W J, The perception of English stops by speakers of English, Spanish, Hungarian and Thai: A tape-cutting experiment, *Language and Speech* 3 (1960), 71–77.

Löffler, H, Deutsch für Dialektsprecher: Ein Sonderfall des Fremdsprachenunterrichts? Zur Theorie einer kontrastiven Grammatik Dialekt/Hochsprache, *Deutsche Sprache* 2 (1974), 105–122.

Mach, V, Comparative analysis of English and Czech phonology and prediction of errors in learning, *Papers in contrastive linguistics*, *ed* G Nickel, Cambridge, 1971, 103–106.

McCarthy, K M, Teaching English prepositions, *TEFL* 6 (1972) 2, 3.

Mackey, W F, *Interference, integration and the synchronic fallacy*. Quebec, Centre international de recherche sur le bilinguisme, 1970.

McNamara, J, The bilingual's linguistic performance: A psychological overview, *Journal of Social Issues* 23 (1967), 58–77.

Madarasz, P H, *Contrastive linguistic analysis and error analysis in learning English and Hungarian*. Diss. University of California, Berkeley, 1968.

Margot, O, On an automated pronunciation—hearing test of French monosyllables for Japanese students, *Annual Bulletin* 6. Research Institute of Logopedics and Phoniatrics, University of Tokyo, 1972, 47–71.

Martin, H, *Untersuchungen zur sprachlichen Interferenz auf der Grundlage finnlanddeutschen Materials*. Turku, 1973.

Martins, E, *Studien zur Frage der linguistischen Interferenz*. Stockholm, 1970.

Marton, W, Contrastive analysis in the classroom, *PSiCL* Vol 1, *ed* J Fisiak, Poznań, 1973, 15–22.

Marton, W, Foreign vocabulary learning as problem No. 1 of language teaching at the advanced level, *ISB-Utrecht* 1 (1977), 33–57.

Marton, W, Pedagogical implications of contrastive studies, *SAP* 4 (1972), 115–127.

Marton, W, Some methodological assumptions for transformational contrastive studies, *Active methods and modern aids in the teaching foreign languages*, *ed* R Filipović, London, 1972, 198–206.

Marton, W, Some more remarks on the pedagogical uses of contrastive studies, *PSiCl* Vol 8, *ed* J Fisiak, 1979, 35–46.

Marton, W, Some remarks on the formal properties of contrastive pedagogical grammars, *Proceedings of the 3rd AILA congress, Copenhagen 1972,* Vol. 1, *ed* G Nickel, Heidelberg, 1974, 182–195.

Marton, W and Preston, D R British and American English for Polish University Students: Research Report and Projections, *Glottodidactica* 8 (1975), 27–43.

Marynowski, S, English phrasal verbs and some remarks on teaching them to Polish learners, *Języki Obce w Szkole* 1 (1976), 7–14.

Mascherpe, M, *Análise comparativa dos sistemas fonologicos do Ingles e do Portugues: Classificação dos erros prováveis com sugestöes para una aplicação pedagógica.* São Paulo, 1970.

Mazzarella, S, Mistakes commonly made by Finnish-speaking people when pronouncing English, *Tempus* 1971, 1, 19–21.

Melchers, G, On teaching English pronunciation to Swedes, *Kontrastiv Lingvistik i sekundärspråkforskning,* ed B Hammarberg, Stockholm, 1979, 41–60.

Melerowicz, A, On the semantics of some English and Polish verbs. *PSiCL* Vol 4, *ed* J Fisiak, Poznan, 1976, 199–204.

Menting, J F, Analyse de fautes dans l'enseignement du français langue étrangère au niveau supérieur aux Pays-Bas, *Proceedings of the 3rd AILA congress, Copenhagen 1972,* Vol. 1, *ed* G Nickel, Heidelberg, 1974, 196–212.

Meriö, K, Mitä interferenssi on vieraan kielen oppimisessa?, *Tempus* 1974, 6, 15–17.

Meriö, K, The psycholinguistic analysis and measurement of interference errors, *IRAL* 16 (1978), 27–44.

Meyer, H-J, Englisches 'up' und deutsches 'auf', *Fremdsprachenunterricht* 17 (1973), 179–187.

Meyer, J, Les tests de perception et leur interpretation: Application à l'acquisition des voyelles anglaises par des élèves francophones, *Travaux de l'Institut de Phonetique de Strasbourg* 2 (1970), 66–81.

Meyer, J, Le traitement articulatoire du groupe occlusive + nasale dans la prononciation de l'anglais parlé par des francophones, *Travaux de l'Institut de Phonetique de Strasbourg* 1 (1969), 51–63.

Meziani, A, The past in English and Moroccan Arabic. *IRAL* 18 (1980), 248–252.

Milon, J, The development of negation in English by a second language learner, *TESOL Quart.* 8 (1974), 137–145.

Mindt, D, Blume H, Cherubim, D and Müller, K L Kontrastive Linguistik: Erfahrungsberichte über ein interdisziplinäres Projektseminar, *Mitteilungen der Technischen Univ. Carolo-Wilhelmina zu Braunschweig* 10 (1975), 32–41.

Mleczak, J, On interference in learning foreign languages: Insights from Polish, *Bulletin phonographique* 16 (1975), 19–44.

Moisio, R and Valento, E, *Testing Finnish Schoolchildrens Learning of English Consonants.* Jyväskylä Contrastive Studies 3. Jyväskylä, 1976.

Molony, C, 'Ich bin sprechen Deutsch aber': the sequence of verb and word order acquisition of an American child learning German, *German in contact with other languages*, ed C Molony, H Zobl and W Stölting, Monographien Linguistik und Kommunikationswissenschaft 26, Kronberg/Ts, Düsseldorf, 1977, 274–295.

Motsch, W, Gedanken zum Verhältnis zwischen Linguistik, Psychologie und Fremdsprachenunterricht, *Deutsch als Fremdsprache* 9 (1972), 213–221.

Moulton, W G, Toward a classification of pronunciation errors, *MLJ* 46 (1962), 101–109.

Mukattash, L, A pilot project in common grammatical errors in Jordanian English, *ISB-Utrecht* 3 (1978), 250–291.

Müller, D, Zu einigen Aspekten der Transferierbarkeit in Bereich der grammatischen Bedeutungen, *Wissenschaftliche Zeitschrift der Humbolt Universität zu Berlin* 23 (1974), 53–66.

Müller, R, Rechtschreibung und Fehleranalyse, *Schule und Psychologie* (1965), 161–173.

Munske, H H, Vorschläge zur multilateralen kontrastiven Grammatik unter Berücksichtigung differenzierter Sprachkompetenz, *Z. Dialektol. Ling.* 39 (1972), 284–299.

Muskat-Tabakowska, E, Some aspects of modification in English and Polish—pedagogical implications, *PSiCL* Vol. 7, ed J Fisiak, 1977, 157–169.

Muskat-Tabakowska, E, Syntactic ambiguity and the teaching of written English to advanced Polish learners—norm and usage, *PSiCL* Vol 4, ed J Fisiak, Poznan, 1976, 319–322.

Muskat-Tabakowska, E, Syntactic ambiguity and the teaching of written English to advanced Polish learners, *PSiCL* Vol 2, ed J Fisiak, Poznań, 1974, 369–384.

Muskat-Tabakowska, E, Syntactic ambiguity and the teaching of written English to advanced Polish learners—grammar or style?, *PSiCL* Vol 3, ed J Fisiak, Poznan, 1975, 99–111.

Muskat-Tabakowska, E, Voiced/voiceless opposition in consonants: A problem in teaching English pronunciation to Polish learners, *Glottodidactica* 5 (1970), 97–106.

Nádasdy, A, Interrogative sentences in English: A language teaching problem for Hungarians, *HCLP* 4 (1973), 45–52.

Nash, R, Phonemic and prosodic interference and intelligibility, *Proceedings of the 7th international Congress of Phonetic Sciences, Montreal 1971*, The Hague and Paris, 1972, 570–572.

Nehls, D, Fehleranalyse versus kontrastive Analysis, *Kongressbericht der 5. Jahrestagung der Gesellschaft für angewandte Linguistik GAL e.V. IRAL-Sonderband*, ed G Nickel and A Raasch, Heidelberg, 1974, 202–208.

Nemser, W Approximative systems of foreign language learners, *IRAL* 9 (1971), 115–123.

Nemser, W, The predictability of interference phenomena in the English speech of native speakers of Hungarian, *Papers in contrastive linguistics, ed* G Nickel, Cambridge, 1971, 89–96.

Nemser, W and Vincenz, I, The indeterminacy of semantic interference, *RECAP Studies, ed* D Chitoran and I Ionescu, Bucharest, 1972, 269–303.

Nemser, W and Vincents, I, The indeterminacy of semantic interference, *Revue Roumaine de Linguistique* 17 (1972), 99–120.

Nemser, W J, *An experimental study of phonological interference in the English of Hungarians*. Indiana University Publications, Uralic and Altaic Series 105, Bloomington and The Hague, 1971.

Nemser, W J, The predictability of interference phenomena in the English speech of native speakers of Hungarian, *Papers in contrastive linguistics, ed* G Nickel, Cambridge, 1971, 89–96.

Nemser, W and Slama-Cazacu, T, A contribution to contrastive linguistics (A psycholinguistic approach: Contact analysis), *Revue roumaine de linguistique* 15 (1970), 101–128.

Ney, J, Two neglected factors in language comparison, *MLJ* 48 (1964), 129–134.

Nichols, A C, Apparent factors leading to errors in audition made by foreign students, *Speech Monographs* 31 (1964), 85–91.

Nichols, A C, English punctuation problems for speakers of Germanic languages, *LL* 12 (1962), 195–204.

Nickel, G (ed) *Applied contrastive linguistics. Proceedings of the 3rd International Congress of Applied Linguistics, Copenhagen, August 21–26, 1972.* Heidelberg, 1974.

Nickel, G, Aspects of error evaluation and grading, *Errata: Papers in error analysis, ed* J Svartvik, Stockholm, 1973, 24–28.

Nickel, G, Aspekte der Fehleranalyse, *PAKS Arbeitsberichte* 7 (1973), 157–165.

Nickel, G, Contrastive linguistics and foreign language teaching, *Papers in contrastive linguistics, ed* G Nickel, Cambridge, 1971, 1–16.

Nickel, G, Contrastive linguistics and some pedagogical implications, *Contact* 15 (1970), 18–20.

Nickel, G, Contrastive linguistics at the second international congress of applied linguistics, *Project für Angewandte Kontrastive Sprachwissenschaft* 3 (1969), 59–62.

Nickel, G (ed) *Fehlerkunde: Beiträge zur Fehleranalyse, Fehlerbewertung und Fehlertherapie.* Berlin, 1972.

Nickel, G, Grundsätzliches zur Fehleranalyse und Fehlerbewertung, *Fehlerkunde, ed* G Nickel, Berlin, 1972, 8–24.

Nickel, G, Kontrastive Sprachwissenschaft und Fehleranalyse, *Fragen der strukturellen Syntax und der kontrastiven Grammatik, ed* H Moser, Düsseldorf, 1971, 210–217.

Nickel, G, Kontrastive Sprachwissenschaft und Fremdsprachenunterricht, *Neusprachliche Mitteilungen* 25 (1972), 77–80.

Nickel, G, Linguistics applied, *Inc. Linguist* 11 (1972) 29–34.

Nickel, G (*ed*) *Papers in contrastive linguistics.* Cambridge, 1971.

Nickel, G, Problems of learners' difficulties in foreign language learning, *IRAL* 9 (1971), 219–227.

Nickel, G (*ed*) *Proceedings of the 3rd AILA congress, Copenhagen 1972,* Vol 1: *Applied contrastive linguistics.* Heidelberg, 1974.

Nickel, G, Project on applied contrastive linguistics: A report, *Active methods and modern aids in the teaching of foreign language, ed* R Filipović, Oxford, 1972, 217–226.

Nickel, G (*ed*) *Reader zur kontrastiven Linguistik.* Frankfurt, 1972.

Nickel, G and Raasch, A (*ed*) *Kongressbericht der 5. Jahrestagung der Gesellschaft für angewandte Linguistik GAL e.V. IRAL-Sonderband.* Heidelberg, 1974.

Nickel, G and Wagner, K H, Contrastive linguistics and language teaching, *IRAL* 6 (1968), 233–255.

Nilsen, L F, Contrastive semantics in vocabulary instruction, *TESOL Quart.* 10 (1976), 99–103.

Noblitt, J S, Pedagogical grammar: Towards a theory of foreign language materials preparation, *IRAL* (1970), 313–331.

Novikov, L, Lexikalische Interferenz in Forschung und Unterricht, *Praxis* 1 (1976), 65–77.

Nygård, A, *Some remarks on contrastive analyses of the pronunciation of two languages.* Engelska institutionens vid Åbo Akademi publikationer 1, 1967.

Ohannessian, S and Gage W W (*eds*) *Teaching English to speakers of Choctaw, Navajo and Papago: A contrastive approach.* Washington DC., 1969.

Oksaar, E, Sprachliche Interferenzen und die kommunikative Kompetenz, *Indo-Celtica, ed* H. Pilch and J Thurow, Munich, 1972.

Oller, J W, Jr, Contrastive analysis, difficulty, and predictability, *Foreign Language Annals* 6 (1972), 95–106.

Oller, J W, Jr, Transfer and interference as special cases of induction and substitution, *Linguistics* 89 (1972), 24–33.

Oller, J W, Jr and Redding E Z, Article usage and other language skills, *LL* 21 (1971), 85–95.

Oller, J and Richards, J (*eds*) *Focus on the learner: pragmatic perspectives for the language teacher.* Mass., 1975 (2nd printing).

Oller, J W and Tullius J R, Reading skills of non-native speakers of English, *IRAL* 11 (1973), 69–80.

Oller, J W, Jr and Ziahosseiny, S M, The contrastive analysis hypothesis and spelling errors, *LL* 20 (1970), 183–189.

Olsson, M, Intelligibility: A study of errors and their importance, *GUME Research Bulletin* 12 (1972), Göteborg.

Oskarsson, M, On the role of the mother tongue in learning foreign language vocabulary: an empirical investigation, *ITL* 27 (1975), 19–32.

Palmberg, R, Bibliography additions, *ISB-Utrecht* 3 (1977), 91–99.

Palmberg, R, A select bibliography of error analysis and related topics, *ISB-Utrecht* 1 (1976), 340–389.

Palmberg, R, A select bibliography of error analysis and related topics, *Errors made by Finns and Swedish-speaking Finns in the learning of English*, *AFTIL* 5, ed H Ringbom and R Palmberg, Abo, 1976, 139–162.

Palmberg, R and Ringbom, H (*eds*) *Papers from the conference on contrastive linguistics and error analysis, Stockholm and Åbo. 7–8 February 1977*, Publications of the Research Institute of the Åbo Akademi Foundation 19, Åbo, 1977.

Pascasio, E M, Predicting interference and facilitation for Tagalog speakers in learning English, *LL* 11 (1961), 78–84.

Paterno, A, English sounds difficult for Tagalog learners of English, *MST English Quarterly* 20 (1970), 358–372.

Peck, A, Die Bedeutung der kontrastiven Analyse für den Fremdsprachenunterricht, *Fragen der strukturellen Syntax und der kontrastiven Grammatik*, ed H Moser, Düsseldorf, 1971, 228–235.

Pergnier, M, Pour une contribution de la linguistique à la pédagogie des langues vivantes: le groupe nominal simple en anglais et en français, *Langues Modernes* 63 (1969), 39–45.

Perrot, J, Problèmes méthodologiques en description contrastive, *Etudes Finno-Ougriennes XI* (1974), 219–227.

Péter, J, Pitfalls for Hungarians, *ELT* 28 (1974), 159–165.

Peters, D I, *A contrastive analysis of selected English and Spanish written verb forms which present difficulty to native speakers of Spanish*. Diss. New York University, 1973.

Phillips, B S and Bouma, L, The acquisition of German plurals in native children and non-native adults, *IRAL* 18 (1980), 121–130.

Pillai, M S, Problems in teaching Tamil to foreign students, *IRAL* 5 (1967), 201–209.

Plaister, T, Contrastive analysis and materials adaptation, *Bulletin of the English Language Center* 1 (1971) 3, 54–64.

Politzer, R L, Language development in two bilingual schools: A study in contrastive psycholinguistic analysis, *IRAL* 16 (1978), 241–252.

Politzer, R L and Ramirez, A G An error analysis of the spoken English of Mexican-American pupils in a bilingual school and a monolingual school, *LL* 23 (1973), 39–62.

Py, B, Analyse des erreurs et acquisition des structures interrogatives du français, *Bulletin CILA* (1973), 21–29.

Raabe, H, Interimsprache und kontrastive Analyse, *Trends in kontrastiver Linguistik 1*, ed H Raabe, Mannheim and Tübingen, 1974, 1–50.

Raabe, H (*ed*) *Trends in kontrastiver Linguistik 1*. Forschungsberichte des Instituts für deutsche Sprache 16, Mannheim and Tübingen, 1974.

Raabe, H, Zum Verhältnis von kontrastiver Grammatik und Übersetzung, *Reader zur kontrastiven Linguistik, ed* G Nickel, Frankfurt, 1972, 59–74.

Ravem, R, Language acquisition in a second language environment, *IRAL* 6 (1968), 175–185.

Reibel, D A, Language analysis, *IRAL* 7 (1969), 283–294.

Richards, J C, Error analysis and second language strategies, *Language Sciences* 17 (1971), 12–22.

Richards, J C (*ed*) *Error analysis: Perspectives on second language acquisition, applied linguistics and language study.* London, 1974.

Richards, J C, A non-contrastive approach to error analysis, EL T 25 (1971), 204–219.

Richards, J and Sampson, G, The study of learner English, *Error analysis— perspectives in second language acquisition, applied linguistics and language study, ed* J Richards, London, 1974, 3–18.

Riegel, K F, The nature of second language learning and bilingualism, *Studies in Language and Language Behavior* 6 (1970), 1–7.

Riegel, K F, Some theoretical considerations of bilingual development, *Psychological Bulletin* 70 (1968), 647–670.

Riegel, K F and Zivian, I W M A study of inter- and intra-lingual associations in English and German, *LL* 22 (1972), 51–64.

Riley, P, Towards contrastive pragmalinguistics, *PSiCL* Vol 10, *ed* J Fisiak, 1979, 57–78.

Ringbom, H, The influence of the mother tongue on the translation of lexical items, *ISB-Utrecht* 3 (1978), 80–101.

Ringbom, H, What differences are there between Finns and Swedish-speaking Finns learning English, *Errors made by Finns and Swedish-speaking Finns in the learning of English,* AFTIL 5, *ed* H Ringbom and R Palmberg, Åbo, 1976, 1–13.

Ringbom, H and Palmberg, R (*eds*), *Errors made by Finns and Swedish-speaking Finns in the Learning of English.* AFTIL 5. Åbo, 1977.

Ritchie, W C, On the explanation of phonic interference, *LL* 18 (1968), 183–196.

Ritchie, W C, Some implications of generative grammar for the construction of courses in English as a foreign language, *LL* 17 (1967), 45–69; 111–131.

Rivers, W M, Contrastive linguistics in textbook and classroom, *Contrastive linguistics and its pedagogical implications, ed* J E Alatis, Washington DC, 1968, 151–157.

Roach, P J, Phonetics in pronunciation training, *Audiovis. Lang. J.* 10 (1972), 34–40.

Rockey, R E, *Contrastive analysis of the language structures of three ethnic groups of children enrolled in head-start programs.* Diss. Cornell University, 1970.

Rojas, C, L'analyse des fautes, *Le Francais dans le Monde* 81 (1971), 58–63.

Roland, L, An experiment in a pronunciation problem, *IRAL* 4 (1966), 255–259.

Roos, E, Kontrastive Lexikologie, *Contributions to Applied Linguistics I*, ed Ch Gutknecht, Bern, 1975, 89–103.

Ross, J, The habit of perception in foreign language learning: insights into error from contrastive analysis, *TESOL Quart.* 10 (1976), 169–175.

Rossipal, H, Zur Struktur der sprachlichen Fehlleistung, *Errata: Papers in error analysis*, ed J Svartvik, Stockholm, 1973, 60–89.

Rusiecki, J, Latent bilingualism, *PSiCL* Vol. 12, ed J Fisiak, Poznań, 1980, 79–98.

Sacks, N P, A study in Spanish pronunciation errors, *Hispania* 45 (1962), 289–300.

Sah, P P, Towards a theory of error analysis, *York Papers in Linguistics*, Vol 1 (1971), 29–56.

Sajavaara, K, Contrastive linguistics past and present and a communicative approach, *Jyväskylä Contrastive Studies* 4 (1977), 9–30.

Sajavaara, K, Äidinkieli ja vieraat kielet, *Äidinkielen opettajain liiton vuosikirja* 23 (1976), Helsinki, 1976, 81–97.

Sampson, G P and Richards, J C, Learner language systems, *Language Sciences* 19 (1973), 18–25.

Saporta, S, Some likely areas of difficulty for Spanish students of English, *English—a New Language* 13 (1973), 34–52.

Saporta, S, Brown, R E and Wolfe, W D, Toward a quantification of phonic interference, *Language and Speech* 2 (1959), 205–210.

Schachter, J, An error in error analysis, *LL* 24 (1974), 205.

Schaeder, B, Die Analyse der Inhalte deutsch und englisch Präpositional-phrasen und ihre Synthese im maschinellen Übersetzungsprozess, *IRAL-Sonderband* 2 (1971), 209–216.

Schane, S, Linguistics, spelling and pronunciation, *TESOL Quart.* 4 (1970), 137–141.

Schlect, G, Der Vergleich deutscher und englischer grammatischer Erscheinungen als Grundlage für eine Verbesserung des Englischunterrichts, *Moderner Fremdsprachenunterricht*, ed W Apelt et al, Berlin, 1968, 75–99.

Schmidt, K, Schwierigkeiten der Realisierung deutscher *e- und o-Laute für Finnen, Deutsch als Fremdsprache* 8 (1971), 242–245.

Schneider, A and Wambach, M, Das System der Fehler und die phonetische Korrektion der Frankophonen in der deutschen Sprache, *Revue de Phonetique Appliquée* 5 (1967), 35–73.

Schneiderbauer, A M, Schwierigkeiten der deutschen Worstellung für Englischlernende, *Deutsch für Ausländer* 16 (1966), 153–167.

Schnitzer, M, Applied generative phonology: A methodology for teaching pronunciation, *IRAL* 12 (1974), 289–305.

Scholes, R J, Phonemic interference as a perceptual phenomenon, *Language and Speech* 11 (1968), 86–103.

Schourup, L C, A cross-language study of vowel nasalization, *OHIO Working Papers in Linguistics* 15 (1973), 190–221.

Schulte-Pelkum, R, Interferenzfehler bei deutschsprechen Japanern, Deutsch–Japanische Kontraste. *Vorstudien zu einer kontrastiven Grammatik, Forschungsberichte des Institus für deutsche Sprache* 29, ed G Stickel, Tübingen, 1975, 59–112.

Schumann, J H and Stenson N (eds) *New frontiers in second language learning.* Rowley, Mass., 1974.

Sciarone, A G, Contrastive analysis—possibilities and limitations, *IRAL* 8 (1970), 115–131.

Scott, M S and Tucker, G R, Error analysis and English-language strategies of Arab students, *LL*24 (1974), 69–98.

Scovel, T, Foreign accents, language acquisition and cerebral dominance, *LL* 18 (1969), 245–253.

Sederquist, A, Methodische Voruntersuchung zum Problem der sprachlichen Interferenz, Teil I, *Phonetica* 27 (1973), 129–149.

Sederquist, A, Methodische Voruntersuchung zum Problem der sprachlichen Interferenz. Teil I, *Phonetica* 27 (1973), 219–251.

Selinker, L, A brief reappraisal of contrastive linguistics, *SAP* 4 (1972), 15–21.

Selinker, L, Interlanguage, *IRAL* 10 (1972), 209–230.

Selinker, L, Language transfer, *General Linguistics* 9 (1969), 67–92.

Selinker, L, Swain M and Dumas, G, The interlanguage hypothesis extended to children, *LL* 25 (1975), 139–152.

Setian, R, Grammatical interference in the teaching of English to Egyptian students, *ELT* 28 (1974), 253–257.

Sharwood Smith, M, Contrastive studies in two perspectives, *PSiCL* Vol 2, ed J Fisiak, Poznań, 1974, 5–10.

Sharwood Smith, M, English word order, error analysis and pedagogical solutions, *SAP* 6 (1974), 129–134.

Sharwood Smith, M, Imperfective versus progressive—an exercise in contrastive pedagogical linguistics, *PSiCL* Vol 3, ed J Fisiak, Poznań, 1975, 85–90.

Sharwood Smith, M, Interlanguage and intralanguage paraphrase, *PSiCL* Vol 4, ed J Fisiak, Poznań, 1976, 297–302.

Sharwood Smith, M, Pedagogical grammar, *ISB-Utrecht* 1 (1976), 45–57.

Sharwood Smith, M, Strategies, language transfer and the simulation of the second language learner's mental operations, *ISB-Utrecht* 4 (1979), 66–83.

Sharwood Smith, M, Strategies, language transfer and the simulation of the second language learner's mental operations, *LL* 29, (1979), 345–362.

Sheen, R, The importance of negative transfer in the speech of near-bilinguals, *IRAL* 18 (1980), 105–120.

Shillan, D, An application of contrastive linguistics, *Meta* 15 (1970), 161–163.

Shillan, D, Contrastive linguistics and the translator, *Inc. Linguist* 10 (1971) 1, 10–13.

Sjöholm, K, A comparison of the test results in grammar and vocabulary between Finnish- and Swedish-speaking applicants for English, *Errors made*

by Finns and Swedish-speaking Finns in the learning of English, AFTIL 5, ed H
Ringbom and R Palmberg, Abo, 1976.

Slama-Cazacu, T, The concept of 'acquisition corpus', 'aberrant corpus' and
'hierarchical system of errors' in contrastive analysis, Proceedings of the 3rd
AILA congress Copenhagen 1972, Vol 1, ed G Nickel, Heidelberg, 1974,
235–251.

Slama-Cazacu, T, Contrastive study 'in abstracto' or function of the meeting of
linguistic systems in the learner, RECAP, Reports and studies, Bucharest,
1971, 57–70.

Slama-Cazacu, T, Kontrastive Analyse 'in abstracto' oder Funktion spraclicher
Systeme beim Aufeinandertreffen im Lerner, Trends in kontrastiver Linguistik
II, ed H Raabe, Mannheim and Tübingen, 1974,

Slama-Cazacu, T, Psycholinguistics and contrastive studies, YSCECP Studies 4
(1971), 188–206.

Slama-Cazacu, T (ed), The psycholinguistic approach in the Romanian–English
contrastive analysis project, 1, Bucharest, 1975.

Slama-Cazacu, T, The Romanian–English language project, YSCECP Studies 4
(1971), 226–234.

Slama-Cazacu, T, Theoretical interpretation and methodological consequences
of 'regularization', Further Developments in Contrastive Studies, RECAP,
Bucharest University Press, 1974, 5–36.

Slama-Cazacu, T and Chitoran, D, Report of the working group of psycholinguistic research; stage of establishing the hierarchical system of errors,
RECAP, Reports and studies, Bucharest, 1971, 31–48.

Spillner, B, Kontrastive Semantik: Inhalts-Faktorenvergleich und übersetzung,
IRAL -Sonderband 2 (1971), 35–42.

Sridhar, S N, Contrastive analysis, error analysis and interlanguage; three
phases of one goal?, Studies in Language Learning 1 (1975), 60–94.

Stanley, G E, Linguistic relativity and the EFL teacher in South Africa, ELT 25
(1971), 284–287.

Stendhal, C Investigating oral and written proficiency in English as a foreign
language at university level: A pilot study. MUP Report 18, English and
Pedagogical Departments, University of Göteborg, 1970.

Stendhal, C, The relative proficiency in their native language and in English
shown by Swedish students of English at university level. SPRENG Rapport 6,
Göteborg, 1972.

Stendhal, C, A report on work in error analysis and related areas, Errata:
Papers in error analysis, ed J. Svartvik, Stockholm, 1973, 115–123.

Stenström, A B, Grammatical errors in teacher trainees' written work, SECS
Report 7 (1973).

Stephanides, E A, A contrastive analysis of English and Hungarian textbooks of
English, HCLP 4 (1973), 53–65.

Sternemann, R, Konfrontative Linguistik und Einzelgrammatik, Deutsch als
Fremdsprache 8 (1971), 156–160.

Stevens, K N, Liberman A M, Studdert-Kennedy, M and Öhman S E G, Cross-language study of vowel perception, *Language and Speech* 12 (1969), 1–23.

Stratton, J, *The sounds of English*. Helsinki, 1970.

Strevens, P, Two ways of looking at error analysis, *Zielsprache Deutsch* 1 (1971), 1–6.

Stubelius, S, *Engelsk fonetik*. Stockholm, 1968.

Sunesson, M, *Deliberate and spontaneous speech: A study of the evaluation by several correctors of certain pronunciation mistakes in two types of oral tests.* SPRENG Report 11 (1972), University of Göteborg.

Suseendirarajah, S, Some pronunciation problems of Tamil speakers learning English, *Indian Linguistics* 33 (1972), 59–66.

Svartvik, J (ed) *Errata: Papers in error analysis*. Stockholm, 1973.

Svartvik, J et al, A typology of grammatical errors, *SECS Report* 1 (1973).

Szulc, A, Die Haupttypen der phonischer Interferenz, *Z. Phon.* 26 (1973), 111–119.

Sörenson, K, Understanding English: Difficulties confronting Danes, *Moderna Språk* 60 (1966), 388–393.

Tabacu, M., Contrastive aspects (Romanian-English) in the code of computing technology texts, *2nd international conference of English contrastive projects, Bucharest, 20–23 November, 1975*, Bucharest, 1976, 333–341.

Tarone, E, Interlingual identification in pronunciation, *TESOL Quart.* 6 (1972), 325–330.

Tarone, E, Speech perception in second language acquisition: A suggested model, *LL* 24 (1974), 223–234.

Tarone, E, Cohen, A D and Dumas G, a closer look at some interlanguage terminology: a framework for communication strategies, *Working papers on bilingualism* 9 (1976), 76–90.

Tataru, A, On the specific character of pronunciation, *ELT* 24 (1969), 26–27.

Taylor, B, The use of overgeneralization and transfer learning strategies by elementary and intermediate students of ESL, *LL* 25 (1975), 72–107.

Taylor, L L, Catford, J C, Guiora, A Z and Lane, H L, Psychological variables and ability to pronounce a second language, *Language and Speech* 14 (1971), 146–157.

Terbeek, D and Harshman R, Cross-language differences in the perception of natural vowel sounds, *UCLA Working Papers in Phonetics* 19 (1971), 26–38.

van Teslaar, A P, Learning new sound systems: Problems and prospects, *IRAL* 3 (1965), 79–93.

Tezer, P, A contrastive approach to teaching English, *Research in the Teaching of English* 4 (1970), 157–167.

Theivananthampillai, K, A comparative study of the English and Tamil auxiliary verb systems and prediction of learning problems for Tamil students of English, *IRAL* 8 (1970), 21–47.

Theivanantham Pillai, K *Contrastive linguistics and language teaching*. Annamalai University, Tamilnadu, India, 1974.

Theivananthampillai, K, *An empirical test of contrastive linguistic analysis as applied to the teaching of the English auxiliary verb system to Tamil speakers*. Harvard, 1965.

Thomaneck, J K A, A contrastive sociolinguistic analysis of students of German as a foreign language, *IRAL* 18 (1980), 135–138.

Tinkler, T, Interlanguage and error analysis—some simple questions and answers for teacher trainers, *ISB-Utrecht* 1 (1976), 117–127.

Titone, R, A plea for experimental studies in applied contrastive phonology, *Etudes de linguistique appliquée* 4 (1966), 151–160.

Todenhagen, C, English and German possessional adjectives: a linguistic explanation for an error of omission, *PSiCL* Vol 4, *ed* J Fisiak, Poznań, 1976, 231–240.

Tomosoiu, N, The prepositional and adverbial particle in post verbal position in English and implications for the study of English by the Romanian student, *RECAP, Contrastive studies in the syntax and semantics of English and Romanian*, Bucharest, 1974, 173–194.

Townson, M, Zur Fehleranalyse, *Linguistik und Didaktik* 2/3 (1971), 235–238.

Tran-Thi-Chau, Error analysis, contrastive analysis, and students' perception: a study of difficulty in second language learning, *IRAL* 13 (1975), 119–143.

Truus, S, *Sentence construction in English and Swedish in the writings of Swedish students of English at university level*. SPRENG Rapport 7, Göteborg, 1972.

Tucker, G R, Lambert, W E and Rigault, A, Students' acquisition of French gender distinctions: A pilot investigation, *IRAL* 7 (1969), 51–55.

Turover, G, Übersetzung und kontrastiv-konfrontative Forschungen, *Linguistische Arbeitsberichte* 14 (1976), 74–80.

Uhlisch, G, Zum Verhältnis im konfrontativer Linguistik und Typologie, *Wissenschaftliche Zeitschrift der Humbeldt Universität zu Berlin, Gesellschaft- und Sprachwissenschaftliche Reihe* 22 (1973), 165–169.

Upshur, J A, Language proficiency testing and the contrastive analysis dilemma, *LL* (1962), 123–127.

Ure, J, The mother tongue and the other tongue, *Ghana Teachers' Journal* 60 (1968), 38–55.

Uusivirta, P, Kvantitet och tvåspråkighet, *Folkmålstudier* 22 (1972), 145–171.

Valdman, A, L'interrogation en français et en anglais: Considérations comparatives et pédagogiques, *Le Français dans le Monde* 81 (1971), 35–39.

Vandamme, F J, Comparison of some English and Dutch vowels: Their interrelation when both are uttered by native Dutch speakers, *Z. Phon.* 22 (1969), 66–76.

Verner, Z and González, J, English language teaching in a Texas bilingual programme, *ELT* 25 (1971), 296–301.

Vielau, A, Kognitive Wortschatzdidaktik, *Dik Neueren Sprachen* 24 (1975), 248–264.

Vihanta, V, Ranskan vokaalikestosta ja sen suomalaiselle aiheuttamista vaikeuksista, *Fonetiikan paperit, Oulu 1973*, Oulun yliopiston fonetiikan laitoksen monisteita 3, 31–34.

Vilke, M, Teaching problems in presenting modal verbs, *YSCECP Ped. mat.* 1 (1971), 81–97.

Vilke, M, Teaching problems in presenting relative pronouns, *YSCECP Ped. mat.* 1 (1971), 98–111. .

de Vriendt, S, Interferenzen einer ersten Fremdsprache beim Erlernen einer zweiten *PAKS: Papers from the international symposium on applied contrastive linguistics*, Stuttgart, Oct. 11–13, 1971, ed G Nickel, Heidelberg, 1972, 43–50.

Wagner, J, Hach, G and Petersen, U H, Danish learner's acquisition of a morphological rule in German, *ISB-Utrecht* 4 (1979), 95–113.

Wagner, K H, Contrastive linguistics and language learning, *IRAL* 6 (1968), 233–255.

Wandruszka, M, L'aspect verbal, problème de traduction, *Travaux de linguistique et de littérature* 6 (1968), 113–129.

Wardhaugh, R, The contrastive analysis hypothesis, *TESOL Quart.* 4 (1970), 123–130.

Wardhaugh, R, An evaluative comparison of present methods for teaching English phonology, *TESOL Quart.* 4 (1970), 63–72.

Wardhaugh, R, Some current problems in second language teaching, *LL* 17 (1967), 21–26.

Wardhaugh, R, Three approaches to contrastive phonological analysis, *Canadian Journal of Linguistics* 13 (1967), 3–14.

Watts, R J and Homberger, B W, Proposals concerning the teaching of the English progressive aspect, *Proceedings of the 3rd AILA Congress, Copenhagen 1972*, Vol 3: *Applied Linguistics, Problems and Solutions*, ed J Qvistgaard et al, Heidelberg, 1974, 619–639.

Weinreich, U, *Languages in contact: Findings and problems*. Publications of the Linguistic Circle of New York 1, New York, 1953. (Reprinted: The Hague, 1963).

Weinreich, U, Mechanisms and structural causes of interference, *Psycholinguistics: A book of readings*, ed S Saporta, New York, 1966, 381–395.

Weinreich, U, On the description of phonic interference, *Word* 13 (1957), 1–11.

von Weiss, A, *Hauptprobleme der Zweisprachigkeit*. Heidelberg, 1968.

von Werner, O and Fritz, G (*eds*) *Deutsch als Fremdsprache und neuere Linguistik*. München, 1975.

Whitman, R L, Contrastive analysis: Problems and procedures, *LL* 20 (1970), 191–197.

Whitman, R L, *Interference in language learning: a theory of contrastive analysis with examples from Japanese and English*. Diss. University of Pennsylvania, 1969.

Whitman, R L and Jackson, K L, The unpredictability of contrastive analysis, *LL* 22 (1972), 29–42.

Wienold, G, Einige Überlengungen zur Theorie der kontrastiven Grammatik, *Folia Linguistica* 5 (1971), 36–45.

Wienold, G, Kontrastive Grammatik und gesteuerter Zweitsprachenerwerb, *PAKS: Papers from the international symposium on applied contrastive linguistics. Stuttgart, Oct. 11–13, 1971, ed* G Nickel, Heidelberg, 1972, 67–78.

Wierzchowska, B, Zur Frage konfrontativer phonetischer Untersuchungen des Polnischen, des Deutschen und des Englischen. Theoretische und metodischpraktische Probleme ihrer Erforschung und Optimierung, *Halle-Wittenberg Wissenschaftliche Beiträge* 24, Halle/Saale, 1976.

Wigforss, E, Foreign accent and bilingualism, *LUND Working Papers* 10 (1975), 155–171.

Wiik, K, *Finnish and English laterals: A comparison with special reference to the learning problems met by native speakers of Finnish learning English*. Turun yliopiston fonetiikan laitoksen julkaisuja 1, Turku, 1966.

Wiik, K, *Finnish and English vowels: A comparison with special reference to the learning problems met by native speakers of Finnish learning English*. Annales Universitatis Turkuensis B 94, Turku, 1965.

Wiik, K, Suomen ja englannin vokaalien eroista, *Suomen uusien kielten opettajain liiton (SUKOL) vuosikirja* 2 (1961), 7–15.

Wikberg, K, Lexical competence and the Swedish learner's problems with English vocabulary; B Hammarberg (ed), *Kontrastive Linguistik i sekundärspråkforskning*, Stockholm, 1979, 157–170.

Wilss, W, Probleme der Fehleranalyse Fremdsprache Grundsprache Englisch–Deutsch, *Deutsche Sprache im Kontrast, ed* U Engel, Tübingen, 1977, 23–51.

Wilss, W, Probleme und Perspektive der Übersetzungskritik, *IRAL* 12 (1974), 23–41.

Wode, H, Natürliche Zzeisprachigkeit: Probleme, Aufgaben, Perspektiven, *Ling. Berichte* 34 (1974), 15–36.

Wode, H and Schmitz T, *Some developmental trends in the acquisition of negation in several languages*. Arbeitspapiere zum Spracherwerb 3, Kiel, 1974.

Yarmohammadi, L, Contact analysis of English and Persian measure words for pedagogical purposes, *IRAL* 18 (1980), 1–20.

Yarmohammadi, L, English consonants and learning problems for Iranians: A contrastive sketch, *TESOL Quart.* 3 (1969), 231–236.

Yarmohammadi, L, A note on contrastive analysis, *ELT* 25 (1970), 76–78.

Yarmohammadi, L, Problems for Iranians learning English vowels, *J. ESL* 4 (1969), 57–62.

Yarmohammadi, L, Problems of Iranians in learning English reported speech, *IRAL* 11 (1973), 357–368.

Ylönen, M, Riikinruotsin sana-aksenttien tunnistamisesta, *Fonetiikan paperit, Tampere 1974*, Tampereen yliopiston puheopin laitoksen julkaisuja 1 (1975), 61–68.

Zabrocki, L, Die Methodik des Fremdsprachenunterrichts vom Standpunkt der Sprachwissenschaft, *Glottodidactica* 5 (1970), 1–35.

Zierer, E, Lautbildungsschwierigkeiten spanischeprachiger Peruaner im Deutschen, *Deutschunterricht für Ausländer* 1961, 26–29.

Zierer, E, The test of aural perception in foreign language teaching from the standpoint of interpretation theory, *IRAL* 9 (1971), 125–130.

Zobl, H, The formal and developmental selectivity of L1 influence on L2 acquisition, *LL* 30 (1980), 43–58.

Zydatiss, W, Die Bestimmung der interimsgrammatik von Fremdsprachenlernern mit Hilfe von Fehleranalyse und elicitation procedures—dargestellt am Beispiel der Progressive Form und des Present Perfect, *Die Neuen Sprachen* 1 (1977), 14–36.

Zydatiss, W, Fehler in der englischen Satzgliedfolge, *IRAL* 11 (1973), 319–355.

Zydatiss, W, A 'kiss of life' for the notion of error, *IRAL* 12 (1974), 231–237.

Zydatiss, W, Some instances of 'over-indulgence' and 'under-representation' in German learners' English, *Ling. Berichte* 33 (1974), 47–53.

Index of Names